CW01432182

Reasons to Rebel

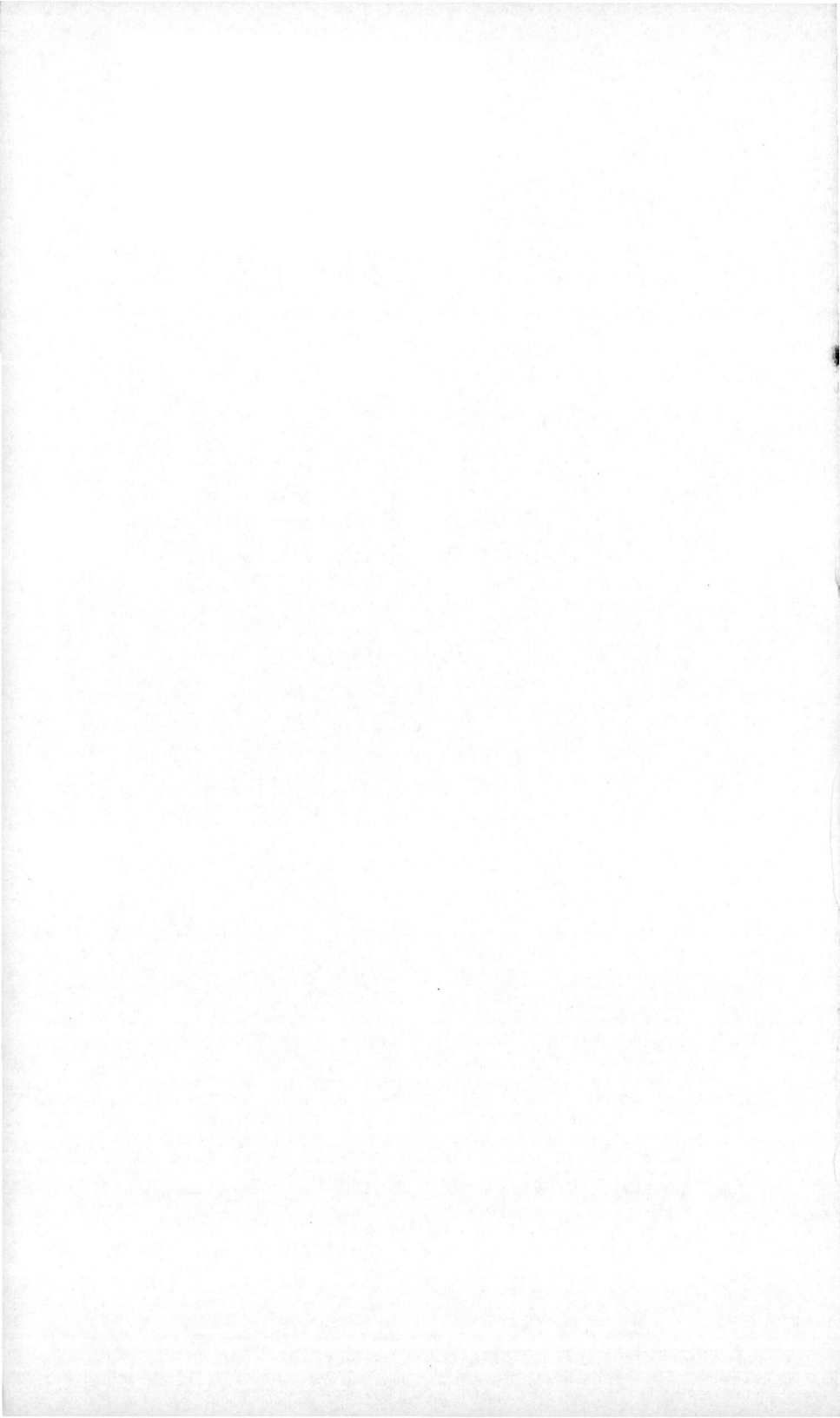

Reasons to Rebel
MY MEMORIES OF THE 1980s
Sheila Rowbotham

MERLIN PRESS

First published in 2024 by
The Merlin Press Ltd
50 Freshwater Road
London
RM8 1RX

www.merlinpress.co.uk

© Sheila Rowbotham, 2024

The moral right of the author has been asserted.

All rights reserved. No part of this book may be reproduced, stored
in a retrieval system, or transmitted in any form or by any means,
electronic, mechanical, photocopying, recording, or otherwise,
without the prior permission of both the copyright owner and the
publisher.

A catalogue record for this book is available at the British Library.

ISBN: 9780850367911

Printed in the UK by Imprint Digital, Exeter

Contents

List of Illustrations

between pages 128 and 129

1. Sheila Rowbotham in the kitchen at Powerscroft Road, c1980
2. Marc Karlin in his office, Berwick Street, Soho. Early 1980s
3. Lynne Segal & Sheila Rowbotham © Christopher Whitbread
4. Hilary Wainwright at the GLC
5. Sheila Rowbotham at the GLC
5. John Hoyland, mid 1980s © Elizabeth Woodeson
7. Peoples' Planners preparing their Centre
8. Newham Out of Work Centre
9. Members of Brent Black Music
10. Workplace Co-operative Nursery
11. Vivian Bell, bus conductress, Chalk Farm Garage, 1984
© Val Wilmer
12. Barking NHS Cleaners protesting against privatisation, 1984
© Gina Glover, Photo Co-op
13. Knottingley banner, 'Miners' Wives', March 1984
© Maggie Ellis
14. Joan Bohanna at home in Liverpool
15. John Bohanna with Will Atkinson and a member of the Bolton Whitmanites, drinking from the Loving Cup on the Whitman Walk
16. Swasti Mitter, Sheila Rowbotham and Marja-Liisa Swantz at WIDER, UNU seminar, late 1980s
17. Women at WIDER, UNU, late 1980s. Left to right Radha Kumar, (not known), Kumudhini Rosa, three members of 'Les Femmes Mahgreb', Val Moghadam, Fatima Mernissi, Kumari Jayawardena, Swasti Mitter
18. Miners and their families with Sheila Rowbotham and mining officials at Dhanbad, late 1980s
19. Women surface workers at Dhanbad, late 1980s
20. Miners at Dhanbad, late 1980s

All photographs are supplied by the author unless indicated otherwise. Every effort has been made to contact copyright holders. The author and publisher will be glad to recognise any omitted holders of copyright in subsequent editions.

Acknowledgements

In writing this book I was able to draw on papers I had deposited at the London School of Economics' Women's Library, and I am most grateful to the staff there for help. Special thanks are due to my agent Faith Evans who read several drafts of the manuscript, sent detailed comments and encouraged me as I wrote. I also wish to thank my publishers at Merlin Press, Anthony Zurbrugg and Adrian Howe, for all their help in producing the manuscript, and Glenda Pattenden for the photo pages.

Lola Dickinson, Nigel Fountain, David Musson and Lisa Vine read early drafts. I am exceedingly grateful to them all for their interest and comments. Shelley Adams, Françoise Barret-Ducrocq, Sue Finch, Julian Harber, Hermione Harris, Radha Kumar, Frances Murray, Julian Putkowski, Lynne Segal, Martin Stott, Hilary Wainwright and Michael Ward kindly helped me with information and source material. My beloved partner Michael Richardson lived through my travails and somehow remained cheerful amidst my groans and my enthusiasms. He has given me much valued help in editing the final version of the text.

For permission to quote from letters from Ros Baxandall and Swasti Mitter I thank Phineas Baxandall and Partha Mitter, and for permission to reproduce images my thanks go to the following photographers: Maggie Ellis, Gina Glover, Christopher Whitbread, Val Wilmer and Elizabeth Woodeson. Their work, which visually communicates the varied activism of the 1980s more directly than words can do, is of inestimable historical value.

Every effort has been made to find all copyright holders. The author and publisher will be glad to recognize any holders of copyright who have not been included above.

Abbreviations

BFB	*Beyond the Fragments Bulletin*
CAITS	Centre for Alternative Technological Systems
CPAG	Child Poverty Action Group
GLC	Greater London Council
ICA	Institute of Contemporary Arts
JFAC	*Jobs for a Change*
LSE	London School of Economics
MARHO	Mid-Atlantic Radical Historians Organisation
NCCL	National Council for Civil Liberties
NHS	National Health Service
RB	Rosalyn Baxandall Papers, Schlesinger Library, Harvard, Cambridge, MA
7 SHR	Sheila Rowbotham Papers, Women's Library, London School of Economics
SR	Papers of Sheila Rowbotham to go to Women's Library
SRD	Sheila Rowbotham, Diary
SRJ	Sheila Rowbotham, Journal
SWP	Socialist Workers' Party
TAM	Tamiment Library, New York
UNU/INTECH	United Nations University /Institute for New Technologies
UNU/WIDER	United Nations University/World Institute for Development Economics Research

Introduction

The 1980s were a shock. The changes introduced by Margaret Thatcher's Conservative government battered left movements, painfully disrupted working-class peoples' livelihoods and pressed down on many groups who faced discrimination.

There was no shortage of reasons to rebel. Along with thousands upon thousands of others I opposed not just the repressive laws, but the fundamental tenets of the new right. Hanging on to visions of creative utopias, we strove for new ways of organizing and relating to others and we sought to connect a liberatory sexual politics with rebellions against many kinds of inequality. We argued, wrote, campaigned, demonstrated, picketed. We established alternative co-operative projects, secured reforms through local government and made direct international links.

Resourceful resistance slowed down the onslaught but we were contending not simply with the doctrinal resolve of a right-wing government. We faced something larger, something that could not be voted out – a more ruthless global capitalism, geared to profits, which was prepared to dump hard-won social provision and neglect to conserve even basic infrastructure.

We learned what it meant to experience defeats. By the end of the 1980s many projects and radical administrative innovations had either collapsed or were drastically depleted while vital pockets of cultural egalitarianism were to be lost. Subsequently even to remember them seemed to stretch credibility.

But in 1979 I knew none of this. I still carried the confident rebellions of the 1960s and 1970s within me. I had become a socialist as a student in the early 1960s because I opposed the injustices and waste that capitalism thrived upon. Early influences were Civil Rights, anti-colonialism, the Campaign for Nuclear Disarmament (CND) and my own amalgam of the nineteenth-century anarchism of Emma Goldman and the communism of Karl Marx. After graduating in 1964 I had become a teacher in East London, where the injustices of race and class were evident all around me; I was stirred by talk of workers' control and by the broader dialectics of human liberation.[1]

I called the book in which I remembered the 1970s *Daring to Hope,* for it did seem in those years that social transformation, however faintly delineated, was within reach.[2] Throughout the seventies I was happily absorbed in the Women's Liberation movement. By translating personal experience into a new feminist politics we had devised ways of seeing and organizing that could strengthen our confidence and courage as individuals, and something more, the inimitable understandings that come from doing things together. This combination enhanced possibilities. It reached into society and culture, taking root in unions, community groups, the public sector, the arts, academia and the media. We sought not just to oppose but to create.

Ours was a personal and passionate politics. The deep friendships that cohered amidst activism pierced to the bone of feeling and cut new swathes of perception. It was to be a profoundly educative love affair for me and for many other women and generated a heartening sense of collective power, augmented because women's liberation emerged in many countries amidst other movements for liberation. We did not escape distressing conflicts, but their repercussions did not seem insuperable, for resistance in one area exposed and weakened the hold of oppression in others.

Nonetheless, many of the loose organizational structures supporting Women's Liberation in Britain were dissolving by the late 1970s. It was a loss, for our hopes had been so high. Yet external circumstances were forcing many of us to look outwards. During the desperate strikes of the winter of 1978 to 1979, along with other socialist feminists, I had seen the Labour government turn against low paid workers, including many women on strike.

Aware that there had been repeated attempts to think through alternatives to the Labour Party, with its long history of caving in once in office, I had also come to reject the plethora of revolutionary groups keen to emulate the Bolsheviks as tight-knit vanguards. I doubted their claim to assimilate and transcend understandings that arose from experiencing specific kinds of oppression.

I certainly did not know the answer but, being steeped in the history of late nineteenth and early twentieth-century socialism and anarchism, I was aware that we women liberationists were not the first to argue for a democratic left in which everyone's individuality could flourish. The militant Welsh miners, in their pamphlet *The Miners' Next Step* in 1912 had put it pithily, 'Sheep cannot be said to have solidarity'.[3]

Moreover, having taken part for several years in an innovative politics which had sought to make space for individual expression, I had come to see how specific movements might carry wider implications for social change. I thought how we had organized as feminists could be relevant to others by contributing differing approaches to contesting capitalism. Perhaps by voicing what I had observed, others would add more insights. I began consulting with friends and wrote a long screed in a large black notebook while my son, Will, was at his baby minder's.

Several local socialist societies were bringing people together and, stimulated by meetings in London and Newcastle, in March 1979 Lynne Segal, Hilary Wainwright and I put together a small, but hefty booklet called *Beyond the Fragments: Feminism and the Making of Socialism*.[4] In differing contexts, the three of us were preoccupied with changing how socialism was conceived and acted upon through a combination of feminist and grassroots perspectives.

Lynne had been deeply involved in local community politics, as well as in feminism in Islington, and was searching for a national sphere of action which could extend and develop the ideas of the revolutionary libertarian left. Hilary had been researching *The Workers' Report on Vickers* (1979) with the industrial sociologist Huw Beynon, chronicling how the shop stewards had developed dispersed forms of leadership. The direct participatory forms of democracy she documented, connected with similar impulses within the women's movement.

The election of Margaret Thatcher in May 1979 sharpened polarities. Initially unable to act as decisively as she wished, she rejected the 'false prudence' of retreating 'to a defensive redoubt' and was resolved to change the 'signals' ideologically and practically.[5] Such overt declarations of unrelenting combat were not customary for British prime ministers. Conservatives were inclined to operate *sotto voce* and Labour, if rather more circuitously, had tended to adopt a similar path.

* * *

From the autumn of 1979, when Merlin Press issued an enlarged edition, *Beyond the Fragments* started to make its way to many countries, causing much commotion in its wake. As the decade ended the call for 'beyonding' had become a wider cause. Socialist feminists, diverse left activists and trades unionists were disputing and discussing what we had written. But this presented us with an awkward tangle. People assumed that we authors had answers hidden up our sleeves. It was a misapprehension which we were keen to counter.[6]

Galvanized by living under a destructive new right government, we decided we must try to test out ideas with more people. In December 1979 Hilary, Lynne and I drafted a letter to discuss how stronger connections on the left could be fostered.[7] Two friends who had influenced our thinking contributed and added their names. Jean McCrindle, a feminist and a socialist since the 1950s, was teaching trade union students at Northern College near Barnsley. Kenny Bell, a community activist, had become a friend of Hilary's through left politics in Newcastle. He was working with council tenants to establish closer links between them and the Direct Labour Council workers who did their repairs. The five of us each sent our letter to around ten people. Kenny's housing group put a question I had often wondered about, but could not answer: 'How does consciousness change?'[8] I would return to it repeatedly over the course of the decade.

1

January to July 1980

At the beginning of the 1980s most people on the left were, like me, involved in radical movements, campaigns, trade unions and community groups or the numerous imaginative cultural and media alternatives. Known as the 'non-aligned', we interacted with the small, relatively new, revolutionary parties, with the burgeoning Ecology Party and with older institutions like the Labour and Communist Parties.

Changes were evident in the unions partly because of pressure from the social movements and partly because of grassroots militancy. Innovative ways of organizing like the shop stewards' combine committees had emerged, while activists were providing research through the Trade Union Resource Centres. Interconnections were being fostered because older labour institutions like the Trades Councils were being revived.

In January some trade unionists and socialist feminists in Brent in north-west London asked me to speak about *Beyond the Fragments* and I travelled across London from Hackney where I had settled in 1964. It was my first contact personally with left-wingers in Brent, though I was aware its Trades Council had supported several strikes during the 1970s involving women workers, notably at Trico and Grunwicks.[9]

I explained that Lynne, Hilary and myself had written from our particular perspectives because we wanted to share what we had observed with others. Aware that the obstacles we confronted as women seeking liberation were not just economic, but were embedded in relationships, in customary behaviour and in language, I described how feminists had taken up ideas from

American new left women about linking personal experience to a politics of social transformation. We had, moreover, come to see that *how* we organized for change affected outcomes and had tried to steer away from both the top-down leadership that characterized the vanguardist Marxist groups and the kinds of anarchism which dismissed the specific aptitudes and skills of individuals.[10] I hoped that *Beyond the Fragments* would enable us to compare our understandings with people in other movements.

I was speaking about ideas I had literally lived within, and not just through Women's Liberation. There had been innumerable attempts in Hackney to prefigure a radical co-operative future with alternative schemes ranging from do-it-yourself photography to food coops. Moreover, the borough was replete with clusters of experimental left-wingers devising new forms of collective living. Some were idealistic absolutists, who wanted to turn personal relationships around completely. Others were more pragmatic, like our household in Montague Road where communal life had evolved ad hoc, surviving through an eclectic mix of good company and convenience sustained by a gruff undercover idealism.

For several years, Will's father, Paul Atkinson, had been living there, and towards the end of 1979 we had all moved from Montague Road to Powerscroft Road so Will, who was two, could have his own room. In January 1980 we were still settling in, putting up bookshelves and painting the walls. However, the domestic communality to which I had become accustomed was unravelling. Shortly after we moved, the journalist Nigel Fountain, whose intractable adherence to shopping rules and rotas could incense me, but whose laconic irony never failed to make me smile, went to live in another house. I was saddened to see him go and so was Will, who ran after him down the road as he departed. In March the two other members of the household, Sue Sharpe and Dave Phillips, went for a long stay in Mexico.

Will had just started at Market Nursery in Wilde Close and was very happy there. It had developed from a playgroup in the mid-1970s, initiated by Sue Finch and Carol Boatswain with support from a network of feminists and socialists. Like other alternative community nurseries, it was run by parents and workers and eventually acquired some council funding.[11] The desperate need for childcare made it very popular with local women. But its maintenance remained a constant effort and in 1980 an early supporter, Andrew Puddephatt (later to lead the Council and become a human rights campaigner), had to appeal for donations.[12]

I trusted and admired the childcare workers, Hermine Anderson and Kathy Jenkins, the fees were modest and it was only about one and a half miles away from Powerscroft Road. So, Paul would take Will in our old Morris Traveller if the weather was bad, and when it was fine I could walk with Will in the pushchair and wander slowly back through Broadway Market and across London Fields. The nursery allowed me precious time to write and think and I felt profoundly grateful to it.

Nevertheless, the next few months proved so hectic that there was little time for either. That February I went to several Fragments meetings in London and travelled north to my hometown, Leeds, for another. The socialist feminists, members of community groups, supporters of CND and anti-racist groups, tenants and trade unionists who turned up for this, decided we should call a conference in Leeds during the autumn. Encouraged by their response, I assured a young Fragments sympathizer in Oxford, Martin Stott, 'We were thinking of an event which would not only take the form of talks & workshops but would be fun'.[13]

Leeds became a regular Fragments gathering place. A former occupant of our Hackney communal house, Caroline Bond, had gone there and several old friends lived nearby in Halifax. Two were from my student days: Gloden Dallas, who had been involved in the early days of the women's liberation group in Leeds, and the playwright Barry Collins. All three helped to plan the Fragments conference and so did the historian of Chartism

Dorothy Thompson, who I had known almost as long.

I had been nineteen in 1962 when I had first gone by bus from Leeds to Halifax to visit Dorothy and Edward Thompson. Dorothy's organizing skills had been honed by the 1930s Young Communist League, which she had joined in her early teens. After leaving the Communist Party in 1956, Dorothy, along with Edward, had become a key figure in the non-aligned New Left. She possessed sharp eyes for bullshit, a biting tongue, a store of reassuring political wisdom and an irreverent sense of humour. I was soon reading Edward's *The Making of the English Working Class* in proofs with delight and excitement and discovering late nineteenth-century activists in their library who felt very recognizable – Isabella Ford, the middle-class feminist who had supported working women strikers and Tom Maguire, the working-class poet and trade union organizer who wrote ironic ballads for them.[14] Over the following decades I was to spend many hours with them both, talking about social and labour history, politics and their own lives.

March 1980 proved even busier than February. My diary records I was painting Market Nursery on the 1st and 8th of March, then going to the birthday party of Will's contemporary Jess Cartner-Morley at a Hackney communal house. On Sunday the 9th I joined the Trade Union Congress (TUC) demonstration against the Employment Bill. Inflation had soared and harsh economic and social policies were in the offing. The mood was defiant. Steel workers marched covered in badges and stickers supporting their national strike.[15] Women tobacco workers carried a banner proclaiming 'Smoke Maggie Out'. Then on the 12th I was at Birmingham University, delivering on the history of socialism and feminism at Dorothy's seminar; on the 14th I went to a newly formed Socialist discussion group in London, by the 15th I was back in Leeds at a *Beyond the Fragments* planning meeting.[16]

Only two days afterwards, came the far grander 'Debate of the Decade', in the Methodist Central Hall, Westminster. The Edwardian domed structure mixed French Renaissance,

Viennese Baroque and early twentieth-century Wesleyan Methodism under one roof and its ethos was redolent of innumerable meetings. Indeed, in 1969, at a previous left debate of the decade, I had run up and down the aisles selling the newspaper edited by Tariq Ali, *Black Dwarf*.[17] That time the topic had been 'Reform v. Revolution?', but in 1980 it was more downbeat – 'The Crisis and Future of the Left'. Nonetheless, 2,600 tickets had been sold in advance and long queues waited patiently outside hoping to get in.

Peter Hain, who had been active in the Anti-Apartheid movement, was in the chair. The speakers were Tony Benn, who had bucked historical tradition by moving leftwards as a Labour minister, becoming a leading voice in opposition; the left economist and Labour MP for Vauxhall and Lambeth, Stuart Holland; Paul Foot, the journalist and wit from the Socialist Workers' Party; my fellow fragment, Hilary Wainwright; Tariq Ali, who I had met when we were both students at Oxford; and Audrey Wise. Dorothy Thompson had put us in touch in 1969 when Audrey was active in the shopworkers union (USDAW). She had played a key role in the left-wing Institute for Workers' Control and been elected as a Labour MP, strongly defending both abortion and maternity rights.

Decisive in debate, she argued against an exclusive focus on change coming from below. Agreeing that women's mobilization outside Parliament had been crucial in protecting the right to abortion, she stressed opposition within Parliament had been equally crucial.[18] The two wings needed to combine. Heckled on the state, Audrey's crisp, insightful riposte struck me forcibly and, long afterwards, I would turn it over and over in my mind. 'I don't believe that the state is some sort of abstraction. I believe that the state itself depends on the acquiescence at least, if not support from ordinary people. And so the big question to which we've got to find the answer is how to persuade ordinary people not to acquiesce while they are prevented from achieving the transfer of wealth and power towards themselves.'[19]

When it came to contributions from the floor, I followed

Paul Acaster from South Yorkshire who had appealed for donations for the striking steel workers. I stood up with legs like jelly to announce the forthcoming Beyond The Fragments Conference, whereupon more fierce heckling erupted from the back. Lacking Audrey's political nous, my experience as a schoolteacher kicked in. I waited in silence, staring severely in their direction. This was folly; the hecklers noisily heckled my minutes away. Peter Hain intervened, allowed me extra time and I blurted out my announcement.[20] The hecklers departed and Lynne Segal managed to assert the need for an alternative vision of socialism which would enable everyone to gain confidence individually and together.[21] As I listened to the speakers, I knew that in relation to society at large, there was only a hair's breadth difference between us. Yet still we were divided.

By 1980 this was true of feminists as well as the left. On 21 March I was back in Leeds again giving an historical account of socialism and feminism at the Communist University, an ecumenical yearly gathering.[22] Three separatist feminists had strategically arranged themselves in a combative triangle. Before I spoke, one vehemently opposed talking about women's history with men present and the other two chimed in with alacrity. My heart sank, this was mind-manacling and absurd, but it could be lengthy and we only had three quarters of an hour. Whereupon the unruffled young woman in the chair swiftly announced in modulated tones, 'All those who have no objection to discussing the history of socialism and feminism with men can come to the room next door.' The whole meeting stood up and departed, leaving the three objectors alone, looking flummoxed.

Thankfully women's movements open to left social movements were growing outside Britain. My early books had been translated into many languages, including Greek, and a persuasive Eleni Varikas had come to visit in the winter of 1979 with an invitation to speak in Athens. I had agreed, lured partly by the thought of sea and sun, but also because I felt an immediate affinity with the young woman sitting on my bedroom floor. She selected her words carefully, shifting her long black hair and smiling as she spoke about socialist feminism.[23]

When I went there in April, I met Eleni's friends, Mimi Votsis, from a pioneering women's publishing group, and Costoula Sclavenitis, a translator, who enunciated a far more precise and grammatically perfect English than we native speakers. They wanted to develop an autonomous women's movement while avoiding entrenchment in a separatist enclosure.

Eleni theorized from an extensive knowledge of history and I listened with a powerful sense of recognition when she observed that autonomous movements around specific identities realized their potential in seeking to go beyond their specific form of oppression. I stayed with Costoula and we talked into the night about politics, love affairs and our problems of earning a living, surfacing each morning by drinking Greek coffees on a tiny balcony in her flat. Costoula did not seem to cook, instead we went out for exceedingly late meals, apart from one unforgettable day when Eleni took me to her mother's for lunch where I tasted a moussaka which contrived to be filling yet mysteriously light at the same time. Despite seeking to recreate it ever afterwards, that wonderful Varikas moussaka has always proved beyond emulation.

I attended a meeting which included women linked either to the social democratic Pan Hellenic Socialist Movement (PASOK), or to the various wings of the communists and the Trotskyists, along with members of the autonomous women's movement. I sat listening to them all discussing in Greek and was puzzled when I kept hearing a word that sounded like 'kinema'. Eleni, Mimi and Costoula laughed when I enquired why there were so many references to the cinema? The word I was hearing meant movement. They laughed even more when I could identify 'tendencies' from body language, distinguishing Eurocommunists and Trots amidst the cacophony of voices.

In Britain we had adopted 'consciousness raising' from the Americans, with the aim of fusing our personal experiences with a new politics. But the Greek feminists I met seemed unenthusiastic and responded to my questions by muttering vaguely about some 'apolitical' women's group consisting of Americans, Australians and New Zealanders. So, I was amused to discover a recognizable clutch of radical women with an ecological bent, many of whom had small children. For their part they were utterly bewildered by the Greeks' stamina for long argumentative meetings debating differing interpretations of Marxism and shocked by their attachment to smoking cigarettes throughout. I felt caught between the two.

It appeared to be unusual to have a public meeting called by a non-aligned grouping and an expectant crowd turned out to my talk on socialist feminism. Among then was Margaret Papandreou, active in the Women's Union which campaigned for social provision for working-class women. She was married to Andreas Papandreou, the leader of PASOK; they had met when he was a political exile and working as an economist in the US.

The meeting was extremely lengthy, partly because of the translating from English to Greek then back again and I was unsure whether what I said was particularly useful to them all. But I treasure the wonderful poster advertising the event which shows a nineteenth-century Greek woman crushing a top hat with deft elegance. Underneath, looking curious indeed in Greek script, is the Yorkshire/Lancashire name of 'Rowbotham'.

The weather seemed so warm that I asked if I could go swimming. Everyone considered it far too cold; but politely accompanied me. My hopes of a sun tan were dashed, for as soon as I emerged from the water, the Greeks withdrew to a shaded café for a political debate over a long lunch.

There were to be no sunny beaches in Belfast, where I spoke in May on Beyond the Fragments. Bill Rolston, who taught sociology at what was then Ulster Polytechnic (later the University of Ulster) and contributed to the local trade union resource centre, had asked me over. I wanted to learn more about the conflicts which had taken so many lives in Northern Ireland and through Bill I met socialists and feminists who were trying to look with clarity and honesty at the tragedies around them without being daunted or encompassed by grief and loss. I wondered at their inner strength and capacity for irony amidst such grim circumstances.

Bill gave me a guided tour of the city's history from the eighteenth century to the present. We had much in common. But when I told him I had been to a Methodist school and, despite ceasing to be a Christian when I was sixteen, had been influenced by the anti-materialist values I had encountered there, I saw him grip the steering wheel so tightly that his knuckles whitened. His response was overtly sardonic: 'I never thought I'd be driving a *Protestant* socialist round Belfast'. Yet I sensed an edge of incomprehension beneath the humour. Belfast was both familiar and indecipherable.

Assumed meanings jumbled dramatically on my flight home. I had bought a record of Campaign for Nuclear Disarmament (CND) songs. To my surprise it was seized by poker faced security guards at the airport, wrapped in special tape and stowed away. Whereupon, out of the upper corner of my eye, I noticed an exceedingly tall man with a long ruddy face who looked familiar. It clicked. I was travelling on the same plane as Ian Paisley, the hardline Protestant leader of the Democratic Unionist Party – perhaps they thought I might belabour him with my CND record!

CND, protest songs and the direct action of the Committee of 100 had been intrinsic parts of the left politics I had encountered in the early 1960s. Indeed, even before my first visit to the Thompsons, I had seen Edward striding along on the CND march from Aldermaston to London talking intensely with a left-wing farmer friend of his from Wales.

Once again, consumed by the threatening international situation and convinced of the need for broad resistance, he had thrown himself into the reawakened peace movement. His influential pamphlet *Protest and Survive* (1980) lampooned the government's civil defence bulletin *Protect and Survive*, pointing out how nuclear weapons made Europe an obvious target in the event of war between the Soviet Union and America. Noting how protests were already stirring in Holland, West Germany and Belgium, Edward asserted that we should be putting on our gum boots and going off to talk with the Americans on their bases. Opposition *'need not wait upon governments'*.[24] He wrote *Protest and Survive* as a socialist, but wanted to call upon a wider constituency.[25]

In April 1980 the Appeal for European Nuclear Disarmament (END) was launched at a press conference at the House of Commons; among the speakers were the Labour MP Tony Benn, Bruce Kent from the Campaign for Nuclear Disarmament and Mary Kaldor, who was studying the economic and social basis of the arms trade. Edward and Dorothy were to play important roles within END and the wider peace movement which revived in many countries from the early 1980s.

* * *

The decision to hold a Fragments conference meant that it no longer felt as if Lynne, Hilary and myself were three women against the world. Among the many new friends that its planning brought into my life were the creative socialist feminist Marina Lewycka (later to become well known as a novelist) her partner, Dave Feickert, already alert to the significance of new technology and Joanna de Groot, socialist feminist, active trade unionist and specialist in the history of Iran, from York University. And through Hilary I came to know the remarkable Bohannas from Liverpool. Both were shop stewards, John at Ford Halewood, Joan at the pharmaceutical company Glaxo, and both were great raconteurs.[26]

Joan, who became a staunch Fragments Conference organizer, used to relate with mischievous delight how they had fallen in love while in the navy. In 1965, when John was posted away, she had realized he was the only sailor she continued to miss when he was gone. So, impulsively, she had headed up after him to Scotland. Not only did Joan's flight leave the admiral she was allocated to chauffeur around stranded, this was desertion and serious stuff. It was thus fortunate that the admiral took it on the chin and sprang to her defence, gallantly rescuing her from being clapped in irons or whatever terrible fate might have awaited her.

While the psychological pressure on Hilary, Lynne and myself was reduced through comradeship, the conference meant our organizational responsibilities increased. Thus, an unintended result of planning for a more personal kind of politics was that Paul and I had begun to resemble the weatherman and woman. When one was at home, the other was out and over the last few months I had been more out than in.

For several years Paul had been researching his PhD on medieval peasant land ownership in Cheshire while sporadically earning money by doing electrical wiring with his friend James Swinson. They were both in a men's group and thinking through manifestations of masculinity socially, psychologically and historically. They were also involved in the magazine *Achilles Heel*, which James designed.

Paul and I shared a similar approach to left politics, however our preoccupations were beginning to diverge. He was becoming more and more interested in various forms of radical therapy and his thesis had been abandoned, along with copies of the Cheshire records he kept rolled up in large cardboard boxes in the cellar next to my study. They documented field and family names and occasionally crimes and village disputes, along with innumerable economic transactions of the long forgotten. But now these faint chronicles of medieval lives were beginning to gather new layers of twentieth-century dust.

* * *

During May my journeyings northwards increased because I had written a play and the rehearsals were being held in Doncaster. In 1979, a letter had arrived from Ron Rose asking me to do a play for the Doncaster Arts Cooperative Theatre Company (DAC). This was a new challenge, but I had just read Ray Challinor's account of Alice Wheeldon, a socialist and feminist in Derby accused during World War One of a macabre plot to kill the Prime Minister, Lloyd George, with a poisoned arrow while he was playing golf. In the atmosphere of wartime panic, she was found guilty and went to prison on evidence collected by informers linked to the Ministry of Munitions. Released after the war, but weakened by incarceration, she had died during the Spanish influenza pandemic, leaving three daughters.[27]

I could imagine the devastating impact this must have had upon those close to her and indeed, learned subsequently from her Australian great granddaughter, Chloë Mason, how a profound distrust of the British state had resonated down the generations.[28] I was intrigued too by the left wingers who surrounded the Wheeldons in Derby during World War One. They included revolutionaries from the shop stewards' networks, socialist feminists in the suffrage movement, along with earnest members of the Independent Labour Party concerned to match their politics with how they lived personally.

Luckily Ron Rose, who had been radicalized as a student at Warwick University in 1970, when they had discovered files revealing the surveillance of left-wing members of staff, quickly understood the implications of Alice Wheeldon's story.[29] In a leap of faith, he told me to go ahead and managed to obtain an Arts Council grant through a small loophole the government had not yet managed to block.

I wrote the script in my study, the semi-basement room next to Paul's Cheshire manuscripts. Sitting surrounded by books, boxes and papers, still only partially stacked from the move, with light coming through from the small window which opened out to the garden, accents resounded in my head. Doing dialogue proved to be sheer joy. Creating characters and making them speak meant I could stretch imaginatively in ways that were taboo in historical writing. I called my play *Friends of Alice Wheeldon*, echoing the more recent support groups who had defended rebels against the state.[30]

Going to the rehearsals was revelatory. Listening to the actors made it clear which lines worked out loud. Their voices added new inflections and so did the songs, while the self-assured director, Penny Cherns, quickly saw how to shift scenes for greater dramatic effect. Watching how they worked, I glimpsed the convergent creativity that makes working in the theatre so electrifying.

When *Friends of Alice Wheeldon* was previewed at Rotherham Arts Centre on 28 May,[31] I was seated next to my socialist feminist friend Sally Alexander and, when it ended, peeped furtively, trying to gauge her reaction. As Sally had studied drama and remained close to many actors, I regarded her as a discriminating judge. The lights were still dimmed in the theatre, but I could detect a tear tracing a glimmering path down her cheek and experienced a flash of elation.

The play created a small stir, generating disputatious discussions as it moved from place to place. Friends supplemented the Doncaster Arts Cooperative's contacts; John Bohanna got the Liverpool Socialist Society to put it on and Jean McCrindle's determined lobbying persuaded Sheffield's Crucible Theatre to show it 'upstairs'. *Friends of Alice Wheeldon* culminated at the Old Red Lion pub in Islington from 17 to 22 June, where it was packed with socialist feminists who surprised the actors by greeting jokes they had not noticed with guffaws of recognition.[32] Chuffed by my new persona as a playwright I bought myself a trendy purple boiler suit I could not afford and was photographed smiling cat's-whiskers-like in an interview in a Northern local paper.

***

Aware that our communication with one another had become predominantly about the externals of determining who was where when, interspersed with my constant worries about money, Paul and I decided to head for rest and peace. A few days after *Friends of Alice Wheeldon* finished at the Old Red Lion, we travelled north to Whitby in the Morris Traveller with Will and Emma, the nine-year-old daughter of a Hackney feminist friend.

I loved Whitby, which I had visited as a small child. In the mid 1970s, encouraged and helped by Gloden Dallas, I had bought a three roomed cottage, 20 Blackburn's Yard, at the bottom of the hill leading up to the ruins of Whitby Abbey and a short distance from the sea. Gloden and I became co-owners. After becoming friends as students at Oxford, we had remained close, sharing an interest in labour and women's history as well as similar socialist and feminist politics.

The Yard was full of small children. Living opposite were two Americans, Laureen Shaw and Pete Gannarelli, with Che, a few months younger than Will, and their toddler, Luke. Pete had been able to find work on a fishing boat and Laureen, whose mother had come from a Whitby fishing family, was struggling to set up a pottery in an old wash house in Blackburns Yard.[33] In the winters Whitby women's liberation group ran a playgroup in number 20 and many friends used the cottage, including workers from Market Nursery, who even persuaded Hackney Council to let them take local children to it for holidays.

Sorties to Whitby had become part of the pattern of my life with Paul and Will and were our parental recovery periods. But on this occasion our weariness went deep. On 1 July, when we packed up to return home to London, we were both still tired and frazzled.[34] It was a grey day and rain was falling as we crossed the moors. Paul's shoulders had a familiar hunch that I knew meant he just wanted to be back in London. We were so close, yet I could not reach him. Nor was I able to drive. I sat in the back with Will on my knee and Emma by my side.

Then the unexpected struck. The car spun round and we were facing the ongoing traffic. The flash of time that followed seemed like an aeon and an instant simultaneously. I saw the clenched, horrified faces of the men in the lorry hurtling towards us and, for a fraction of a second, was somehow aware that they would not be able to stop in time.

Next, we were turning in the air. Paul, in the front, was the only one with a seat belt for there were none at the back. Without thinking, I folded myself around Will. I felt my back and shoulders hit the top. Emma was also up in the air. The car overturned and landed upright, mercifully off the road in a ditch. Will's face was black, his eyes wide open. I felt a momentary panic, before realizing he had been covered with the cocoa we were thriftily taking back to London with us.

The men in the oncoming lorry had stopped and surrounded the car protectively, their faces at the windows. They had the professional roadsters knowledge of accidents and their eyes were brimming with loving relief upon seeing that we were not seriously harmed, especially I think because children were in the car. Paul and I both started to rejoice in that utopian moment of affinity and our luck at being alive, whereupon an exasperated Emma, who had seen cars explode in accidents on TV dramas, took charge, shouting, 'Get out of the car'. Luckily the blue Morris Traveller just sat there stolidly, its wheels in the mud. We were bruised but intact, apart from Will who was not bruised at all.

We were bundled up in rugs by the lorry driver and his mates; the police arrived and carried us off to the local station. I gathered we were near Doncaster. They were gracious rescuers, carefully collecting all our belongings, giving us tea and telling us the accident had been caused by a tyre blow out and that the sturdy structure of the Morris Traveller had saved our lives. A modern car would have buckled.

I did not experience shock immediately, fussing instead over everyone else and musing on the multifarious contradictions of the state. Then, shortly after our crash I bit my lip at the dentists, came home, felt ill and went to bed. When a peculiar bump appeared by my ear I went to see my GP, Michael Leibson, a philosophical and unflappable East Londoner, who gave me antibiotics. It subsided, but I remained weak and tired.

On 30 July, Hilary, who was researching the proposals developed by workers at Lucas Aerospace, had arranged for me to meet the trade unionist Mike Cooley.[35] It felt a long journey on the train from Clapton to North Acton, where we were due to meet Mike in a pub, but I was determined to go. I had heard so much from Hilary about him and the other Lucas workers who had come up with their own inventive alternative economic and social strategy, which extended ideas of workers' control beyond the labour process.

During the mid 1970s when management announced redundancies, they had not simply described how the skills they possessed through manufacturing armaments could be diversified to create socially useful products, they had actually developed prototypes: a 'hobcart' so children with spina bifida could be mobile; a portable kidney machine; a simple life-support system to keep victims of heart attacks alive until they reached hospital, along with heat pumps that could conserve energy. The management, apparently undermined by the workers' initiatives, had disregarded their proposals for human-centred products, while some trade unionists who saw their role as strictly oppositional were also suspicious. Instead, the Lucas plan had fired the imagination of innumerable people internationally.

At this first meeting at the Castle pub, as I listened to Mike explaining in his disarmingly soft voice what they had done and why, I had no idea how familiar that lilt, along with his capacity to strengthen others and his inner steely resolve were to become over the course of the decade.

More Beyond the Fragments meetings were followed by a lightning visit from my American socialist feminist friend, Ros Baxandall, who taught women's history in American Studies at SUNY Old Westbury, a college in Long Island. Ros, an indefatigable seizer of contingencies, had devised a cheap way to travel from New York as a courier guarding packages on planes for the DHL express mail service. Since our first meeting in 1974, I had watched in astonishment as she manoeuvred to make things happen.[36] Ros was exceptional, but not alone. Along with another socialist feminist historian, Ellen Ross at Sarah Lawrence College, she was agitating for my play about Alice Wheeldon to be published through the New Feminist Library by the left Monthly Review Press in the US. This hands on, can-do sisterhood of the American socialist feminists I came to know never ceased to amaze me.

2

August to December 1980

The Fragments conference was due to be held in Leeds on Saturday 30 August. Paul and I went to Whitby beforehand. By Friday 29th I had laryngitis and was voiceless. The rain poured down relentlessly that Saturday in Leeds, yet nearly two thousand people turned up. As well as socialist feminists, they included gay groups, anti-sexist men's groups, members of the Socialist Environment and Resources Association (SERA) and the Conference of Socialist Economists, tenants from South Wales and the North East, new technologists from Nottingham, agitators for health care, against hazards and against nuclear weapons. Among those who arrived with stalls were the Union of the Physically Impaired, community arts groups like Bootle Arts and Action, the charity War on Want, the Yorkshire District of the Communist Party, the libertarian left group Big Flame, and Bookmarks, the Trotskyist Socialist Workers' Party's impressive shop.[37]

My whispery croak was barely audible making it impossible for me to say anything at the opening plenary. Kenny Bell and a representative of the South Wales Tenants' Group did speak however and so did Mike Cooley. He described how the shop stewards at Lucas had initially approached 'experts' on developing alternative products. This had yielded little. In contrast, when they turned to the 14,000 workers at Lucas Aerospace, an outpouring of proposals came, not in 'abstract written accounts', but precise sketches and models. Their creativity infused workplace resistance with a far-reaching potential, for the Lucas Aerospace Alternative Workers' Plan demonstrated workers could alter not just how they worked, but what they did with their skills.

Mike stressed how mistaken it was to 'confuse linguistic ability with intelligence'.[38] I had observed what he was saying through teaching working-class pupils, without being able to formulate it. Words are my sustenance and an unceasing source of pleasure, but sadly in the English language they also codify forms of culturally exclusive power, weighted towards the privileged. Mike's supreme skill was making explicit the implicitly known.

I had made organizing the conference crèche my specific area of responsibility, envisaging an exciting prefiguration of the socialist future; an interactive experience of beauty, play, ideas, happiness, fun and inflatables that children and teenagers would recall for ever. I have no idea what they remembered, but for me the day was stressful indeed. We had about eighty children registered and well over double that number turned up. The crèche was in a building some distance from the conference, so contact between the two sites in the pounding rain was difficult.

Along with Gloden Dallas and Hilary's sister, Tessa Wainwright, in the morning I looked out at what seemed like chaos. We quickly realized we had to abandon our careful plans and improvise. By mid-morning we were having to tell new arrivals we were full up; the reality was that we were spilling over. I ruefully reflected on how wrong we had been to assume parents would book in advance! Making such crucial requirements explicit was an organizational lesson I never forgot.

I had commandeered several teenagers to help, including the Bohannas' son John, then aged 14. They saved the day because the children loved hanging out with them and they also constituted vital lines of communication to the conference by braving the rain as runners. By the afternoon we had acquired more help. The musician Leon Rosselson sang for the children, the economist Alan Freeman arrived with a video, the artist James Swinson, organized football and basketball games.

Meanwhile, over in the main conference the workshops set up by people who had gone to the planning meetings were so large they floundered. Following the practice of Women's Liberation conferences, we had left space for extra spontaneous workshops. Nevertheless, complaints geysered in all directions: some groups felt excluded, others thought there were too many workshops. We had feared disruption from Trotskyists and Maoists, however they left us to stew in our own juice. Instead protests came from some socialist feminists, lesbians and gay men who felt their autonomy had been eclipsed. This was not at all what we had intended, but such criticisms coming from those we saw as the closest to us politically were exceedingly hard to counter.

During the final plenary Hilary battled womanfully to ensure some positive outcomes, but the Beyond was already sagging like a pie without an egg cup when what young John Bohanna described as 'that commotion at the end', put the kibosh on her efforts.[39] The energetic erupters were a little band of young men in black leather jackets, stiff with rectitude. The rumour was that they were from a mysterious new group called 'Class War'.

In writing *Beyond the Fragments* we had not anticipated how silencing debate can manifest itself in anarchical as well as Leninist forms. Nor had we foreseen how attempts to make horizontal connections might generate tensions amidst movements and grass-roots groups. People's fears of losing a hold on their own identities and issues were entangled with an anticipated threat to their existing, albeit limited, gains. These proved far more powerful than we had imagined.

Implicitly, we had assumed interconnections that had come to seem obvious to us were generally evident. But when a large number of people gathered this proved not to be universally the case. One of the South Wales tenants, Barbara Castle, exposed this particular knot succinctly, 'I felt your personal judgement and experiences actually should have been more "up-front". But maybe that's the essential contradiction your perception throws up.'[40]

In endeavouring to strengthen autonomous movements through links with others, inevitably we had left several blank spaces. The socialist feminist philosopher Kate Soper pointed to a significant gap in our reasoning; if a woman happened to go to a Rape Crisis Centre there was no *automatic* guarantee that she would make connections between sexism and capitalism or proceed to link feminism and socialism, it would depend very much on who was there to help her see these.[41]

Edward Thompson sent a postcard hoping the conference had gone well. But even I, who was generally optimistic, could see its implications had been somewhat murky. Afterwards I watched a very long uncut video a group had made of the event. It was noticeable how many participants in the workshops mumbled, interspersing everything they said with huge intakes of breath and the interpellation 'like'. By being so acutely tentative they detained whatever it was they were trying to say in an exasperating manner. It was a sobering audio-visual demonstration to me of my own recoil from being identified as a leader. Henceforth I told myself: 'Overcome reticence. Try to be clear. Don't mutter.'

It was reassuring that the conference had brought so many Fragments together, but our concern not to dominate others with our own propositions resulted in a paralysis. There had been many tussles within the women's movement over how to put forward ideas of what to do and initiate wider protest without depriving others of their contributions. We had evolved some rule of thumb ways around this over time, but we had no experience of how to transplant tacit understandings into another context.

Nevertheless, ideas did get out and there were unexpected spinoffs. An edition of the Merlin Press book appeared in the United States; complete or partial translations were to appear in Dutch, Spanish, Italian, German, Turkish and Japanese and we learned later that the book had influenced Brazilian exiles who would contribute to the formation of the Workers' Party.

I had compiled the names of the people and groups who

had attended the conference in Leeds, filing them in a box of cards, so we were able to call meetings around the country. Julia Meadows from the Women's Theatre Group nobly agreed to coordinate requests for information and several regional volunteers, including Joanna de Groot in York, came forward.[42] We funded the production and mail-out of the first *Beyond the Fragments Bulletin* (January 1981) from the profits of the conference. After that we charged for copies. These continued for several years, bubbling with ideas about socialism and suggestions for changing everyday life, thanks largely to the skills of Charles Foster, who also worked on *Hackney Peoples' Press*.

Meanwhile various local non-aligned socialist groups and centres went ahead and called meetings to plan joint action. One of the workshops on Socialist Education, led by Robin Blackburn from the *New Left Review* and Steve Haywood from the Publications Distribution Co-operative, resulted in the formation of the Socialist Society with the aim of connecting socialist theoretical work to the grass-roots expertise on specific social policies within the labour movement.[43]

In the autumn of 1980, John Bohanna (the elder) helped by Joan, produced an unusual bulletin for Ford's Halewood workers. Deftly reversing the normal pattern of left groups seeking trade unionists to support their newspapers, they invited the Trotskyists and Maoist groups to contribute along with the libertarian Marxists in Big Flame. Whereupon workers in the Labour Party and Communist Party also wanted to join in. 'The Halewood Christmas Special' duly appeared, its economic and political commentary accompanied by cartoons, poems and stories. It proved such a hit, 'demand far exceeded supply' and people were offering the dizzy sum of a £1 for a copy![44]

More formally, the Lucas Aerospace Workers' Plan for creating jobs by transferring skills was publicized through links with the Centre for Alternative Industrial and Technological Systems (CAITS) based at North East London Polytechnic. In 1980 CAITS published Jane Barker's Workers' Plans for

Better Health, which not only called for more health workers but extended the scope of socially useful work by outlining its implications for caring.[45] Shortly after the Fragments conference I reviewed Mike Cooley's book, *Architect or Bee? The Human /Technology Relationship* and Stanley Mitchell's translation for Penguin of Marianne Herzog's *From Hand to Mouth*.[46] I focused on Mike's awareness of workers' tacit understandings, his recognition of how being undervalued becomes internalized as a diminished sense of self-worth and his deep conviction of the transformatory impact of seeing 'the social results and usefulness' of one's labour.[47]

From Hand to Mouth was an account by Marianne Herzog of the lives of German women piece workers in an engineering factory, translated by Stanley Mitchell with an introduction by Sally Alexander. Unable to assert the skill in their work or to take collective action, Herzog documents how they survived through their imagination. Frau Winterfield dreams of owning an ice cream parlour and dwells on recipes for pastries and sundaes; Frau Lange drifts back through the sexual relationships she had before marriage. They create a fragile culture of mutual care, exchanging clothes and advice on children.

Herzog juxtaposes this with the explicit mutuality forged among French women workers who took part in the occupation of the Lip watchmaking factory in Besancon in 1973-4. She quotes 'Reine J.' recounting how 'the great friendship which arose out of the struggle is still alive'.[48] *From Hand to Mouth* showed how human beings require not simply fulfilling work and control over life and labour; our perceptions of self-worth, pleasurable imagining and loving friendship also intimate what might be.[49]

* * *

Ros Baxandall and Ellen Ross had arranged for me to be paid for several lectures in the US and towards the end of September, I departed on one of the cheap Laker flights from London to New York for a week.[50] Ailments dogged me when I did too much and I had not cast off the laryngitis. I sat slumped in the taxi from the airport, weary and looking forward to reaching Ros, but the cab driver who took me from the airport got lost. As we wound our way through Lower Manhattan, he explained he was from Haiti, so I enquired if he knew of the great rebel against slavery, Touissant L'Ouverture. Of course he did, and he had read CLR James's book *The Black Jacobins* about him too, which an English teacher had brought into his school. Declaring that I reminded him of this teacher, he turned off the meter and talked non-stop, with me grunting happily in reply.

We meandered through the winding streets, arriving exceedingly late at Ros' apartment at 2 Washington Square Village, one of the four tall blocks which made up the 'Village'. In Britain they would look impersonal, but in New York they assumed a homely feel amidst all the other skyscrapers. Ros had one large room and two smaller ones; their walls were lined with bookcases and each time I visited new exciting additions would have appeared. Through listening to Ros and reading the books on her shelves, over the years I learned about the history of American radical women, along with much else besides.

I was due to lecture in the US on the history of socialism and feminism and the women's liberation movement in Britain from 1969.[51] My first talk was at Ros' college, SUNY Old Westbury, which attracted both black and white working-class students. We picked up her close friend and fellow historian, Elizabeth (known as Liz) Ewen, on the drive out there. Both were inspirational teachers and good organizers, running the American Studies Program in complementary ways. Ros was demonstrative, impetuous and a passionate speaker, while Liz was strategically minded with a dry perspicacity. These contrasts, along with their shared tenacity, made them a powerful combination.

The following day Ellen Ross drove me to Sarah Lawrence, the private liberal arts college in Yonkers where she taught, regaling me with an illuminating account of the hidden dress codes for women teaching at various East Coast universities. As an oblivious Brit I tended to see Americans as uniformly casual and informal in style; Ellen's wryly funny account uncovered the complex nuances. Evidently a denim skirt, like the one she was wearing, was acceptable at Sarah Lawrence, but not at Harvard, and jeans were generally taboo for women college teachers. It was a revelatory introduction to the implicit boundaries hemming in American women who seemed so assertive and confident.

I went by bus to speak at Ithaca College and Cornell University, where a pioneering Women's Studies program had been started in the early 1970s. At Ithaca I met Zillah Eisenstein, whose edited collection *Capitalist Patriarchy and the Case for Socialist Feminism* (1979) had helped me think through the interconnections between male domination and capitalism.[52] Zillah was witty and sparky, as well as having an incisive grasp of political thought, and we bounced ideas together excitedly, walking through the campus in the sun. I returned to New York and Ros, cheerful, but tired.

* * *

Back in England the talks and meetings continued, but I could not rid myself of a persistent exhaustion. By mid-October I was in pain; again my doctor in Bethnal Green, Michael Leibson, decided I had an infection and gave me more antibiotics.[53] I had had a coil fitted in the 1970s and, aware that they could contribute to infections, decided to have it removed. The young man at the Marie Stopes Clinic tugged away but could not get it out. He told me to go to University College, so off I tottered. They removed it. I was due to have lunch with Tony Gould, the Books Editor from *New Society*. I had no way of reaching him to cancel our meeting and so I staggered on to Covent Garden. He was always full of interesting stories of books and authors, but this time I sat in dazed silence. Splashing out on a taxi, I flopped into bed at home and resumed work on the card index from the Beyond the Fragments conference.

Within a few days I became feverish, then a large lump swelled up by my hip. I was given more antibiotics, but I grew weaker and weaker until I could not lift a plate. In despair I wrote to Peter Huntingford, the gynaecologist who had delivered Will. When he examined me at Mile End Hospital, he explained I had endometritis and changed the antibiotics. He had been influenced by feminist writing on women's health and combined his medical skills with a committed empathy towards his patients. I began to feel better, my spirits rose, and I ascribed to Peter the mystical powers of a healer.[54]

By the end of November news that I was ill had circulated and convalescing turned into a veritable social whirl. On one particularly busy day Martin Stott came from Oxford, where he was arguing for alternative projects within the Labour Party; the historian of Jewish East End anarchism, Bill Fishman who, in the mid 1960s, had given me my first job teaching at Tower Hamlets College of Further Education, arrived and so did Liz Waugh. She and I had stalked the city streets in a Women's Liberation campaign to unionize night cleaners in the early 1970s.[55]

Another former leafleteer, Sally Alexander, made the journey a few days later from Pimlico with her young son, Daniel. 'Very nice day,' I wrote in my diary.[56] Indeed, it was such a nice day that I wrote a poem about it.

'Sally on Saturday'.

Two friends
sit on a Saturday
at the crossroads
with sons
playing with trains.
'I think it's our age,'
you said.

I'd thought
it was rather the times
we live in,
colliding my psyche

with
the state
of the nation.

We chat
of this one and that one,
sketching quick outlines
of what can be known
amidst interruptions.

You go out shopping
and return.
We search for tea –
and when you leave
anxious
because Daniel's cold
is making it hard for him to breathe,
I feel a loving sadness.

A Saturday spent
at the crossroads
without time
to journey between outlines.[57]

By early December I was back into the routines of daily living, recording in my diary that 'Kelly' came to stay the night on 5 December.[58] This was Kelly Barrie, the son of two artist friends, Mary Kelly and Ray Barrie. They had lived with Sally and her then partner, the Cambridge historian Gareth Stedman Jones, in the Alderney Street Collective in Pimlico, but had moved to Clapton. Kelly was older than Will, and being more worldly-wise about boy-stuff, took a dim view of Will's politically correct black and white dolls, after which the dolls, poor things, were to be dumped forever. Gender-bending socialist feminist mothering was rather more complicated in practice than we had anticipated.

Mary had helped to make the experimental film by the Berwick Street Film Collective, 'Nightcleaners', and had held innovatory exhibitions featuring women's work and motherhood, but in 1980 she and Ray were about as broke as Paul and I were. On one occasion Ray mentioned a recipe for a pie from potato peelings, which made our lentils look like wild hedonism.

Mary was sweetly charming on all matters to do with daily life and sons, but exceedingly principled about political art. When Ray had finished a painting of Paul's arms holding Will and feeding him with a bottle, Mary had said it was too romantic. Being a romantic, I thought it was powerfully moving, but kept quiet. Though I never fathomed the premises from which her elaborate conceptual approach derived, I considered that as a socialist feminist artist, Mary surely knew more than I did.

* * *

Towards the end of the year, I was doing a review of *In and Against the State* for *New Society*.[59] The book's authors, 'The London to Edinburgh Return Group' (they eschewed individual names) were associated with the Conference of Socialist Economists and included several socialist feminists.[60] The title brilliantly compressed a dilemma, which with the advent of Margaret Thatcher was looming large. How to defend existing social welfare, while exposing the biased assumptions and power ingrained within the state? I was split. I had a libertarian Marxist's suspicion of the capitalist state, but I was also a mother and comprehended the truth of a remark Sally Alexander had made in a discussion on welfare, 'But Sheila, women *need* the state'. I could see she was right, though the aloof control and coercion that often came with it made me ill at ease.[61]

For socialists and feminists in my generation the nature of the state was not an abstract issue, many of us worked within it and all of us were affected by it, for better or for worse. Contrary approaches had coexisted within Women's Liberation. In practice we had campaigned for legislative changes and for increased social provision, while resisting the sexism, racism and patronizing class assumptions embedded in state institutions.

Ours was not, of course, a recent quandary. Over the years reformist socialists, revolutionary followers of Marx and anarchists has raised warring flags. These had marked out a theoretical terrain and over time the slogans and dogma, hardened in isolation, had been used to bludgeon opponents. It seemed to me that each had carried off partial insights.

Optimistically, during the late 1970s I had come to think possibilities of overcoming the impasse over the state were emerging. Our defence of equal access to health care frequently had been accompanied by challenges to the hierarchical demarcations of authority within the structures and assumptions of the NHS, which, bizarrely, could still be headed by retired military men. I was also aware of innumerable attempts to connect the users of state services with rank-and-file workers and to parry authoritarianism within the state.

Moreover, a campaign for democracy was burrowing away in the Labour Party and Hilary was in close contact with trade unionists challenging Labour leaders' habit of obeisance to establishment prerogatives once in power. In November 1980, Trades Councils in Coventry, Newcastle, North Tyneside and Liverpool issued the *Workers' Inquiry into State Intervention,* which criticized the Labour Party's response to strikers during the 1970s.[62] Published by the Newcastle Centre for the Unemployed, this *Inquiry* aroused interest among various other Trades Councils, including Sheffield, Preston and Bristol.[63]

I remained unclear about how the harder edge of state power might be democratized. Black feminists were among those exposing the racist treatment of both immigrants and of young people from African, Afro-Caribbean and Asian families born in Britain. My own anti-statism had been viscerally reinforced by living in Hackney, where sections of the police were overtly racist and there had been several deaths in custody.

Yet I knew police attitudes and behaviour varied. I had also seen that police could be attacked with sudden violence themselves. In March, when I had gone to speak in Birmingham at Dorothy's seminar, while sitting in a café, I had seen a lone policeman hurled through the window by a group of young men of South Asian descent. As the glass smashed around me and the policeman lay near my feet, I sat, petrified and irresolute. I could imagine what terrible wrongs the incensed young men were revenging, yet the injured man was alone. For a fearful moment I thought I ought to stand up and try to defend him. Then, as more police arrived with remarkable alacrity, I started to worry about what they would do to their captives.

I had still been shaken when I reached Dorothy. But when I agonized over a cup of tea on the moral and political choices the incident raised, a tough-minded Dorothy had swept my ineffective scruples off the table by remarking with sparky, sardonic humour that she did not think 'middle-aged ladies could be expected to defend the police'. This had absolved me from cowardice, settled my angst about rescuing policemen and enabled me to deliver on 'The Relationship between Socialism and Feminism, 1880-1914'.[64] However, it also shredded my illusions of remaining forever young. I had just turned 37. Surely middle age could not begin quite so early!

The unease appears to have lingered as on 8 December I jotted in my diary 'wrote on passion (!)'.[65] There was a personal irony in my choice of topic, hence the exclamation mark. Paul and I were not getting on very well. We both were consumed with the effort of earning money, caring for Will and by differing types of activism. Moreover, my illness had made me anxious, angry and depressed. The joy of our loving had somehow shoved off. Neither of us knew how to summons it back.

On 9 December, I recorded, 'John Lennon shot'.[66] Of course, I did not know him, but he symbolized a questing spirit from the 1960s with which I had identified. His death hovered like a portent.

3

1981

I had invested £5 in a *Big Red Diary* for 1981. Its theme that year was 'Utopias': hence each week was strewn with inspiring historical examples. At the back were thirty-one reassuring pages with long lists of diverse contemporary groupings, outlets and publications seeking visionary change: Brixton Black Women's Group, Greenpeace, Sheba Feminist Publishers, Rank and File Teacher, *Achilles Heel, Cornwall Diggers' Newsletter, Saorsa* in Scotland. Alternative sustenance for body and mind was being proffered by Beano Wholefoods shop in Leeds and a host of radical bookshops like News from Nowhere in Liverpool, Preston's Fly in Amber, London's Gay's the Word and New Beacon Books, started by the Caribbean campaigning poet and intellectual John La Rose.[67]

The survival of these disparate alternatives testified that much had been accomplished and maintained. The values they espoused repudiated the depressing misconception that Margaret Thatcher's perspective was the only one conceivable. I was glad they all existed. But how an earth were they to act in concert? The Beyond the Fragments Conference had left me stumped.

In case readers were tempted to shelter complacently behind them, Aidan White's introduction to the diary detailed the government's cuts in health, welfare and education, amidst inflation and rising unemployment. He concluded, 'Life under the Tories is bad – and getting worse. but Labour must never be let off the hook for paving the way'.[68] This was true but sobering. Where then should we turn?

The inflation was dismally recognizable to me; rates for the articles and reviews I did remained low, and innumerable unpaid diversions kept arising. Moreover, I was guiltily aware that I was meant to be writing a book for Penguin on the women's movement. I had spent the advance several years ago and the manuscript kept being deferred.

My economic predicament was not helped by a fateful phone call from Raphael Samuel, the persuasive proponent of 'history from below'. For over a decade Raphael, and the History Workshops he started with his trade union students at Ruskin College in Oxford, had been vigorously encouraging radical 'histories from below' and chipping away at the impounding of the past by those at the top.[69] The large gatherings had sprouted the exploratory *History Workshop Journal* and Raphael wanted me to write up research I had done in the mid 1960s for my unfinished PhD on the responses of working-class students to University Extension courses during the late nineteenth and early twentieth centuries.

In the early 1980s this work seemed remote. But Raphael was attuned to an awakening interest in class and education. Peoples' History, Autobiography, or 'Lifetimes' groups' had appeared in London, Liverpool, Brighton, Bristol, Manchester, Newcastle and Aberdeen and in 1976 they had grouped together to form the Federation of Worker Writers and Community Publishers, known as 'the Fed'. By the early 1980s they were battling with the Arts Council for literary recognition.[70] Raphael's blandishments were ineluctable. I did do the article, and, when it appeared later in the year in the *History Workshop Journal*, I felt glad the aspirations of those adult students I had pursued through old newspapers and magazines were being aired at last.[71]

Another historical request had come from Faith Evans, who was then editorial director at the publishers Andre Deutsch. In 1979 we had corresponded over Ruth First and Ann Scott's biography of the South African writer Olive Schreiner and she now wanted me to write an introduction to a collection of Marx's daughters' letters, which she had translated and annotated.[72] My ears pricked up on hearing I would be paid £100.

When we met to talk it through on 17 March, Faith, and the poignancy and thoughtfulness of the letters between Eleanor, Laura and Jenny, lured me back into the late nineteenth century, a period I could almost imagine myself as living within.[73] I loved writing that introduction; I had long been fascinated not simply by Marx and his ideas, but the history of the Marx family. I empathized most of all with Eleanor, the defiant New Woman and socialist activist, but could also identify personally with Laura and Jenny's anxieties as mothers.[74]

Nevertheless, the Tory government was beginning to make my fascination with the past feel like a kind of indulgence. I knew too that I must find a longer-term solution to my own wobbly economic predicament. Amazingly, one was in the offing. I had been invited by the Women's Studies Department at the University of Amsterdam to fill a part-time professorial post for a year. I went to meet them briefly on 28 April, unsure what to expect.[75] I was welcomed by an interesting interdisciplinary group of feminist historians and social scientists and their impressive administrator, Jarti Notohadinegoro.

The post as visiting professor was for one day a week, but, because I was based in London, the thoughtful Dutch women had carefully added up the days, allowing time for me to prepare lectures and seminars at home and dividing my teaching at the University into blocks of time so I would not be away from Will too long. Accustomed to the rates for part-time adult education in Britain, I could hardly comprehend that I was to be paid £2,500. Indeed, it was so unbelievable that I wrote it down in the back of my *Big Red Diary* for 1981 '2 1/2 thous. + travel'.

Hearing that workers at Ford Amsterdam had occupied their factory, I was eager to visit so that I could report back to friends like John Bohanna and the Ford Combine Committee. Jarti Notohadinegoro volunteered to accompany me to it. If the trade unionists from the Ford's Participatory Committee were surprised by visitors from women's studies they did not reveal it. With a solemn scholarly gravitas, they took us with them to a meeting where Turkish immigrants spoke about being under stress because of continuing pressure to increase productivity. The elaborate arrangements for translating to and from Turkish and Dutch were impressive.

Boosted by the visit to Amsterdam, I intensified my efforts to earn money through freelance journalism. Sanguinely, I headed off to the offices of *Cosmopolitan* with a proposal inspired by the anarchist Colin Ward's book *The Child in the City*. Instead of a dangerous environment geared to cars, Colin argued for design that started from the needs of children.[76] Like the Lucas Aerospace Workers' Plan, he connected specific wrongs to a wider interrogation about how we lived. His book showed we did not just need childcare, or even adventure playgrounds, but a rethinking of the planning of urban spaces, public buildings and indeed the transport system.

Trying to fold a pushchair in the London Underground with one hand and grip Will with the other, while bags and bottles collapsed onto the floor, had taught me how moving through the city with a small child was very different from going about on your own. I could comprehend all too well the desperation of a young Afro-Caribbean mother I met on a bus in Hackney when she related her daily struggle on buses and tubes. She had to take one child to a nursery and another to a play group, then hasten from Hackney to Holborn by bus to work part-time in a café, retracing the whole procedure in reverse each day. I estimated that she lost at least five hours of life time every day. She was one among millions.

The article I did for *Cosmopolitan* was a scrappy mish mash and was rejected. Anyway, it was the wrong pitch; they were interested in modern career women's commutes not Afro-Caribbean working-class mothers. My unsuccessful bid for a popular media outlet did, however, stimulate a spate of scattered ideas about the design of the everyday. I became aware how dominance was monumentalized in buildings, how priorities were imprinted by the choice of routes and continually inscribed and reinforced by the selection of criteria through which peoples' time is valued. Also, I was beginning to reveal flickers of a belated green awareness, noting that lorries battering down inner city roads were contributing to air pollution and endorsing proposals for bicycles and walking, as well as improved public transport.[77]

Needless to say, there was no crèche at a meeting of Ford trade unionists at Halewood, when Will and I went to stay with John and Joan Bohanna in Liverpool that May.[78] Undaunted, John Bohanna, well drilled by Hilary in the personal and political, took Will off with him so I could have a rare lie in. John was laughing when they came home. Will had evidently sat quietly surveying the meeting, until suddenly a puzzled piercing four-year-old voice was heard from the back enquiring, 'Where are all the ladies?' Meetings for Will meant a crowd of women.

* * *

Having a child, combined with Margaret Thatcher's abrasive up-by-your-own-bootstraps policies, had forced me to focus on bread-and-butter issues. My numerous meetings now included discussions with socialist economists about the Alternative Economic Strategy (AES).[79] Confusingly, the AES seemed to shape shift, making it hard to grasp. Sometimes it manifested itself as a version of Keynesian proposals to stimulate growth, at others it emphasized altering the balance of resources and power by democratizing the state, which in Britain was creaking with assumed privilege. A vagueness enfolded implementation. Even the apparently moderate propositions from the Labour left for a more egalitarian approach to growth were clearly going to face enormous political and economic obstacles.

Disagreements intensified. The differing guises of the AES were denounced from various perspectives as insufficiently revolutionary, as too top down and for assuming that the main agents of change were to be the male militants who spearheaded the organized trade union movement. I inclined to the socialist feminist economists and political thinkers who had examined women's paid work and mothering, some of whom were arguing that extending the social resources going into caring should be the objective of policy, rather than increasing productivity. This represented not only a challenge to the purposes of an economic alternative, it subverted the assumptions prevailing in economic theory.

When the socialist feminist journalist from the *New Statesman* Anna Coote spoke on an economy geared to care, I noticed how quickly a young Lucas worker from Burnley picked up on the idea. Was he a father, I wondered? Or was he open to the idea because the Lucas workers had developed socially useful prototypes and, in the process, recast customary mindsets. I was shocked when the obdurate Lucas management, apparently threatened by the conversion of arms to hobcarts, sacked Mike Cooley.[80] Now even strong groups of trade unionists were vulnerable. Something more was evidently needed.

During May, the Peoples' March for Jobs had arrived in London. The recently elected left Labour councillors at the Greater London Council (GLC) had gone to greet them as they entered the city, putting them up in County Hall. The welcome from the left councillors had not only been a statement of respect and solidarity, it was a symbolic declaration of intent. Led by Ken Livingstone, who possessed an acute awareness of how power was held and wielded in British society, they were resolved to show from the start that this was Labour local government with a difference, one that intended to shift the axes of entitlement to public resources.

On 10 June, Michael Ward, the GLC councillor responsible for economic policy, came to speak on 'Jobs and Workers' Plans' in Hackney's Labour and Trades Hall. I had been to many rather fusty meetings there, but my attention was aroused when Michael, a labour historian, as well as a politician, told us how they had searched through old records at County Hall and discovered not only that the GLC had the legal power to fund social provision but also held long neglected public assets. Amazingly, Londoners, collectively through the municipality, owned both valuable land and unused buildings. He then went on to describe how he and a group of councillors had got in a van and set off to examine all this unrealized social wealth. They wanted to activate their findings by enabling them to serve needs. That van trip was at once ingeniously uncustomary and such an obvious thing to do. It proved far reaching.[81]

In July I met Michael again at a meeting on the GLC where he spoke about developing economic policy by involving Londoners. Michael was familiar with discussions at the conferences of the Institute for Workers' Control on promoting direct links with trade unionists and communities and was applying these ideas to local government.[82]

This time he shared the platform with a young GLC councillor, Valerie Wise. Like Michael, Valerie was interested in the wider implications of the Lucas Plan.[83] Her mother, Audrey, had imparted her commitment to both women's emancipation and socially useful production to her daughter. Still in her early twenties, Valerie Wise was soon to go on to form the GLC's Women's Committee, an initiative that was to be adopted in other cities.[84] Listening to her I understood how important London-wide action could be for women's equality at work and for the struggling under-funded community childcare projects like Market Nursery. I saw too that instead of just talking of an alternative economics in the hope of influencing Labour, through the GLC Michael and Valerie could make changes happen.

I had left the Labour Party during the Vietnam war in the late 1960s. In the seventies, through the women's movement, I had collaborated with Labour women in campaigns, but while I admired several of them, especially Audrey Wise, I had stayed non-aligned. By the early 1980s promising shifts were evident nationally within Labour. Michael Foot had been elected leader and Tony Benn had become convinced of the importance of workers' plans. The GLC councillors helped me to make up my mind. Like many other fragmented socialists, I rejoined the Labour Party.

Even so, I still hankered for ecstasy and anarchical utopias, penning the verses of 'Reclaim the Moon'.

Well we the wise ones
have disowned the moon,
to spoon
in June
is not our tune.

And as for Hecate's pale spell,
the healing glade
or loving dell,
they are the patriarchal sell,
just signs and symbols of our plight.
So nymphs take flight,
abandon myth,
objective science is the tryst
for feminist materialists.

And yet, and yet and yet and yet,
there is the odd moment of regret.
This mumbo-jumbo moonish stuff
Is ideologically pretty tough.

Or do I lapse
to think that p'raps
the moon and love
are not all guff.
If lapse I do
then I should rue
this world we hew.

Let us lay claim
to our birthright,
liberty, love
and delight. [85]

* * *

In a flash of utopia that summer we had decided that our next Beyond the Fragments meeting would take the form of a creative weekend close to nature. More specifically, the plan was to camp at the home of Hilary and the radical philosopher Roy Bhaskar in Herefordshire.[86] Paul, having been a Queen's Scout and more into the salutary aspects of alternative outdoor lifestyles than I was, liked this proposal. In 1974 we had spent a damp holiday in Cornwall in a plastic tube which condensed our breath and in 1976, when pregnant, I had dodged wandering bears by camping with him at Yosemite National Park.

As Paul expertly hammered tent pegs into the lawn, I milled around with Will, trying to look supportive but feeling secretly envious of Joan Bohanna who was settled in one of the bedrooms. Paul volunteered to cook on the first evening and had arrived prepared with nutritious bulgur wheat. Joan's face, usually alive with mirth, fell at the first mouthful. Protesting vehemently, she departed in haste to a nearby fish and chip shop and returned in triumph laughing about 'proper food'.

Tent life and bulgur wheat might not be everyone's utopia, but an unintended consequence was that Joan met Alan Hayling, who Paul and I knew from the radical film group, Newsreel. In 1976 he had started a manual job at Ford and was active in the workers' combine there. The favourable report she took back to John helped to overcome the North-South wariness between the Ford plants.

After the camp we headed for Whitby listening to reports on the car radio of violent conflicts between young black people and the police. Toxteth, an area in Liverpool with extremely high unemployment, had erupted and within a few days Hackney followed. The police poured out of coaches and vans and hit out wildly. Charles Foster, reporting for *Hackney People's Press*, was struck on the head with a police truncheon in the doorway of the Rio cinema. It was one among many clashes in Britain that summer.

Anger about poverty, poor housing and lack of opportunity had been brewing for several years among both white and black teenagers. The severity of the Thatcher government's monetarist policies intensified this. The police were also using their powers to stop, search and arrest intensively. Violence had always been likely in their dealings with young working-class men and this was greatly magnified by a pervasive racism in the police force. Resentment against the impact of 'swamping' by large numbers of police in inner city areas, provoked a series of uprisings. Many people in black communities had come to the shocking realization that the law was biased and that neither the media nor the police would defend them.

People of Afro-Caribbean, African and Asian descent were in physical danger too from racists and from organized groups of fascists; several deaths occurred, including a horrifying petrol bomb attack on 1 July in Walthamstow, London which killed a mother and her four children. When twelve members of the Bradford United Black Youth League went on trial for making petrol bombs in case the fascists attacked their neighbourhoods they were accused of conspiracy. They defended themselves with reason and passion; the jury acquitted them on the grounds of legitimate self-defence.[87]

Asian and Afro-Caribbean women active in anti-racist and black feminist groups, began to organize legal and financial support for those who were arrested on the streets, including children who were being taken forcibly into care.[88] When Paul and I returned to Hackney, outraged parents at the nursery who had not been previously involved in organizing against racism were helping to form defence committees for young people who had been arrested. Rumours were rife. Law-abiding black and white working-class mothers at Will's nursery assured me the rioters had all come up from Brixton, echoing claims of troublemakers coming from elsewhere that I had come across in eighteenth century records of the French revolution.

The mood of disaffected rage had contributed to the revival of a new, mainly white, skinhead subculture. Inclined to street risings, they, too, did not love the police. Friendships and music could create bonds with black and Asian youth, though others were racist and sympathetic to the extreme right. One day on the underground I found myself surrounded by a group who were much taller than the skinhead apprentices I had taught in East London during the 1960s. They had enormous boots and their leather jackets were elaborately bedecked with studs and chains. Suppressing a flicker of apprehension, I hailed them by telling them about their Stepney forebears. They listened with respectful interest.

Being an historian can be handy for making comparisons. But neither my research as a historian or my own experience of politics had prepared me for the direct, desperate confrontations against the state in Britain that summer.

* * *

In August I flew with Will to Athens, invited for a holiday by Costoula, Eleni and Mimi. Athens lacked London's municipal parks and the green gardens around houses were being devoured by new tall apartments. I used to walk with Will to one precious park and sit in front of a large tree to watch streams of ants going busily up and down, wondering how they coordinated.

My friends announced with excitement that they had found the perfect holiday refuge, a small island called Koufonisi, formed by an extinct volcano. The previous year they had met two brothers called 'Mavros' (Black) there. They were building workers in Athens in the winter, but during the summer they would return home to Koufonisi to run a café by a beautiful white beach. Giving me a letter for the brothers, they wrote some basic Greek words on a card for me.

Will and I departed on a slow boat, settling ourselves on two green slatted wooden seats in third class. We called at many islands. Night fell and the waves became higher. I examined the back of our seats, there were no safety jackets. Will slept but I could not. I felt sick and went on deck, the boat was lurching wildly. I was too ignorant to feel fear.

After twenty-four hours we scrambled ashore at the port in Koufonisi where a man with wild grey hair on a tractor awaited visitors. Weary but relieved, I waved my letter, saying 'Mavros,

Mavros'. He beamed and tucked it away. Off we bumped on his trailer. He deposited us at an isolated café where we sat and waited for what I thought was to be our turn. It never came. When all the other Greek guests had been shown to a room, Will began to urge me, 'Ask Mum, ask'.

But how? Dizzy with the heat, I tried in English, explaining I had given a letter to the man on the tractor from my Greek friends who had booked us a room. This was met with incomprehension and much shaking of heads. No room. The last vestige of organized-mother-abroad crumbled as a tear made a rivulet through the suntan lotion on my cheek. The Greek building worker-cum-waiter, gave me a concentrated look, then beckoned and shrugging off my thanks, led us to a small white concrete structure containing two beds. I would later learn he had given us his room.

The kind twinkly woman cook befriended us. She approved of my card full of Greek words and of Will, especially when he started to pick up some Greek. Whenever she could, she put aside one of her few eggs for him, so he could have it with chips; otherwise he lived off feta cheese and salad. I swam and he splashed in the waves.

After about ten days a terrible affliction struck the café, for which the waiters blamed campers in the surrounding woods. Thankfully Will never caught it, playing with his tiny toy soldiers on the floor while I lay in bed with a fever completely unable to move. When I recovered, I had lost track of time.

It was not until Eleni Varikas accompanied by Mimi Votsis and her family arrived that I learned the café owners and the elderly man on the tractor were all called 'Mavros'. Unable to read, our driver had sought help in deciphering its contents, only to be bemused why unknown people in Athens were sending him an English mother and child. The Greeks all laughed mightily as the enigma was unravelled. And I watched the man who had given up his room dancing in a circle with gratitude; £60 for three weeks board in Koufonisi had been a good bargain, regardless of scares and fever.

To my relief the boat to Athens stopped less frequently than on our outgoing journey and the sea was calm. At one island men were herding cattle on to another boat, when a huge dark brown bull made a bid for freedom, racing along the sand and up over a slight incline covered in scraggy grass. A man lassoed it, tugging desperately. When it seemed as if he would be dragged along through the brush, another ran to join him and they managed to pull it towards the line of docile cows mounting the plank, skilfully manœuvring the wild creature behind a cow. It promptly abandoned escape. I was amazed both by the swiftness of the men's reaction and the dramatic transformation in the bull's behaviour at the smell and touch of the cow.

I returned with a small piece of ancient pumice stone from Koufonisi; whenever I held it I would vividly recall those weeks in Greece. But a remote island alone with a young child had been too adventurous; ever afterwards I opted for package holidays or the homes of friends.

* * *

The National Child Care Campaign Conference, held in Loughborough that September felt like a breakthrough. All those arguments about the state appeared to have settled themselves into a sensible consensus.[89] In place of the absolute dichotomy between state provision and the community nurseries set up and run by local groups, we now had a broad campaign that coupled the democratization of state provision with a recognition that community projects for children also required funding from public resources.

Similar connections were being made in different contexts. Hilary proposed that parents' and workers' active combinations in nurseries could be equally relevant for patients in the NHS and for those claimants confronting the Department of Health and Social Security.[90] In September 1981, inspired by the Lucas workers, she helped a group of trade union combine committees and Trades Councils to produce a declaration called 'Popular Planning for Social Need'. This rejected 'competitive success as the objective of industrial reconstruction'. It argued instead for linking 'the social needs still unmet as a result of the rundown of public services with the resources (particularly human resources) of the manufacturing, energy and construction industries'.[91]

Other feminists were recasting women's sphere while engaging with areas of policy which had been a male domain. Aware that women as service workers as well as carers in the home were serving human needs, Ursula Huws, who worked in the Leeds Trade Union and Community Resource Information Centre, extended the scope of skill beyond manufacturing production into daily life at home. She also linked feminist discussion of information technology to the critiques of bias in the design of both medical and military technology.[92]

We held a Beyond the Fragments fringe meeting at the Labour Party Conference in Brighton in October 1981 with an all-woman panel which attracted an audience of around a hundred people. The revival of anti-nuclear agitation was bringing the democratization of military strategy to the fore, and Meg Beresford, from the Campaign for Nuclear Disarmament and European Nuclear Disarmament, shared the platform with myself, Jean McCrindle and Audrey Wise, no longer a Labour MP, but a feisty member of Labour's National Executive Committee.[93]

Alternatives were coming out of my ears that autumn. On 18 October Hilary and I spoke at the conference on 'Alternative Strategies for the Labour Movement' organized jointly by Beyond the Fragments, along with members of the Socialist Economists Conference. It aimed to connect theory and 'experience of struggles'.[94] I saw the importance of formulating an opposing socialist economic strategy and did not deny the need for certain forms of state intervention from the centre. What I could not work out was how these might interact with 'the decentralized release of initiative and imagination' which could make transformative moves towards socialism. I feared the rise of another 'set of planners designing our lives in their wisdom from on top again'.[95]

The words of two speakers stayed with me: the socialist environmentalist Victor Anderson queried growth as an overarching aim and Anna Coote, from the *New Statesman*, argued that improving how we cared as a society for children should be a central concern.[96] Both perspectives disrupted how 'economics' was usually construed.

Over the summer I had been talking with a member of Hackney Trades Council's women's sub-committee, Betsy Brewer, and with Jeannette Mitchell, who was involved in both the Politics of Health and the In and Against the State groups. Betsy and I decided to co-ordinate a Hackney Workers' Educational Association (WEA) class at Centerprise, the radical bookshop in Kingsland Road, bringing together ideas and projects for 'Alternatives'. Beginning in autumn 1981, these continued for a second term in January 1982.

The speakers included Jeannette Mitchell on *In and Against the State*, Anna Coote on why caring for children should be at the core of economic and social policy and Mike Cooley on Technology and Science.[97] Alternative approaches to work, health, food and culture all featured, but the two hot issues proved to be transport and energy.[98] The GLC had reduced fares by a third on public transport but faced a legal case from the Conservative Bromley Council which threatened to reverse the cut, while energy loomed large nationally partly because of the strength of the revived anti-nuclear movement along with the growth of environmental awareness.

From Halifax Gloden Dallas reported in the Fragments Bulletin that hundreds had joined European Nuclear Disarmament in Calderdale and 250 of them had gone to the 1981 London CND march on 24 October.[99] That October demonstration was estimated at a quarter of a million strong. Two veterans from CND in the 1950s and 1960s, Michael Foot, leader of the Labour Party and Tony Benn, who had narrowly missed becoming his deputy, spoke to the crowd. So did a new public voice, Ann Pettitt, one of the first contingent of women who had walked in protest to the Greenham military base.[100]

The resolve of the women who took direct action at Greenham by camping around its perimeter fence year after year raised awareness with their bodies, not simply with words. At the same time the feminist and socialist Mary Kaldor was engaging with the existing political structures, tackling the international arms industry and the complex political and technological machinery that sustained it.

* * *

At the end of the month, I went to Toronto to lecture on 'Women, Power and Consciousness' for a large Women's Studies Conference at the University of Toronto. The topic was much on my mind, but exceedingly hard for me to summarize. I wrestled with it, shaking and stretching ideas as I went along, elaborating on how women's movements had sought 'to break down concentrated forms of power' and to 'redistribute power among the powerless'.[101] I saw both impulses as arising from specific approaches to politics rather than as innate to womankind.

I rejected assumptions that women were somehow biologically wired for egalitarianism, co-operation and nurture, along with the opposite stereotype of the mythic all-conquering Amazon, because I regarded both as restrictive dead ends.[102] In an interview, Simone de Beauvoir had warned of the dangers of enclosing ourselves in our 'difference' and her words had stayed with me.

In agreement with the American feminist Joan Kelly, I thought we should aim to be equally valued within social existence. This meant changing relationships between the sexes *and* challenging other forms of domination. Both aspects would mean 'a prolonged contest for power' and require devising 'practical alternative strategies' along the way. However, I stressed the significance of the multiple sites of power that feminists had already set out to confront.[103]

This kind of combined resistance was under pressure. As it was becoming harder to make radical social changes, some feminists I knew were focusing on inner feelings; therapy groups, spirituality and diverse forms of cultural expression. Others were concentrating on bringing feminist perspectives into a wider left endeavour to defend trade union gains at work and maintain collective alternatives in communities around childcare, health, the environment, legal defence, bookshops or literacy schemes.

I argued that both wings were contesting prevailing values implicitly by demonstrating that personal *and* economic and social alternatives were needed by women and by people within other oppressed groups.[104] It was vital that they did not become detached from each other so that the transformatory impulse which had characterized women's liberation in the early 1970s could acquire new resonances. Somehow, we had to enable those realizations arising from differing types of resistance to gain strength through mutual exchange.[105]

I was busy in those five days in Canada, meeting socialist feminists, doing interviews on the radio and lecturing around Toronto, not simply on women and power in general, but more specifically on the rise of Margaret Thatcher and on the British women's movement and working-class women.[106] I found a more concerted left and socialist feminist movement in Ontario than in Britain and was moved by Canadian radicals' interest in *Beyond the Fragments*. It was the beginning of a lasting interconnection. They were generous with their strength when we in Britain were struggling.

I flew from Toronto to New York where I stayed once again with Ros Baxandall in her flat perched on the 11th floor of the university housing block in Washington Square Village. While I was there Ros showed me an article by Barbara Ehrenreich and Annette Fuentes, 'Life on the Global Assembly Line', published in the January issue of the feminist *Ms* magazine. She also introduced me to Annette, who was just beginning her journalistic career. Our meeting and that revelatory article prompted me to learn more about the international exploitation of women workers in poor countries. I had met socialist feminists in Britain and in Canada who were focusing on 'Women and

Development', and I began to wonder how their work related to the exploitation of women on the global assembly lines.

The stringencies of the Thatcher years made me increasingly dependent on other countries for survival; though this put me under pressure, it also meant I benefited from exposure to perspectives outside Britain. As my own country moved to the right these international links became more and more crucial, personally as well as politically.

* * *

In 1979 and 1980 it had seemed that a new kind of non-aligned movement might emerge. Instead, by the end of 1981, the Beyond the Fragments conference had contributed to an extended left network with multitudinous offshoots. I was helping Charles Foster with the production of the Bulletins, which despite their small and slender format, were packed with information and ambitious propositions. No. 1, called 'Life After Leeds', dated January 1981, reported on the spate of meetings and conferences springing out of the conference. No. 2, produced in June 1981, included me struggling with 'A New Kind of Socialism' and Dave Feickert on 'Liberating Time and Energy' through new technology. Given our bustling agenda, his title was somewhat ironic.[107]

The Wednesday WEA class on alternatives at Centerprise bookshop brought me into contact with groups and organizations connecting specific forms of agitation with a wider radical vision, such as the Hackney Law Centre, the British Society for Social Responsibility in Science and the Socialist Environment and Resources Association (SERA). Inspired by people from these and by a friend, Dave Welsh, a worker on the underground who produced the rank-and-file magazine *Close Encounters on the District Line*, I became involved in planning a conference on 'alternative ground floor plans for London'.[108]

The 'ground floor' image came from an old London tenants' organizer called Bert Scrivener, who had been a mainstay of the Agit Prop silk screeners at Camden Poster Workshop in the late 1960s.[109] Borrowing too from William Morris, we

called the conference, 'London As It Might Be'. The idea was
for community and trade union activists to work through the
problems and possibilities of London as a place to live, work,
grow and learn.

* * *

Despite being preoccupied with so many 'might bes', when
Tony Gould asked me to write a review for *New Society* of a
magnificent book, *Käthe Kollwitz: Graphics Posters Drawings*
(1981), I agreed.[110] The combination of starkness and compassion
in Kollwitz's art had impressed me since I had first seen them
in a 1960s exhibition and in 1980s Britain they had assumed a
new pertinence politically. But it was her self-portraits depicting
aging that most affected me by reawakening buried grief.

I wrote 'Loss' around this time:

'Think back,'
my mother said, –
'What was it
you were doing?'

'Think back',
my mother said, –
'When you lost
it.'

Think back
when I lost …
'Think back',
my mother said,
'To what it was'.

Was I doing
was I doing
what it was.

What is loss?
what was ...
my mother said

what was
in my head
is loss.

Think back.

What was
my mother
doing
dead?[111]

Towards the end of 1981, Ursula Owen from the feminist
publishers Virago suggested I should put together a collection
of my writings. We had become friendly in women's liberation
during the early 1970s and Ursula was aware how much had
vanished from view. During 1982 we would go through my
carrier bags sitting in the cellar, stuffed with articles and poems,
to produce *Dreams and Dilemmas* (1983). I put 'Loss', written
in autumn 1981 about my mother's death in 1965, at the front.

4

1982

At the beginning of 1982 Paul told me our relationship was over. On 14 January, I wrote in my diary, 'Paul ending' and the following day, 'realise Paul ending'.[112] That realization would take a great deal longer to take root, for it required a reorientation at the nub of my existence. I had perceived how our love was being hollowed out under the pressure of our circumstances and sensed that he was pulling away from me. However, I had been so sure of my love for Paul and of our decision to have a child that I was heedless of the force of *his* inner emotions. Theoretically, I continued to believe in freedom in love, yet I had been hanging on to him with the desperation that accompanies that semi-conscious moment of awakening after a nightmare of imminent extinction. Now he had met someone he really wanted to be with and we were no longer together sexually.

Otherwise, though, we were together. For nearly a year we would continue to live in the same house because both of us dreaded upsetting Will. This may well have resulted in even more confusion for a puzzled five year old. On one occasion when Paul was away, Will discovered a man with whom I formed a brief relationship. When Paul returned, he remarked sagaciously, 'Dad, you know Mum, she's got married'.

Various friends wrote to commiserate. But Ros, whose relationship with her son's father, Lee Baxandall, had broken up in the late 1970s, took a more abrasive approach. After receiving 'a gloomy Paul letter' she responded,

On Paul, & I hope this doesn't sound harsh. You, I think, became dependent on him. Some of it is inevitable a child, no other men around, but I think dependence is a burden on men & relationships & leads to guilt in the man, jealousy in woman – or at least it works this way in me & makes me real afraid after Lee of having a monogamous type relationship, although I have longings for it. Men can't take it for good and bad reasons.[113]

While I could see outer factors contributing to our break-up, I never fully comprehended the inner ones, apart from an intimation that Paul needed to grow away from me in order to find himself. Ostensibly I was not particularly dependent upon him, but Ros had spotted the concealed, intangible trope of my need. Dorothy Thompson surprised me too, reflecting thoughtfully, 'Of course women of your generation are asking entirely new things of men in your relationships'.

As disbelief faded, the pain hit. I swabbed it by keeping on doing what I was accustomed to doing. On 17 January I wrote a review of a biography of Ellen Wilkinson, the red-haired independent woman who had supported hunger marchers, become a Labour minister and was mysteriously attracted to Herbert Morrison.[114] A few days later I went to listen to Sue Finch, one of the founders of Market Nursery, talk at the Workers' Educational Association 'Alternatives' class in Centerprise on 'Community controlled Child Care'.[115]

More meetings were in the offing after Lords Wilberforce, Diplock and Scarman upheld Bromley Council's appeal against the GLC's reduction in bus and tube fares. Lynne Segal and James Swinson, who had shared a squat with Paul in Brixton, bundled me off, one on each arm, to the Fares Fair meetings. These excursions with them helped to bring me back into an external realm and stopped me from dissolving into my own grief. Our cheers for the GLC hit the roof, but could not alter the fares increase, though the innovatory travel cards survived. The GLC's thwarted efforts nevertheless aroused an awareness that changes for the better *could* be made in the conditions of daily life. This most subversive of messages was getting through. I had lived in Hackney since 1964 but had never before witnessed queues at the bus stops bearing placards and stickers for a radical cause.

Not only were passengers disgruntled. Bus workers had been hit by privatization. OPO (One Person Operation) meant they had to drive and issue tickets without a conductor. When a group of workers in Leeds alerted Dave Feickert and Marina Lewycka, who had helped to organize the Fragments conference, to the resulting stress, they prompted Marina to speculate what kind of socialism could make both workers and passengers happy, while inducing buses to turn up on time.[116]

Convinced that moving around should be freely available to all, a group of us in Hackney hired a bus and, with the help of a sympathetic socialist bus driver, collected amazed passengers and delivered them to their destinations without fares. The mood became jovial and festive, turning into an unstoned Magical Mystery Tour without any Beatles.

Radical imagining was an invaluable antidote to gloom. Marc Karlin, a close friend who had lived in our communal house in the 1970s, was making a documentary commissioned by the BBC called *For Memory* with the screenwriter Don Macpherson. It explored how heritage constructed and preserved what was remembered and how unprotected memories were cast aside and thus endangered.[117] Marc would mull over the ideas behind his films with friends. I used to enjoy these long conversations about imponderables in which he sifted through thoughts and took off into the stratosphere. His films approached themes from unexpected angles, weaving slow, complex kinetic tapestries. He finished *For Memory* in 1982, only for it to be shelved and forgotten by the BBC until 1986. From the late 1970s it was becoming harder and harder for left film makers to get their work onto the BBC. Some went to Hollywood, while others, including Marc, began campaigning for an independent channel.

* * *

From the end of February, references appear in my diary to meetings at the Greater London Council and on Tuesday 2 March I note attending a lengthy employment planning meeting between two and five in the afternoon.[118] While all the publicity surrounding the conflict over fares was raging, Michael Ward, in collaboration with Valerie Wise, had contrived to form a small GLC group to research a London-based alternative economic strategy.

Sharply critical of Wandsworth Council's trial run of the monetarist policies which Margaret Thatcher had adopted nationally, Michael was resolved to reorientate London's ailing economy through the GLC's brief to serve the welfare of Londoners. He drew on his historical knowledge of municipal socialism and the Fabians' attention to administrative detail, along with the more recent example of Italy's Red Bologna. Its left local council had combined elected and direct democracy, putting radical measures, such as free mobility and the provision of educational courses for low-paid workers like cleaners, on their agenda.[119] The aim was to involve Londoners in developing an alternative London Industrial Strategy (LIS) and the Industry and Employment Committee was set up to consider proposals and help them to materialize. In 1982 the GLC provided resources for a Greater London Enterprise Board (GLEB) with funds that could be invested in firms and co-operatives.

When Valerie Wise was first elected as a GLC councillor for Battersea South she found the ethos of County Hall both challenging and exciting. Ideas of extending socially useful production, participatory democracy and reshaping the state all made sense to her, yet she had remained watchful because she was aware how women's specific needs and perspectives could be overlooked. During 1981 she had gathered a women's advisory group together and in spring 1982 this led to the creation of the innovatory Women's Committee.[120] Interacting with all the GLC's work, it funded much needed projects and generated awareness of the economic and social needs of women in London.[121]

Robin Murray, who I knew from the May Day Manifesto Group's attempt at left unity in the late 1960s, had been appointed Chief Economic Adviser at the GLC. He applied a wide range of understandings he had gained as an economist at the Institute of Development Studies *and* as a community activist in Brighton's QueenSpark. Initially they had published a series of working-class memoirs, but as the cuts began to hit locally, they had devised a local alternative plan which combined economic and social analysis with personal testimonies.[122] Robin's position at the GLC enabled him to develop his approach on a London-wide basis. His intellectual enthusiasm was infectious; he would immerse himself in details and then surface with some illuminating insight in great sweeps of excitement. He was able to theorize specific circumstances into a series of interconnecting, practicable utopias and his charismatic confidence could make what seemed impossible, possible.

The lessons of the Lucas Aerospace Workers' Plan were brought directly into the GLC's economic policy by Mike Cooley, the design engineer who became the GLC's Technology Director and founded the Greater London Enterprise Board (GLEB). Sacked by Lucas, Mike contributed his knowledge of human-centred technology, along with his profound comprehension of the social potential of workers' skills.[123]

Hilary, as the Deputy Economic Policy Adviser, carried into County Hall her socialist feminism and a commitment to participatory democracy, gained partly through working with shop stewards.[124] Aware of the theoretical debates around the differing interpretations of alternative economic strategies, she also grasped the extended ramifications of the Lucas Workers' Plan in showing the latent power released through combining individuals' tacit skills. The amalgam she configured, 'Popular Planning to meet social need', thus had its roots in her own experiences in the women's movement and a sustained collaboration with trade unionists.[125] The Popular Planning Unit she headed was an integral part of the broader Economic Policy Unit and both were linked to the GLC's Industry and Employment Committee.

On 28 April Hilary took me to Romford to meet women clothing workers who had formed a co-op they called 'Poco' to make children's clothes.[126] When I met them, they were struggling with a divisive problem, for they were ruefully aware that they could not make their co-op viable if they had to provide childcare. On the way back Hilary and I tried to think through the implications of this for the London Industrial Strategy (LIS). She was in touch with several women at County Hall who, like Valerie, wanted caring for children to figure in the economic strategy and I began going to meet with them. The slogan 'Jobs from Child Care' emerged, encompassing the need both for wider provision and improved opportunities for a range of childcare workers. This link between employment and social need was a significant advance. But I was conscious something was missing.

Becoming a mother had made me understand that childcare was certainly partly material labour, but observing so intimately the intricacies of a child coming to awareness made this equally a labour of love. My socialism was rooted in the nurture of 'human life and growth' as well as 'artistry in making'.[127] Yet I struggled to compress this doubled vision in a succinct slogan that moved from what was into what could be.

* * *

Historical memory, economic strategizing and re-envisioning socialism restored and strengthened me personally as well as politically, but the decisive salve became my work in Amsterdam. My first session as a visiting professor there began in late March and the second one early in May.[128] Being in the company of people who did not share my past brought a welcome sense of release. The attentive, internationally minded students and teachers in Women's Studies not only listened to lectures in English, they critiqued and complemented what I had learned through the women's movement with their ideas. And the historical lectures I gave on campaigns in Britain for childcare, birth control and abortion, along with theoretical feminist debates on motherhood, the state, democracy and utopias, enabled me to clarify ideas that had been milling around in my head over the last few years.[129]

Moreover, I was able at last to focus on how to structure that long-delayed manuscript on women's liberation in Britain commissioned by Penguin back in the 1970s. I wanted to tease out how concepts had developed 'in movement' in an effort to reveal dynamically how thoughts are conceived and disseminated through social action.[130]

The mirthful Dutch feminists restored me emotionally too. I was enveloped in friendliness. They pedalled me along, sitting side-saddle on the back of their bicycles, down narrow tracks by the water, waiting patiently while I searched for quaint bargains in a market. They took me into cafés serving delicious coffee and cakes where tall and graceful ferns in enormous pots melded with the green, fawn and yellow décor. I seemed to have been wafted into an idyll with time and space for cycling, reciprocal relationships and calm well-being.

Of course, this was not the only Amsterdam. As I wrote my lectures in the hotel room at night, the frantic screams of a sex worker, interspersed with loud altercations between the women or with their clients and pimps resounded from the street below. Grim reality intruded again on 7 April when I went to visit Bhasker Vashee at the Transnational Institute and he enquired, 'Did you know your country was at war Sheila?' I had not seen any English newspapers for over a week and listened in shock when he told me of the conflict with Argentina over the Falklands.

I had first met Bhasker in the late 1960s through a friend, Vinay Chand, who had studied with him at the London School of Economics (LSE).[131] As a young anti-colonial activist, Bhasker had been deported from what was then 'Rhodesia' and, once in London, took a part in student militancy at LSE. Subsequently one of the founders of the radical Counter Information Service (CIS), he was doing similar research on a global basis at the Transnational Institute along with Mary Kaldor, the END strategist.

During May the women's studies group decided to invite me for a second academic year. I was chuffed they thought I had done a good job and delighted that Jarti Notohadinegoro and I could continue to meet. Jarti operated informally as a kind of diplomat on behalf of Women's Studies in the University. Though overtly a benign tolerance appeared to rule, the interdisciplinary experimental approaches to knowledge and the links to a feminist social movement meant that some of the more conservative male academics were apt to view its doings askance. Jarti artfully established crucial channels of communication within the structures of the university. I speculated that her perceptive intelligence, combined with her dazzling but unselfconscious loveliness no doubt disarmed much potential opposition. Jarti emanated a deep radiance which effortlessly transmitted courage.

As she related to me the circumstance of her birth in German-occupied Holland during the war, I decided she had been marked with bravery from the beginning. Jarti said her father was a student from an Indonesian upper-class family who became an opponent of colonialism; her mother was the daughter of a Jewish diamond merchant. When her mother became pregnant, the Dutch Communist underground had persuaded a prostitute called 'Jarti' to shelter her in the basement. While German soldiers visited the prostitute upstairs, her mother went into labour in the basement. She named her baby 'Jarti' after the brave woman who had protected them both.

Her family heritage had left her with conflicting emotions towards the left. They were at once rescuers and bringers of terrible dangers. In Holland, Communists had saved her mother and herself. But in 1965, her father's anti-imperialist politics had led him to be involved in the attempted coup d'état in Indonesia which was brutally suppressed leading to the death of many thousands in Indonesia. By this time her parents had separated and Jarti was hazy on the details. All she knew was that her father had been killed on the spot and the peasant woman with whom he lived was imprisoned for many years.

The Communist Party was held responsible for the failed coup and met with harsh reprisals from Major-General Suharto who came to power as a result.

* * *

In between the sessions that spring at the University of Amsterdam, on Saturday 1st May I had gone to Doncaster where I was to give a speech along with the left Labour MP Michael Meacher.[132] We both had to walk at the front of the May Day march. I had never done this before and discovered that setting the pace and keeping in step, especially if you had shorter legs than your companions, was harder than it might appear. The trade union steward tried to teach me, and I managed a shuffle, hop, skip.

The police looked down their noses at the march and one made derogatory remarks about us. Whereupon our steward straightened his back, drew himself up to his full height, fixed the policeman in his gaze and issued a ringing reproof in tones of utter conviction, 'These people are the salt of the earth'. He was not *resisting* the police, he was reprimanding them. I saw the face of the state under its helmet dissolve momentarily into a confused discountenance.

The meeting turned out to be tricky. It was a predominantly male gathering and my beady eyes spotted bundles of porn magazines in brown cardboard boxes under a table, which were being sold for funds. Despite being decisively in favour of sex and desire, I could not help being dismayed to discover the Labour Party being fuelled by commercial sleaze. The topic I had been given was 'freedom', which I extended beyond political and social rights to include the cultural context in which a sense of personhood developed. I pointed out that how we were regarded and defined profoundly affected our expectations. Beginning with class and race I went on to gender and thus to the impact of being portrayed in magazines as 'porn'. This brought a few resentful stares, but I got off relatively lightly.

I thanked my lucky stars I did not have Michael Meacher's subject of 'peace'. His well-informed and measured speech against Britain's military intervention in the Falklands was received with deep growls of disapproval from patriotic Labour supporters in the audience. I admired how he answered every question with calm reason, but I do not think the growlers were convinced. As for 'freedom', at least the porn was relegated back into the boxes, waiting no doubt until the feminist was back on the train to London.

* * *

In the first half of June, I was happily working with Ursula Owen on the Virago collection of my articles and poems. One sunny day in the garden I can remember us moving pieces of paper back and forth into piles as we debated what to cut.[133] I must have written the concluding section, 'Against the Grain', around this time, for 'the salt of the earth' make an appearance in it, marching with bands playing and people singing.[134] I had been teaching Charlotte Perkins Gilman's utopian novel, *Herland* (1915), that May in Holland and remained sure 'that all human beings can be more than present circumstances allow'.[135] Nonetheless, I was a feet on the ground, eyes on the stars kind of utopian, warning that we must not ignore 'the humdrum' or scorn 'the handiness of the patch or darn'.[136]

Alert to the hitches of hubris, I knew we feminists had not achieved as much as we had hoped. Splits had left us without any cohesive women's movement in Britain. Nonetheless, I noted how ideas and organizing had extended in other ways. 'There are black feminist groups, groups of Filipino and Asian women, Latin American women's groups, feminist theatre, film, poetry, publishing, groups, magazines and journals'.[137] I was aware too how many feminists were asserting specific 'women's issues', while also combatting the impingement of right-wing policies upon women's lives. I described us as 'helping to develop workers' plans, contesting the allocation of council housing, creating alternative forms of heating, forming co-operatives'. We were thus 'part of the attempt to democratize welfare, halt the cuts, make local government more responsive to people's needs'.[138]

* * *

That summer Will and I went for a holiday at Ros Baxandall's house in Truro, Cape Cod. I had visited Ros at the Cape in 1974, but this was my first trip there with Will. Ros's ebullience extended to children and adults alike. She presented Will with a baseball hat and plastic helmet and whisked him off to the tennis courts in the early mornings to ball boy for her. Ros's son Phineas (Phinny) and his friend Marc Perry, being in their early teens, were sterner and insisted the small British visitor learned how to be a thorough American, not only by wielding a baseball bat, but by saying 'candy' before they allowed him sweets. He submitted partly because of the bribes, but also because the two older boys were heroic figures to him.

Truro had been a fishing community and grown out of two villages. Long ago Ros's house, lined with wooden panelling, had been the village store and it was visible from the road leading to the Pamet River, but most houses were scattered through woodlands, hidden down tracks. The oddly named 'Truro Center' was a parking space with a Post Office, a grocery store and a few other shops. However, neighbouring Wellfleet contained an excellent library, a book shop and a small supermarket.

Portuguese settlers in the nineteenth century had been followed in the early twentieth century by bohemians and socialists who had discovered the peace and stark beauty of the Outer Cape. During the 1930s some unemployed workers had migrated there and built wooden houses in the woods. Ros knew several older leftists, including Max, known as Manny, Granich, a former Communist. Manny's family had been Jewish immigrants living on New York's Lower East Side and his older brother Mike (Gold) achieved fame for his novel *Jews Without Money* (1930).

Manny had studied journalism and worked on cattle ranches before journeying first to the Soviet Union and then to China, where he and his wife Grace encountered left-wing writers like Edgar Snow and Agnes Smedley. After World War Two they established a left-wing summer camp for children, Higley Hill Camp in Vermont, which they ran until 1964. In the 1970s Manny was active in the Chinese-American Friendship Association and used to lead tours to China.[139]

We visited Manny, who lived in a tall round house, which Ros said he had built himself, walking round its circumference and tracing the smoothness of the grey, wooden walls. I was struck by how at ease Will aged five was with Manny, then in his mid-eighties, listening wide-eyed to the old man's tales of riding on the tops of trains when he had been a member of the anarcho-syndicalist Industrial Workers of the World (IWW).

Numerous historians and activists radicalized by the 1960s new left holidayed near Truro in the summer, including Linda Gordon and Allen Hunter, who I had met on my visit to the US in 1974. Both were involved with the journal *Radical America*, which probed historical as well as contemporary resistance, and their daughter, Rosie, was around Will's age. Liz Ewen, who taught with Ros at Old Westbury, and her husband, Stuart, were social and cultural historians who specialized on the media and it was Stuart who invented the sybaritic 'Marxist Institute', which mysteriously conducted its 'meetings' in swimsuits seated on towels on the beaches near Truro.

Even less clad were the nude beach enthusiasts who used to gather further down the shore. Ros's former husband, Lee Baxandall, who had written the *World Guide to Nude Beaches and Recreation* (1980), was a key organizer of what became a large-scale popular movement. Much to Ros's exasperation, supporters used to ring for Lee on her telephone number. 'Another nude beach person for Lee,' she would exclaim, slamming down the phone. Nevertheless, it must be admitted that the naturists acquired a broader reach than the 'Marxist Institute'.

* * *

I was travelling again in September to speak at a panel in Madrid on 'What is Socialist Feminism?'[140] The euphoria of the immediate post-Franco years had died down and Spanish socialist women were trying to connect the left-wing members of the women's movement with working-class women. I am not sure whether our panel proffered a solution. One woman told me she was confused because all the speakers had been so different. I think this was because 'socialist feminism' was not a political doctrine. It had arisen out of radical cultures in contexts that differed internationally; our assumed starting points were not always explicit and could be baffling.

I was feeling strained on this visit to Spain because Paul had just moved out. I had pressed my distress inward, forming a cover for my emotions and enabling me to carry on, so when Paul actually went, apart from worrying about Will, I was numb. Paul was not exactly going far away, settling in a communal house a short walk from Powerscroft Road. Still, his physical departure constituted a major marker of separation. It was the loss of close companionship that gnawed most of all. Over time, spasmodically, connection would be resuscitated. We were friends after all, and even deeper bonds persisted through our love for Will. When we all three assembled for school events or pantos at Hackney Empire, I would revert to the old happiness and then feel a wave of sadness when it was time to go home.

Nevertheless, friendship survived, and we continued to share caring for Will. This was so ingrained in our political outlook and our personal relationship that I did not question it and was startled when Dorothy Thompson observed that I would not have been able to do what I did without Paul taking responsibility for Will.

It was important to me that the two friends who had lived with me since the 1970s, Sue Sharpe and Dave Phillips, were back in the household after their stay in Mexico. We had many overlapping interests, they were closely involved with Will, and we were reassuringly familiar with one another's habits and foibles. Sue had written a study of London school girls, *Just Like a Girl*, and was doing research into the lives of working mothers, which would be published in 1984.[141] Dave was working in the Survey Research Unit of the Polytechnic of North London (later

London Metropolitan University) and had just produced a guide for 'community workers, students, tenants, trade unionists and others' called *Do-it-yourself surveys: a handbook for beginners*. Ahead of its time, along with practical advice it demystified 'the uses and common misconceptions about surveys'.[142]

Theoretically I was all for demystifying, but I was less happy personally when Dave mentioned in an off-hand way that at my age it was statistically unlikely I would form another new long-term relationship. Dave, who tended to approach the future with a dry humour, mixed with cautious pessimism, appeared to find a certain calm in the removed objectivity of statistics. But as far I was concerned, such a dismal calculation was better left mystified and I most adamantly refused it.

Aged 39, I tried to emulate the resilience of those roly-poly wooden brightly painted Russian dolls. When you took the head off one, there, inside, sat yet another. I had to admit though that there *were* certain obstacles. Time for romantic canoodling seemed most definitely to have diminished and breaking up with Paul exposed a fear that I was no longer physically desirable. Distressed by my atrophied sexual nerve, implicitly I pared down to just fancying and being fancied. But it proved remarkable difficult to get these in sync. The men I fancied who were around my age were invariably with someone else and, though love affairs with younger men offered passion and desire, they tended to have an inbuilt impermanence.

It was impossible for me to imagine how some new encompassing relationship could ever be fitted into my existing preoccupations – Will, work and politics. Perhaps, too, I feared being hurt and/or the inner control of another person over my being. As a love that could be lived with came to seem inconceivable, sexual longing settled into a small, concentrated part of me, buried amidst the innumerable daily doings that absorbed most of my energies.

* * *

The first trip of my second year at Amsterdam University coincided with Will's half term at Gayhurst Primary School, so he could accompany me. We stayed with Jarti, her partner Hans and her two sons, fourteen-year-old Raafi and little Tomas who played with Will. One day Jarti led us all off on an expedition to the zoo where the children gazed at the animals while she and I walked contentedly around meditating on the vagaries of love.[143] Jarti was extremely happy for she and her partner, Hans, were busy converting an old warehouse into apartments with a group of friends. When she showed me around what appeared to be a building site, saying how much she looked forward to having space, I was amazed by the range of skills the little group of practical and aesthetic Dutch converters brought to this vast task.

I went back to the University of Amsterdam for a longer period alone in November and Will stayed with Paul. Meeting up again with everyone made me feel at home, especially with Jarti, who fed me delicious Indonesian food, took me with her to buy silks of brilliant colours and laughed subversively about pomposities of all kinds. This time I expanded my lectures from the women's liberation movement to women and politics more generally, with topics such as 'The Background to the Rise of Thatcherism' and 'Feminism and the Left'.[144]

On this trip I went to speak at the International Institute of Social Studies (ISS) at the Hague on women's history where I met members of the Women and Development programme, along with the writer on international trade unions and grassroots social movements Peter Waterman. These meetings opened up a whole series of new vistas for me. So did an exciting book I bought there called *Feminism and Nationalism in the Third World* by the socialist feminist historian from Sri Lanka Kumari Jayawardena, which introduced me to the history of women's movements in India, Sri Lanka, Japan, Korea, Turkey, Egypt, Iran, Indonesia and the Philippines.[145] Deftly intertwining their struggle for emancipation as women with their commitment to nationalist and revolutionary movements, Kumari recorded women in the East drawing on some ideas from the West, while recasting them through their own exigencies. This brief contact with the ISS made a lasting impression upon me. Peter evangelically sent copies of articles, accompanied by further references and, while Kumari had not been at the Hague when I visited, we were soon to meet and discover we had both historical and political interests in common.

I had been asked to lecture that autumn in Denmark at the Universities of Roskilde, Aalborg and Aarhus. This exchange was funded by the British Council, but they had rejected me as a suitable speaker on the grounds that I was not an academic. The Workers' Educational Association apparently did not count. I could not help wondering whether an unspoken reason may have been because a group of rumbustious anti-Thatcherite miners had preceded me. When my name popped up had someone within the inner bowels of the Council muttered that it was time to get a grip on what aspects of British culture were suitable for export?

Rejection is never pleasant, but my feelings were mixed, for I had quite enough to do in Amsterdam and was worried about leaving Will, especially now that Paul and I had parted. I underestimated the tenacity of Danish socialists. Not only were the radical social scientists, philosophers and historians in the universities who had invited me adamant that I should come, socialist feminists took up my case, which became a political as well as an educational issue. I was not given any information by the British Council, but I was told by the Danes that Denmark had threatened to withdraw from the exchange programme, whereupon my lectures had been abruptly and mysteriously reconsidered and the ban reversed. Given the Danes' extraordinary efforts, it would have been crass to refuse to go.

So, on 22 November, I set off from Amsterdam by plane, in first class and surrounded by businessmen in suits. I was making notes for a review of Rudolf Bahro's *Socialism and Survival*, crouched in the corner of my seat, when the man next to me admonished, 'Have space, use it'.[146] I saw the same ergonomic practicality and attention to detail when I visited a Danish state-funded nursery specially designed for under-fives. I felt like an envious giantess lumbering about in a utopia, devised and constructed for small people.

But when some young Danish feminists later told me they were *opposed* to it because they believed that if they had *less* state welfare there would be more scope for self-activity, I gulped and felt utterly lost for words. How was I to describe what was happening in Britain and the endless weary meetings trying to defend threadbare welfare provision?

They were perplexing and so was the Grauballe Man, sacrificed in a bog for unclear reasons in the third century BC. I gazed at his face contorted by time and suffering in the Moesgaard Museum near Aarhus, unable to comprehend his life or his death. In contrast, I experienced a peculiar sense of familiarity while watching a comedy programme on Danish television; the rhythms of speech, the intonation, facial expressions and gestures were completely recognizable from Yorkshire. I ran downstairs to ask my host, the philosopher Hans Fink, how could this be? Bewildered by my intensity, he replied vaguely that they were conservative fishing people from the far northern coast.

I had never taken a decision to turn into such a wandering worker. My itinerant life had arisen primarily because of economics. Paradoxically, in Britain the sums I could earn from either my writing or teaching in adult education barely covered the preparation time, yet I could make enough to support myself and Will by *not* being at home. Contact with these wider worlds always stimulated my curiosity and wonder, while the friendships I accrued called me back. So, I was left in two minds, searching far afield for sisterhood and comradeship while desiring some rooted connection to a specific spot.

* * *

That autumn we held the conference 'London As It Might Be'.[147] It had taken a long time to plan, partly because we deviated from conventional formats by combining speakers who were workers with users or consumers wherever possible in the workshops. For instance, one session consisted of a pensioner and a childcare worker, along with my friend Dave Welsh from London's Underground, who helped to produce the rank-and-file magazine, *Close Encounters on the District Line*. One of the plenary speakers at 'London As It Might Be' was the socialist economist Stephen Bodington. We had become friendly in 1969 through organizing an attempt at left unity called the Convention of the Left.[148] From an older generation, Stephen had been in the Communist Party and had worked for the Admiralty during the war, where he was an early exponent of applying mathematics to plotting the best routes for ships, laying the basis of linear programming. In the post-war era he became a senior civil servant in the Board of Trade, was influenced by both the Institute for Workers' Control and the Lucas Workers' Plan and did pioneering research on new technology.[149]

Stephen could have acted like an eminence grise but was utterly without intellectual arrogance. At 'London As It Might Be' he cut through the over-simple dichotomy of being for or against the state. Defining a welfare state as a *step* towards meeting needs, he added that to prevent it from being managed by an elite bureaucracy, it required a 'change of consciousness that grasps popular planning for social needs as a feasible replacement for the failures of the market economy'.[150] He left me puzzling how such a consciousness was to come about, be expressed and take effect?

I had observed that person to person democracy did enable divergent views to be aired. But these did not necessarily follow the tracks that I envisaged. For instance, at one of the GLC's East London Assembly meetings I had attended, a group of women had forcefully rejected the proposal of affordable housing and strenuously demanded more office blocks. They wanted 'white collar' jobs in an area where skilled trades for women were declining. On another occasion at Hackney Labour Party Women's Section, I had argued that we needed to oppose how power was reproduced through relations of hierarchy in institutions and daily life, mentioning how those in a 'professional' role could subordinate others. This annoyed an older member of the audience, and she pulled me up sharply. She was a skilled clothing worker who took considerable pride in doing her work 'professionally', by which she meant exercising a specialized craft well. She made me see that it was not the possession of a *skill* that was the problem, but its jealous guarding from others. Both encounters reminded me that wants and worth could not be just assumed.

* * *

These thoughts had ceased to be purely abstract. Encouraged by Hilary, I had applied for a post in the new Popular Planning Unit at the GLC, job-sharing with an old friend John Hoyland. Because of Will I did not think I could do a proper full-time job alone and I knew John and I complemented one another. During the late 1960s, the two of us had started Agit Prop, a network to connect radical artists with left causes, and had helped produce the left paper *Black Dwarf*, edited by Tariq Ali.[151] We were appointed, shortly before Christmas, to inform Londoners about the GLC's research and projects, transposing our mix of anarchical efficiency into the Popular Planning Unit that Hilary headed in County Hall.

I was to help also in developing an alternative economic strategy in which childcare and domestic labour were included. Hilary had drafted a Leader's report which included a commitment, not simply to women's employment needs, but to domestic labour. With Ken Livingstone's support, this had become GLC policy. After so much stravaiging around my life had suddenly assumed a concentrated purpose as a local government worker.

I quickly picked up rumbles of hostility in County Hall to both the left Labour members and to us 'political appointees', a term enunciated with astringent venom by two important-sounding affronted voices in the Ladies. I sat, a silent Mata Hari, on the toilet seat in one of the cubicles while they trounced the lot of us. Then, at a Christmas party, three young men began to tell me about a terrible harridan called Hilary Wainwright, who had been seen wearing dungarees held up by a safety pin. And, just at that moment Hilary arrived, bouncing with delight, declaring 'Look at my glitter'. As she batted her eyelids like Betty Boop to show me the fashionable accoutrements of purple, green and gold sent by her younger sister, I smiled sweetly and announced, 'This is Hilary'. Hilary beamed broadly. The three young men melted away into the night.

1983

The Popular Planning Unit, a glass-fronted building
shaped like the letter 'L' backwards, had formerly been a
showroom. John's desk was against the far wall; mine, by the
window, looked out at a bustling Waterloo; his was stacked with
tidy piles of committee papers, mine with a morass of papers
and publications. These two desks became our base camp.

The resplendent Edwardian building of County Hall was
designed to evoke solidity and awe rather than popular planning
and initially I explored its miles of corridors like a daunted
Titus Groan in Mervyn Peake's *Gormenghast*, trying to get my
bearings, literally and psychologically. I had never worked in
such a gigantic place and destinations have always presented
challenges; my diary reveals nervous instructions about the
whereabouts of offices and committee rooms. Officially I was
searching for people linked to the committee papers neatly
stacked on John's desk. I soon learned that knowledge was not
confined to them.

The brown wooden corridors themselves hummed with
information. Electricians, emerging from a trapdoor, described
to me in graphic detail how they crawled through underground
cavities for miles to fix the wires. I heard from the cleaners how,
before we arrived, only they and staff of a high rank were allowed
up to the Council Members' offices. The floor still preserved a
special smell of polish. Then there were scandalous tales from
porters about secret meetings of a big wigs' drinking club which
used to be closeted in the labyrinthine basement.

County Hall was a domain unto itself, rustling with secrets

and padded with mysterious rules. Someone at some time had devised a hierarchical administrative structure, delineated by military-type titles like 'Director General'; John and I were appointed as 'officers'. I only admitted to this embarrassment of rank once when a security man barred me from entering a meeting I was meant to be in. Even then it stuck in my throat, 'I'm an of-of-officer', I bleated and passed through. We Popular Planners, being uneasy with ceremony, evaded the rituals that remained. John's stratagem was to hang a red tie by his desk. This served as his formal uniform for committee meetings and was eventually collectivized because the other men in the PPU used to grab it and head off down the corridors when their turn came to present a paper to the committee.[152]

John and I both took to one of the GLC's great assets, the staff canteen. It reminded me of the municipal restaurants which had lingered on after the war. John, who had the energy and physique of a greyhound, sometimes used to consume two municipal dinners there.

* * *

Despite living and working in London since 1964, the GLC had remained remote, the looming object of militant tenants' protests or schoolteachers' demonstrations. Even after the election of the new radical members I had mainly heard about what they were doing through the media, supplemented and sometimes contradicted by conversations with Hilary and another old friend in County Hall, Tony Bunyan.

I had met him in the late 1960s when he was transitioning from the Young Liberals into libertarian socialism. In the 1970s we had independently come across the trial during World War One of Alice Wheeldon and her family when they had fallen foul of Special Branch and the intelligence services. Tony had written a classic study, *The Political Police in Britain* (1977), and had recently started working as Deputy Head of the Police Committee Support Unit, which was to morph into the Police Monitoring and Research Unit.

The chair was Paul Boateng, a barrister who had opposed

the 'SUS' (suspect) laws which gave the police the right to stop and search people. In practice they searched mainly young black people, giving rise to many complaints of violence against them. That January, a young black man called Colin Roach had been killed by a gunshot wound in the foyer of Stoke Newington Police Station, and his family, friends and supporters were struggling in vain to find out how this had happened. Their protests and the memory persisted but the precise circumstances of his death remained shrouded.

During Will's half-term I took him into County Hall and he accompanied me on the long treks through the corridors.[153] We visited Tony, who was used to Hackney five-year-olds, but next on my list was a meeting with a GLC worker from the previous Tory regime of Horace Cutler. He was one of several people with whom I was meant to 'liaise' for reasons I never fathomed. He loathed the left Labour councillors and was tucked away in a small office in what seemed like a remote turret.

He looked aghast as we walked through the door. When the phone rang and Will answered it for him, his long, lugubrious face whitened in panic. I contrived to calm him down by listening to his occupational and political woes, along with descriptions of his eight children, far away in the outer suburbs. Eventually he melted sufficiently to impart the distillation of a lifetime's work in local government, 'When writing a committee paper, never say anything explicit, make sure that the wording is always vague.'

This sounded like a line from the hilarious TV satire on Whitehall and the British establishment, *Yes Minister*, yet he spoke as if disregarding his bizarre advice would result in dire consequences. I kept it in mind, though I never followed it through. Ingrained aspirations for exactitude and a deep-rooted commitment to clarity proved too strong. I did, however, slip unexpected phrases into official documents as mind-ticklers to stop committee members from dozing off.

Municipal mores were perplexing. I took courage from Hilary, who was now my immediate boss, imparting her unique compound of trust, humour and conviction. She had put together a booklet entitled *Jobs for a Change*, a slogan derived from Tyneside CND and Newcastle Trades Council. On its cover a black and a white hand gripped a chain with London mapped out beneath them and the words, 'The wealth of London is the skill and sense of its people. This book is about unlocking that wealth.'[154] The text conjured up past socialists William Morris and Ellen Wilkinson, while its design by John Finn from the Artworkers' Collective along with Peter Kennard's photomontages graphically invoked what might be.

Nestling on the pamphlet's inside back cover were the words, 'Printing arrangements by the GLC Supplies Department'.[155] Hilary, too, had gone exploring and had come across a large, open plan office and an arranger par excellence, a Welsh printer called Reg Corke, who produced the bulky catalogue of goods issued by the Inner London Education Authority for the schools. He was a short, rotund, no-nonsense kind of guy, Labour born and bred, who harboured a strong feeling of rivalry towards the GLC's designers who he suspected of looking down on the Supplies Department. He used to shake his head in amazement about Hilary's disregard for customary practices, but he became a steadfast friend and ally.

Adopting *Jobs for a Change* as the name of the newspaper we produced once a month, we used to find out about meetings and what was being funded, decide what to include, visit projects and interview people. We wrote the articles, subedited text and chose the photographs. Then we went up to Supplies to lay it all out with Reg. Together the three of us would design and paste down the pages of copy on tilted boards, deliberating all the while.

Initially we were tense and unsure, while Reg inclined to the format of the compartmentalized Supplies Department Catalogue. Our first issue focused on women's employment and featured Lambeth Toys, an interesting co-operative of Asian and Afro-Caribbean women making multi-ethnic toys, funded by the GLC. But it looked rather stiff; the images were too small and packed amidst the text and the photography was rigid.[156] Municipal imagery mainly concentrated on buildings and mug shots of members. It was technically skilled, but the approach was detached and the work routines alienating. Eventually we complemented the inhouse work with the emotive photographs taken by co-ops and collectives of talented freelancers.

When I went to meet the GLC photographers and heard that they never saw how their photographs were used in Council publications, I started delivering them copies of *Jobs for a Change* so they could look at the results of their work. Keen to show them the topics we were covering that spring, when John and I went off to Brent to find out about the impact of unemployment and factory closures in the borough, we took one of the GLC photographers along.

Tom Durkin, from the Trades Council showed us round, and we put a photograph of him on our front page standing in a vast expanse of concrete emptiness, tall and rock-like, his long, white hair dishevelled by the wind. Tom pointed towards the desolate, puddly wilderness and told us that a few months before a large printing factory had stood on that site, but now the jobs had 'Gone like the snow in summer'.[157]

This was my first introduction to Tom, who was a legendary figure in the Brent labour movement and a poet. He came from a poor Irish family and in the 1930s had tramped from Liverpool to London, managing to find work in construction. An unsectarian Communist, a poet and a member of the Union of Construction and Allied Technical Trades (UCATT), Tom had supported the women strikers at Tricos and Grunwicks during the 1970s and delivered wood for the women's peace camp against cruise missiles at Greenham during the eighties.

A believer in local economic initiatives, Tom had helped to set up the Brent Local Economic Trade Union Resource Centre, which activated imaginative employment schemes. He took us to meet the enthusiastic socialist feminist who ran it, Shelley Adams. Shelley, who bore a strong resemblance to a young Simone Signoret, one of my film star heroines, communicated a reassuring mix of warmth and tenacity. Between them Tom and Shelley possessed an exhaustive knowledge of Brent's local economy and its labour movement.

The situation was urgent. Not only was manufacturing leaving London, privatization had penetrated the public sector. On 20 April I went down to Tooting to interview three former dustbin men, Dave Benlow, Micky Langley and a younger man called Pete. All three had lost their jobs when Wandsworth Council, led by the Conservative Christopher Chope, contracted out refuse collection.[158] Initially they had tried to put forward their own proposals for a better service but to no avail. Then they had gone on strike, only to find themselves isolated. Dave said he thought this was because 'people hadn't realized how serious privatization is'.[159]

The whole pattern of their lives and livelihoods had been shattered and they were still stunned when I met them. Deriding the woeful blunders of the inexperienced private firms, they mulled over family memories. Micky faced me intently from an armchair in his front room, relating how his father had been the first to acquire a regular job as a council worker and how he had followed in his footsteps. Pete was still in his twenties, but he too reached back through the generations. He had been told that before there was any council refuse collection, one of his forebears had lived from whatever he could clean up as a 'scavenger'. His voice was clipped with fear.

Painfully, they had come to recognize what had happened to them was part of a wider scenario. Micky told me that the long period of unemployment had made them aware how northern workers had been hit even harder and to understand why so many young black Londoners, who were the most severely affected in the city, had rioted in Brixton: 'We're all in the same boat, tricked, cheated and bullied.'[160]

We moved on to talking about what their work meant to them and I mentioned an idea I had recently heard put by the French socialist thinker André Gorz. I had been to a meeting at the Institute for Contemporary Arts (ICA) where Gorz, in a discussion with Hilary and the socialist feminist writer Elizabeth Wilson, had proposed a greatly reduced working week.[161] Micky greeted the idea, adding with alacrity, 'I'd be down the races'. I laughed at this. It was my father's idea of leisure too, but no one had suggested it at the ICA.

When my article based on the interview appeared in *Jobs for a Change*, John and I were summoned by the GLC lawyers. The GLC's chief lawyer, John Fitzpatrick, an august and imposing man, asked us in what way did interviewing dustbin men enhance the reputation of the GLC? His tone made it clear that in his opinion it did not. Sparked into replying, and on ground I understood, I delivered an impassioned response about oral history, labour history, Ruskin History Workshops and history from below, the bias in received history, the silencing of working-class experience, the historical contribution of the labour movement to social reforms, local government and the vital role of refuse collection in all our lives.

John Hoyland barely got a word in. He knew me through left organizing rather than radical history and was looking surprised. But the white-haired lawyer no longer looked stern, he was smiling. I thought afterwards that perhaps we would have to see the lawyers over every issue of *Jobs for a Change*, but after that they left us to it – perhaps to forestall further tirades.

* * *

My London had been mainly in the east. Working at the GLC opened up not only the great edifice of London's local government, but the whole of London itself. It felt as if the boundaries between boroughs were beginning to meld as I roamed south, west and north interviewing people in the employment centres funded by the GLC which aimed to identify knowledge and skills locally and to help people to anticipate and combat economic changes that affected them adversely.[162] On Deptford High Street at the Lewisham Women and Employment Project, which had started in 1979, I met Heather Wakefield, a tiny ebullient organizer with thick auburn curls like Lynne Segal's. I was instantly drawn to Heather not simply because of her politics, but by her affirming, sparkling energy. She was well aware not just of the economic but of the personal and social implications of creating jobs, introducing me to three unemployed women who wanted to train to become carpenters. One of them, Lorna, a former dental nurse, stated explicitly what the Tooting dustbin men had implied: being unemployed meant you lost 'your sense of self-worth'.[163] Heather was eventually to become the official responsible for local government in the public service union, UNISON.

Another early contact was Susie Parsons, a resourceful organizer in North Kensington community groups. Through her work on the local health council she had helped a group of women campaign for their municipal laundry and wash-house.[164] From 1926 these had been set up by the predecessor of the GLC, the London County Council, to help working-class women who lacked space for washing clothes. Long an irritant to the Institute of Launderers, with the advent of launderettes and washing machines, they were now being closed by councils. But around 20 per cent of Londoners were without washing machines, so the municipal laundries still provided an important practical service and meeting place, especially for older women.

The North Kensington campaign had resulted in the GLC funding the co-operative, Westway Laundry. Situated under the arches of the motorway, Westway was run by its users, who not only did their own washing, but the laundry of the community nursery next door, another project helped by the GLC. When I visited, I was intrigued to learn how women had rallied long before any municipal provision had existed. A photograph on the wall honoured Catherine (Kitty) Wilkinson, a Liverpool woman who, during the cholera epidemic of 1832 had 'lent freely her kitchen and washing facilities to her less fortunate neighbours'. Her action had inspired a movement for public baths and wash houses, which started to be set up following legislation in 1846.[165]

The funding of Westway and the neighbouring nursery was made possible by the policy initiated by Valerie Wise and then outlined by Hilary on childcare and domestic labour. Though both had been exhaustively discussed in the women's movement, they remained peripheral in economic debates, so Hilary and Robin asked me to give a summary of feminist thinking. I stressed our focus on home as a place where work was done rather than simply a unit of consumption and recommended that they should read Ellen Malos' *The Politics of Housework*, a collection of essays that covered the range of subsequent debates.[166]

Stressing the time and material effort involved in doing housework and childcare and the impact on women's employment, I described how we had sought to alter the sexual division of labour at home by experimenting with larger communal groups of adults taking responsibility for childcare. But just changing personal life was not sufficient, so demands for better social provision for children had arisen.

I related how unease about the persistence of biased attitudes in some state nurseries had held back the formation of a national nursery campaign in women's liberation and described the ad hoc emergence during the 1970s of anti-sexist community nurseries run by the involvement of parents and workers. While these were democratic in structure, they needed funding if they were to extend and improve the services they provided.[167]

I explained that most socialist feminists had decided the demand 'wages for housework', would confine women further and extend the cash nexus, along with intrusive state control, into the home. Instead, we emphasized the importance of funding various forms of social care in order for people with small children to have better and more flexible *choices* about how to balance homelife and paid employment.

These discussions were very much in my mind because I was meeting up with Lynne in the evenings to go swimming, multitasking as we did our lengths by setting the world aright. She had been editing a Penguin on *What Is To Be Done About The Family?* which came out that year.[168] The question mark was indicative. Changes in childcare, personal relationships in families and, indeed, domestic labour, constituted key elements in developing a social economy, but were too complex to be resolved by any single demand. Working at the GLC convinced me that resources were needed to enable people without power to define their own particular needs. After all, public funds customarily went to businesses in the shape of infrastructure.

Because I suspected feminist debates would be new to some of my listeners in the Economic Policy Group, I took a while elaborating them. Robin had called out everyone for the meeting and I became aware, as time went on, that our Finance officer, Chris Duffield, was shuffling somewhat in his seat – envisaging budgets perhaps. Chris was one of the first men I had seen wearing early 1980s fashionable suits. Previously suit styles had tended to turn men into square shaped boxes, his, in contrast, possessed an undeniable elegance. On this occasion he emanated an air of modish discontent, which made me fear I had spoken rather too long and failed to communicate. Nonetheless it would be Chris who rescued me a few months later when the statistics in a committee paper I took to the Council were challenged by the Tories.

* * *

At work I might be Ms Domestic Labour and Childcare, but my own personal domestic arrangements were exceedingly complex. I attempted to impose a coherent structure in a chart at the front of my diary, pencilling in when Paul or I would deliver and collect Will to and from school, helped by Dave Phillips and Sue Sharpe on alternate Mondays.[169] These were supplemented by a series of elaborate swaps with other parents.

Such charts were difficult to maintain, partly because commitments from my life before the GLC kept breaking into my attempts to establish any orderly alignment. The Fragments meetings continued, and I had lectures and talks arranged from the past in my diary. I worried greatly about whether I was doing my full quota of GLC hours, totting them up in my diary, staying on at night when Will was at Paul's and taking work home at the weekends, noting my catch-up hours assiduously in my diary, though nobody ever asked to see them.

GLC work accompanied me on my travels. In February I set off for New York, not only to lecture as usual, but with two GLC missions to accomplish.[170] Robin wanted me to contact the New Yorkers who had introduced more nutritious and culturally diverse menus for school meals and also to track down radical workers at Kodak's parent company in Rochester. Kodak was restructuring; French employees already faced redundancies and relocation and British trade unionists feared that they would be next. The French were backed not only by their union, but by their Communist controlled local council. However, the firm's research was concentrated at Rochester, where Kodak exerted a powerful influence through a long tradition of paternalism and philanthropy. Also, the European workers lacked direct links with their American counterparts, who were not members of any independent, recognized union.

School meals reformers proved relatively easy to locate but Kodak presented more difficulties. By following a daisy chain of this one and that one, thanks to Ros's networking skills and several days of telephoning, I eventually stumbled across an unofficial group of organized workers. Having accomplished both missions, I was able to bring the contacts back to Robin.

Early in March I was in Amsterdam for the final period of my part-time professorship there. The GLC influence is evident in lectures on women, work and local politics as well as in others on the family and the state.[171] On 17 March I travelled up north to Groningen University to pronounce on the more high-flown topic of 'Marxist and Feminist Ideas of Consciousness', after which I noted in my diary simply, 'Sleep'.[172] The following day in Amsterdam, I came back down to earth by speaking about working-class women's autobiographies. I took as my title a poem called 'Shush Mum's Writing', published in a pamphlet by the community group, Bristol Broadsides, based in Knowle West council estate.[173]

This time I stayed with Jarti and Hans in the beautifully converted warehouse on Vierwinden Straat which they had turned into their home. When it was time to leave, Jarti and I were truly sad to part. One consolation was that a kind of continuity had been secured. The Women's Studies Group had invited the socialist feminist historian Linda Gordon, a close friend of Ros Baxandall's, to succeed me as a visiting professor the following academic year.

Some requests to give talks in Britain were impossible to refuse. On 8 April I spoke in Pontypridd at Llafur, the Welsh Labour History's Easter School. Its theme was 'Working-Class Women' and it was the first time their conference had specifically focused on Welsh women's experiences.[174] Shortly afterwards I was recruited by Dorothy Thompson for a huge Virago meeting at Central Hall, Westminster to launch *Over Our Dead Bodies: Women Against the Bomb*.[175] This collection of essays and poems by women writers against nuclear weapons had been Dorothy's initiative and their range was a testimony to her personal reach as well as her organizing skills. She was helped by an editorial group which included Hilary and the left film maker Jill Craigie, who was married to Michael Foot, while contributors ranged from the Greenham activist Ann Pettitt, to the novelist Angela Carter.

One of the connecting themes was women's resistance to militarism and I was particularly interested in Jill Liddington's account of 'The Women's Peace Crusade' in which the redoubtable Ellen Wilkinson surfaced once again in a 1920 women's delegation to Ireland on behalf of the Manchester branch of the Women's International League for Peace and Freedom. She and the other delegates accused the British government of 'force and fraud' in Ireland.[176] Predictably they were ignored.

During May I went to Halifax to talk on Alice Wheeldon and was able to spend time with Gloden Dallas. Though in recent years the practicalities of our shared house in Whitby and the furore surrounding the Fragments conference had tended to consume much of our time together, our longstanding connection was based on a shared interest in women's history.

Gloden had acquired an exhaustive knowledge of socialist suffrage women in the West Riding of Yorkshire and we used to exchange information on them.

But Gloden had a block about writing which caused her considerable distress. With three young children, she had little time and yet would always help and encourage others. Each year she used to judge essays by members of the Women's Cooperative Guild. It took her many days and she was paid £25. In vain, I would remonstrate, 'Think of the hourly rate you are getting'. But Gloden knew how important those essays were to their authors and carried on.

The Beyond the Fragments network continued to meet in 1983 coordinated by Charlie Owen, an unassuming educational researcher at the Institute of Education. When he was young, Charlie had joined a particularly sectarian Trotskyist group, the Workers' Revolutionary Party, and had reacted strongly against its authoritarian structure. Charlie was a tolerant organizer who held us together, but he never shed one ingrained habit from the Leninist left – punctual meetings. Without fail, Hilary, who was invariably late, would upset him profoundly. I tried to explain to Charlie that her lateness derived from her excessive hopefulness – she always imagined she could do more than she could. Charlie would shake his head in incomprehension and give a sideways smile, then get worried all over again when she was nowhere in sight.

Over the course of 1983 we gradually stopped gathering and the Bulletin ceased. I felt guilty about abandoning the small band who had continued meeting, but the pull of other commitments had become too strong. Hilary and I were increasingly absorbed in the work at the GLC, while Lynne was now active in the Islington Labour Party and had helped to vote Jeremy Corbyn in as the candidate.[177]

* * *

On 22 April 1983, the day before a second People's March for Jobs was due to set òff from Glasgow, I was the representative from the Popular Planning Unit at the meeting to accommodate them. Two years before, after being greeted by the Labour councillors, they had camped in County Hall. Now they were coming back.

A mood of disrupted bewilderment was evident among many of the GLC employees at the meeting. However, a slim, dark-haired young man was briskly conducting the ruminations about where to put an unknown quantity of people with sore feet and sleeping bags. Moving with quicksilver confidence through a series of dilemmas and logjams, Damien Welfare proceeded with a combination of amiability and precision, referring to precedent. I was amused to watch practice assuming the status of custom. When the troubling question of whether to allow for the separation of the sexes arose, he reported briskly that the marchers had wanted to stay together in 1981. This appeared to settle it, even though the expression on the faces of several of his fellow officers was aghast.

I stayed unusually quiet at that Peoples' March for Jobs meeting. This was partly because I figured the marchers were going to be fine left to Damien, and partly because I had come to understand that becoming at all noticeable meant more stuff to do. Within a few months my half a job was already expanding at an alarming rate. I feared it would soon be impossible.

I realized I had to prioritize. From 1970 to 1973 I had been involved with a small group from the London Women's Liberation Workshop trying to help cleaners employed in offices by private contractors to improve their pay and conditions. We had leafleted and picketed, and some victories were won, but our efforts had not been able to secure many permanent improvements. We had, however, generated a trail of publicity about what was wrong.[178]

By the early 1980s cleaners in the public sector were mobilizing against privatization and their cause was vigorously supported by a committed researcher, Dexter Whitfield, and the anti-privatization newsletter *Public Service Action*. Attitudes within trade unions had shifted too. A meeting with a sympathetic official at the Transport and General Workers'

Union, Philip Pearson, who was so obviously serious about low paid workers, convinced me that I must raise the conditions of contract cleaners through the GLC.[179]

I had not reckoned with Robin's capacity to inspire and, after one of our meetings on the London Industrial Strategy (LIS), I came away mysteriously responsible not just for thousands of contract cleaners, but for contract caterers, along with all the dry-cleaning businesses in London. I suspect this may have been because I had mentioned being friendly with the Turkish-Cypriot couple who ran my local cleaners in Hackney.[180] I did begin to read on dry cleaners in the excellent GLC library, but, to my relief, along with contract catering they seemed to fade away and be forgotten. Once again, I kept my peace; domestic labour, childcare, contract cleaning and *Jobs for a Change* were more than enough for a mother with half a job.

In early June I took *Jobs for a Change* down to the Crystal Palace Bowl in south London where the People's Marchers were gathering.[181] An election was imminent, but Labour was divided between left and right. The media mercilessly attacked Michael Foot's opposition to Britain being a nuclear power and the tabloids caricatured his demeanour as an unconventional radical intellectual. They peddled deference and spiked it with derision. My heart sank when I failed to convince a young skinhead who reviled the marchers and the long-haired Labour leader, chanting the refrain, 'Worzel Gummidge, Worzel Gummidge' (the dishevelled scarecrow on children's TV).

Margaret Thatcher won the election once again on 9 June. Despite the unpopularity of many of her economic and social policies, she had aroused a wave of patriotic fervour through the Falklands war. Left local government was operating against the grain. Yet the GLC, with its banner recording the number of unemployed wafting in the wind along the banks of the Thames opposite Parliament, represented a galling irritant to the Prime Minister, who was resolved to assail what she called 'the Left's redoubts in the great cities'.[182]

Nevertheless, from the shelter of County Hall, the GLC

retained its unique coordinating capacity because it reached across London; Ken Livingstone and the other left councillors continued to steer it around like some enormous liner, to serve Londoners who lacked assets and power. The range and variety of reforms they effected, shifted the scope of how left politics came to be seen, defined and understood. These were strengthened by the support of myriad creative, swift-moving radical movements. Prominent among these were gays and lesbians, who confronted virulent prejudices. Ken Livingstone had been influenced by the fun-loving Harvey Milk, who had bravely run for election to the San Francisco Board of Supervisors as a gay candidate. The GLC's stand was exceptional and often disparaged, but it reverberated in the labour movement where the rank-and-file could be ahead of their officials.

Under pressure from people with disabilities, the inequalities they faced were also made a priority. However, while an acknowledgement of injustice is important, finding solutions could be tricky. For instance, it was recognized that the design and structures of the city, including County Hall, were exceedingly inhospitable for wheelchair users. So, changes had been decreed and a box had been ticked. But good intentions do not always work in practice, as I found one day when I walked alongside an angry campaigner circumnavigating the labyrinth of corridors that constituted the lengthy and vexatious detour he had been allocated. I came to see that keeping open ways of reforming reforms were vital.

* * *

I spent June and July frantically writing Industry and Employment Committee papers on cleaners, domestic labour and childcare. Not only was I configuring them under intense pressure, the committees themselves were tense affairs. Even though I did not have to grab the requisite red tie, I felt that I was plunged into some hyped up gallimaufry, part gambling session and part oral examination, so I was relieved when my committee papers were defended by Ann Sofer, the Social Democratic Party councillor who was critical of the left, as well as by the Labour members. I chuckled as she pointed out to the bemused Tories around the table that I had quoted two eminent Conservatives, on economics, working conditions and low wages: John Ruskin and Harold Macmillan.

Psychologically, after the committee meetings were over, it seemed like a tremendous achievement. But they were simply the beginning of a much longer process. Once accepted, committee papers were elaborated into duplicated pamphlets to be distributed for debate and comments. So, I no sooner would have done a committee paper when I would be frenetically turning it into a pamphlet and an article for *Jobs for a Change*.

However, the existence of the Economic Policy Group made it possible to link in-depth research with practical projects. On 6 July I brought together a meeting of people who were working on contract cleaning from unions and community groups as well as within the GLC.[183] With the support of Michael Ward and helped by Chris Duffield, I was able to commission an investigation by Jane Paul, which resulted in a comprehensive report on cleaning in London, *Where There's Muck There's Money*.[184]

Within the GLC, a combination of union pressure, the Women's Committee and the efforts of members of the Economic Policy Group, notably the researcher Irene Bruegel, also contributed to improvements in the GLC cleaners' conditions. Cleaners' pay went up and the GLC, along with other public service employers, enabled cleaners to have a paid day off each week for flexible basic skills courses. The groups were small and the topics defined by the cleaners' needs and aspirations. Along with formal learning, they built confidence.[185] These were valued, and cleaners spoke with feeling to me about how crucial these changes were for them.

Housework appeared not to have registered in the Conservative lexicon of menacing loony left redoubts and the Tory men looked particularly nonplussed when pondering my domestic labour committee paper. Its immediate impact was limited because, apart from proposals for some co-operative laundries, there were not many projects seeking funding. However, a precedent had been established by including it in an economic strategy and women in Britain and elsewhere extended it. In London, the most intense agitation for intervention came for childcare provision and through the Industry and Employment Committee we were able to complement the projects of the Women's Committee by funding workplace nurseries.

Ideas of democratic control of nurseries by parents and workers had passed into the GLC through feminists and former community activists while the example of Bologna had shown how direct democracy could *combine* with the election of representatives.[186] Market Nursery had demonstrated to me how, given a shared commitment, participatory and elected representation could function in practice. Conflicts had occurred, but we had remained friendly, because we were happy that the children were happy and we parents valued what had been achieved. After Will had left, he and some friends from Gayhurst Primary School had walked across London Fields, to visit the community nursery they remembered as such a good place to be.

* * *

So, it had been a severe shock that spring to learn of a bitter dispute within Market Nursery in Hackney. For some time, the childcare workers there, Kathy Jenkins, Hermine Anderson and Hermine's daughter Milly, had been unhappy about two new young members of staff who they did not think were caring well for the children and were being biased towards the little boys. Angry complaints from parents were also mounting. The elected management committee was loath to act. Finally, Kathy, Hermine and Milly said they would leave unless the new workers went. This would have been catastrophic as they were all committed and energetic mainstays. In panic, the committee sought to pre-empt this by telling the two new workers that they would have to leave. A minority of parents then asserted that this constituted victimization against lesbians.

Wretched that the original core of nursery workers who had worked hard and conscientiously were being treated unjustly, I spent a long time compiling an account of what had occurred.[187] A group of friends, including two lesbian parents, whose children had benefited from the nursery, started meeting to see how we could counter the inaccurate accusations of anti-lesbian prejudice being spread around about Kathy, Hermine, Milly and the nursery management committee.

The conflict damaged relations between people directly connected with Market Nursery and spread outwards as local schoolteachers and politicians took sides. It cut right into the goodwill that had been generated around the pre-school education of a group of young children growing up in Hackney. A formal resolution of the case was eventually effected and the nursery continued to be funded by the GLC and the borough. Most importantly it survived. But the bitterness continued to divide women who had been active for several years in the women's movement and split local trade union activists.

The conflict struck at the hub of my convictions about feminism, socialism and participatory democracy. Painfully, it led me to acknowledge that a blinkered version of feminism could be as divisive and destructive as any other ideology when exerted in a doctrinaire manner. Market Nursery had operated by engaging in a democratic negotiation with the views of all the parents, regardless of class, gender or race. Participation had worked. It was good. But it was not in itself a panacea for all problems.

* * *

My work at the GLC preoccupied me so intensely that when *Dreams and Dilemmas* was launched at the Institute for Contemporary Arts (ICA), I could not reorientate back to my pre-GLC self.[188] I did manage though to link up with two old friends from the 1970s, Linda Dove and Bruce Green, who visited London that summer from California with their children. I had met Linda in the mid-1970s when she was one of the few women sound editors. She and her partner from the States, Bruce Green, had been part of Newsreel, like Alan Hayling. They had moved from making left documentaries to Hollywood where Bruce had done some of the special effects for 'Star Wars', so, of course, we all went on an outing to see 'The Return of the Jedi'.[189]

On 9 July the tragic news of Gloden Dallas' death crashed right through my preoccupation with committees, policies and local government. The shock was so extreme it took a while to register. We were the same age, had been friends as students and shared so many memories and interests. Two months before it had been evident she was under considerable pressure, I was aware too that she had not been sleeping well and had high blood pressure. Later I would learn she had fainted several times a few months earlier. But I could not imagine how she could die so young. I happened to be reviewing a history of the Women's Cooperative Guild called 'Caring and Sharing' for Tony Gould at New Society.[190] Every time I opened a page, I thought of Gloden and all those co-operative women's essays she read each year. She left two children from her marriage to Duncan Dallas, who worked for Yorkshire Television, and one daughter from her relationship with the historian Steve Caunce.[191] The sadness of her early death hung heavy.

Returning from Halifax on the train after her funeral, stunned, drifting and lost in reverie, my eyes fixed suddenly on the name 'Stuart Hall', the cultural theorist I had first met when he was active in the New Left during the 1960s. A typewritten list was being held aloft by the person on the seat in front of me. From my early teens my gaze has always been drawn irrevocably towards words and as I scanned a potted biography of Stuart, which mentioned him coming from Jamaica as a Rhodes scholar, I alighted on the word 'Marxism'.

When the man holding the papers turned his head sideways, I noticed two unmistakable bushy, greying side burns. It was the bewhiskered Conservative supporter of Margaret Thatcher's government, Rhodes Boyson, and the list was of people he did not favour in higher education. He was surrounded by a noisy, confident group of acolytes talking about a meeting they had been attending. As I sat soberly surveying our surveyors, I knew Gloden would have understood the bizarre incongruity.

* * *

Margaret Thatcher's victory in the election provided her with greater scope to pursue her resolve to eradicate public services and public ownership – which she saw as harbouring socialists and socialism – through the extension of 'privatization'.[192] Contracting out services had the added attraction of diminishing union power in the public sector. Noting the example of Christopher Chope on Wandsworth Council, she had focused on cleaners in the NHS, but encountered sustained resistance from unionized women at Barking and Hammersmith hospitals.[193]

Ken Livingstone's Leader's Report in July 1983 pointed out that the privatizing blazoned by 'Tory local authorities' had transmogrified into 'a key part of monetarist strategy'.[194] In contrast, the GLC aimed to defend public ownership, while improving provision and democratizing working relationships. This did not mean reproducing the old state-run hierarchies; in a special edition of *Jobs for a Change*, announcing 'A Jobs Plan For London', Ken argued that the people who best understood what needed to be done were those actually doing it. He meant not just management, but the rank-and-file workers who were habitually ignored.[195]

Local Health Emergency campaigns were springing up by autumn 1983 and the GLC had funded an all-London Health Emergency Group to give practical support and document the impact of cuts and privatization of services.[196] It publicized a litany of bungling and higher costs that had followed the contracting out of cleaning and catering services.[197] Aware that the government had them next in line for privatization, a group of British Telecom (BT) workers began to develop an alternative plan for their industry.[198] In the evenings they started to discuss developing and publicizing their own counter strategy with one of the new recruits to the PPU, Richard Hallett, who had been involved in the 1980 Workers' Inquiry into State Intervention.

I would be catching up on work in the Popular Planning office and, as my desk was only separated from them by a screen, I used to hear them deliberating as I struggled to concentrate on my subediting. These meetings would result in a public enquiry into the privatization of British Telecom which the GLC held later in the year.[199]

By the autumn of 1983 the Economic Policy Group (EPG) had produced a great wadge of strategy papers and pamphlets on London's economy. John and I set about crafting these lengthy statements and complicated arguments into short summaries for that September's *Jobs for a Change*.[200] I found domestic labour and childcare especially challenging. This was partly because neither were usually regarded in relation to 'economics'. Yet at the same time I did not want to *reduce* human intimacy to politics and the cash economy, instead I wanted to stress that caring for children was at once deeply personal *and* a material and social activity. The headline, 'Just a labour of love?' caught the semi-permeable demarcations.[201]

In my pamphlet, 'Child Care – meeting needs and making jobs', I noted that childcare required resources and was thus partly an economic issue, but stressed it was equally a human relationship. I argued that recognition of how these were entangled, meant that we could interrogate how work is valued in capitalism and raise the fundamental question of how people's time and energy might best be spent.[202]

The implications were extensive. Not only did the 'economy' – the nature of our jobs, buildings, transport, energy, the location of industry, along with where we lived, all affect our personal relationships. By assuming that making profits was not the main criterion for this 'economy' and instead putting human beings' relationships and care at the centre, our established understandings of worth, merit, benefit, esteem, cost and usefulness could be revitalized.

In our 'Stop Privatisation' issue of *Jobs for a Change* that November, I extended the discussion of caring to people with disabilities, emphasizing the importance of the 'well-being' of the carers themselves, whether at home, or employed in the health service, doing social work, providing leisure services or cleaning.[203] I adopted 'well-being' in preference to 'welfare', to avoid the latter's statist connotations, only to see advertisers nobbling it to market purchasable life styles.

Making complicated points clearly in print might be knotty, but I was to learn at the GLC that trying to accomplish a series of changes in practice is even harder. The London Industrial Strategy's aim of combining job creation with alternatives that served peoples' needs was pitted against the policies of the Conservative government. We were thus trying to help defend what was being wrenched away, and, at the same time, seeking to encourage and sustain new democratic and social alternatives.

We learned from Londoners of the extent of the problems they were facing and how much more there was to do. As needs revealed themselves the scope of the Industry and Employment Committee grew, and the Economic Policy Group increased in size; so did our Popular Planning Unit. To my great relief Kath Falcon was able to take over the co-ordination of our links with all the variegated childcare projects, tackling this complex task with reassuring confidence. Among other new recruits to the heterodox PPU bureaucracy were two people I already knew: Dave Welsh, who came to work on London transport and Alan Hayling, from the Ford shop stewards combine.

Hilary and I were part of the panel interviewing Gail Lewis, who had been active in the early black women's groups during the 1970s. We had to fight for her to be given the post, even though her understanding of the interconnecting contradictions of race, class and gender, both theoretically and through the lens of her own experience, was so evident. I would later learn how difficult and complicated this had been.[204]

Gail taught me something I should have seen but did not. One day she came up to Supplies when I was laying out *Jobs for a Change* with Reg and immediately noticed that the photographs in our spread on workers resisting were exclusively white and male. I had often been annoyed by a tendency for socialists and male trade unionists to drop any mention of women when they referred to 'the working class', as if 'class' was the purlieu solely of white men. But I had reproduced the same omission. The images did not convey the reality of the many working-class women and men from black and ethnic minorities in London who were taking action.

Visually I had acquiesced to an absence I opposed so strenuously in words. When Gail and I changed these, the meaning of opposition to the government's policies towards trade unions acquired a new resonance. It also demonstrated that our coverage of projects specifically for black and ethnic minority workers in *Jobs for a Change* should be integrated with acknowledgement of their role in defining the nature and scope of wider resistance. This, too, should have been obvious to me.

* * *

In September, Ursula Owen from Virago and Bill Webb, the literary editor of *the Guardian*, recruited me for a 'Readathon' – twenty minutes non-stop readings by writers for the Campaign for Nuclear Disarmament. This proved unexpectedly perilous. Along with the novelist Ian McEwan, I duly turned up on time, but no sooner had I begun when I was heckled fiercely by a group of homeless men angry because we were not agitating for them. I tried to mediate and a brief calm opened up until Ian McEwan spoke, whereupon fury erupted again, forcing us to retreat as missiles that looked like table legs came hurtling towards us.[205]

Ursula reclaimed me once again from local government by persuading me to rework an essay I had written in the late 1970s as part of a feminist group in Hackney in which we had talked about our fathers and our relationships to them. She was editing a collection, *Fathers: Reflections By Daughters*, which included contributions from writers I revered such as Angela Carter, Sara Maitland, Doris Lessing, Michèle Roberts, Melanie McFadyean and Grace Paley.

Calling mine 'Our Lance' – because this was how he had been known by his sisters on the family's small farm near Rotherham

– I confronted my disassociation and estrangement from him: 'My father was in his fifties when I was born. We were separated in age by half a century and the gulf only seemed to grow wider. Our placings in the world and our relationship to where we found ourselves were contrary and apart.'[206]

Lancelot Rowbotham had died in 1967 but when my son was born in 1977, I had realized I needed to get beyond my passionate resistance to my father's outlook in order to comprehend him as a person, replete with contradictory attitudes. This was a personal quest, but it suggested something more. I believed that the liberation of women required 'not just a redefinition of femininity. It involved turning prevailing understandings inside out, so that being a man was no longer just 'here in the world'.[207] This was the kind of destabilizing sense of becoming that Paul and James Swinson had been seeking to express in the men's group magazine they helped to produce, *Achilles Heel*.

Philosophizing was all very well, but despite over a decade as a feminist I was still apt occasionally to dissolve into hopeless emotion. Working at the GLC resulted in many good friendships with people who had not come across either left sexual politics or women's liberation. Among them was Reg Corke. Doing *Jobs for a Change* with him was brisk, jovial and co-operative and I regarded him as my dear workmate. The three of us learned together through doing and began to devise a better balance between words and visuals, with greater flow in the design. However, while Reg bore me no malice, he retained fixed ideas from his upbringing, his work and his rank-and-file membership of the print union, SOGAT. In Reg's view women were women and newspapers had a single (male) editor.

At a whole day London Industrial Strategy meeting during the summer Reg kept referring to 'John Hoyland' as the editor of *Jobs for a Change*. Not only had I somehow vanished. Reg had exploded my conviction that the three of us were working together in equal cooperation. I erupted in rage and fury, spluttered in protest and rushed from the room where I ignominiously burst into tears causing much embarrassment.

Over time I managed to explain why I had been so upset. Taciturn when it came to emotions, Reg listened. I could see he was not happy about distressing me, but nonetheless unsure what to do. Despite our clash, because Reg and I liked one another and shared an obsession with deadlines, I would still happily make the journey from Hackney, even in the early hours of the morning, to work on *Jobs for a Change* with Reg.[208] Eventually he found a way to cross over to me in his own manner by discovering I possessed a recognizable 'skill'; I could cut words quickly for him while they were on the board. He acknowledged this ability with respectful craft generosity, but I suspect in his own mind John remained the 'editor'. Nevertheless, Reg did not call him that again.

My half a job had made some home improvements possible. I bought a hall carpet to replace a patchwork of surplus bits of differing colours donated in an earlier era by my sister-in-law, Dione. Friends recommended a skilful man from Scotland who lived in an old post office van he had ingeniously turned into a beautiful woody caravan. Before the weather turned, he parked it outside, came in, looked around, diagnosed the Victorian house's pressing ailments and set about repairing them. When eventually he departed, to my great delight, all my vague worries about things I did not understand, but thought I ought to, seemed to have been resolved.

My diary that winter records me moving through sharply contrasting milieux. On 3 November the Industry and Employment Committee decamped in a coach to Docklands to discuss the alternative Peoples' Plan for the docks with local campaigners. When we set off, an elderly Conservative councillor grumblingly mistook me for a 'trainee'; as I was forty, this was flattering in a backhanded kind of way. A clutch of festivities followed: fireworks on 5 November in Hackney's Springfield Park with Paul, Will and Dave Phillips, then on the 10th Virago held a party for the *Fathers* book, where I enjoyed talking with a stroppy and sensuous Jill Craigie. Later that month, at the birthday of the left film director Roland Joffe in Chelsea, I was dazzled when Cherie Lunghi took my coat – she was Guinevere from 'Excalibur' to me.[209]

During December I whirled merrily through parties held by the Economic Policy Group, the Supplies Department, *New Society* and a revamped *Marxism Today*, replete with a crowd of snappily dressed young demi-communists, circulating around the innovative editor, Martin Jacques. They were a puzzling new phenomenon and appeared to have migrated from *The Face* magazine, leaving me wondering whether I had passed over into middle age without noticing.[210]

On Christmas Day Will was with Paul. Peace fell in Powerscroft Road and I could catch up with many overdue letters.[211] I then snatched the pause between Christmas and New Year to ruminate on the differing historical forms of 'feminism' and how the particular emphases we had adopted through the Women's Liberation movement in Britain had arisen. The recent past was beginning to mutate into history.[212]

6

1984

During January and February, I was ostensibly busy preparing for the Economic Policy's Hearing on Domestic Labour and focusing on *Jobs for a Change.* Yet, unaccountably, my mind meandered. 'Write article on desire', I jotted in my diary on 21 February.[213] This note turned into an article, 'Passion off the Pedestal', for *City Limits,* the magazine Nigel Fountain co-edited with John Fordham, in which I pondered how 'to balance sexual passion with freedom of mind and spirit'.[214]

Since my early teens in the 1950s I had been in rebellion against the fear, reprehension and hypocrisy shrouding sex. Then, from the late 1960s, I had written about the marginalization and disaffection of my generation of young radical women, embracing the political, cultural and personal release which had come through women's liberation as a social movement. Initially, I had felt confident that we could straddle earlier feminist divides between love and liberty and also hoped that we would finally eradicate the overt hostility and the furtive prejudices gays and lesbians faced.

But I was to learn change does not advance in a neat line. Instead, there were a series of closures. By 1984 the spread of HIV Aids was intensifying homophobic stigmatization, making it even more vital to contest the restrictive taboos around same sex desire. At the same time, I was also aware that exploring sexual feelings between men and women as we had done during the 1970s in women's liberation, was becoming hard to raise politically. Oddly, a new taboo appeared to have arisen and feminists' discussions about heterosexuality seemed to have gone guiltily to ground. I noticed how unease about these recently ensconced prescriptions was being deflected to novels and poetry or surfaced in a grumpy resistance to being hedged in, 'If anyone tells me again: "Surely you can't feel that as a feminist", I'll explode,' a friend retorted angrily at a meeting.[215]

Unsure quite how these psychological and political barriers had arisen, I wondered if we had assumed too easily that inner feelings would change and ignored how sex and reason tend to nestle uncomfortably together. Yet this could only be a partial explanation, for lesbian friends were adamant that accepting oversimplifications about a neat fix between the personal and the political, was obviously not peculiar to heterosexuality.

I certainly did not wish to return to forms of relating before the emergence of women's liberation. I just wanted to open up space for talking frankly about the impact of feminist politics upon sexuality. Instead, when 'Passion off the Pedestal' was published, it enraged a group called 'Lesbians Against Pornography', who occupied *City Limits* demanding that their denunciatory reply must be published.

Their riposte provoked some brave letters in my defence, including one signed by writers Alison Fell, Liz Heron and Marsha Rowe, by photographer, Maggie Millman and by Lynne Segal, who was to write a series of books exploring the politics of sexuality in depth over the next few years. These letters were so important; they reassured me that I was not alone in perceiving that desire, with all its revelations and surprises is, of course, a risk, but so too is freedom.

Writing about sex involves transposing an awareness from one bit of your brain to another zone of expression. So, it is perilously easy even in the best of times to just sound daft. In the fractious early eighties, it was bound to get you denounced. It was hardly canny of me to hold forth on passion.

* * *

I displayed a similar lack of circumspection when it came to fun. Remembering the festival in Trafalgar Square against the Vietnam war that John Hoyland and I had organized in 1968, I mused whimsically to Robin Murray that a 'Jobs for a Change Festival' would be 'fun'.[216] Robin was predictably enthusiastic, while John Hoyland, who loved music festivals, was an eloquent advocate. Festive resistance was re-emerging. In 1983 there had been a peace festival. Then, early in 1984, thousands of trade unionists had taken the day off, converging with parents and school children in defence of the GLC at the Festival Hall.[217] Moreover, 1984 was the GLC's Anti-Racism Year; the unemployment rates, particularly among young black men in the working class, were shockingly high and Michael Ward was concerned to reach out to yet more young Londoners who were not involved in either unions or community groups.

Unlike me, who was ardently listening to Bruce Springsteen 'Dancing in the Dark' and Annie Lennox singing 'Everybody's looking for something', John had kept up with music outside the mainstream and was in contact with Tony Hollingsworth, whose cousin, Michael Eavis, owned the farm where the Glastonbury Festivals were being held. Tony agreed to handle the entertainment logistics with Sue Beardon, David Bradford and Ken Hulme.[218]

The next thing I knew was that we were to have a Jobs Festival. Because everyone was grumbling about the terrible burden of extra work this would involve, I decided diplomatically, and somewhat sneakily, not to mention having suggested 'fun'. I got my comeuppance anyway for by 28 February I was attending not just the Press Committee, but extra meetings for the Festival Committee, learning the hard way that 'fun', once municipalized, entailed meetings.[219]

The Press Committee was enlivened one day by the arrival of members of the advertising firm Boase Massimi Pollitt. They had been commissioned to create posters against the GLC's abolition and wanted to sound out ideas. I listened to their responses with both ears wagging, hoping to learn from them about getting to the gist. I realized afterwards there is never just one gist. The black and white posters they produced were visually arresting and the succinct words jumped off the page, but their focus was on defending representative democracy rather than contesting economic and social inequalities.

The only other woman at these Press Committee meetings, Pamela Gordon, the Deputy Administrative Adviser, was far more experienced in local government than I was. Before we newcomers arrived at the GLC she had worked her way up to Assistant Director General. But her belief in what we were doing had prompted her to take a step down from this senior position in order to help us. My first encounter with Pam had been her arrival, laughing happily, clad in red robes as 'Mother Christmas', when we had held a children's party in the PPU. I used to watch her with admiration, noticing how she would hold her peace until just before the end of a Press Committee meeting, when she would gather up a consensual thread, draw on her considerable administrative experience and then miraculously point to pathways which enabled things to be done. She did this with an air of supreme serenity.

But just once I saw another Pamela and realized what a long, long march she had made through the institution as a woman. When she and I were on an interviewing panel together and all the candidates were men, I remarked to her with a smile how we were reversing the norm, for at that time it was rare indeed for women to be determining the fate of men at work. Pamela startled me by responding with quiet vehemence, 'The boot is on the other foot'.

I felt a similar respect for our conscientious PPU administrator, Trevor Richardson, a man of great tact and wisdom. Steeped in the procedures of the old County Hall, like Pam, Trevor was a skilled facilitator. A loyal Sidcup Labour supporter, he enjoyed what the GLC had become, though sometimes his dark brown eyes would shadow over with anxiety at some act of iconoclasm. He regarded Hilary with a warmth, edged with a degree of exasperation, for she was doing so much at once and could be a distracted kind of boss. Yet in combination the two of them were our nubs of security. Trevor kept the records and Hilary nurtured adhesion and commitment, not by trying, but by being. As we were a gang of libertarian Stakhanovites who believed in our work, we did it with zeal.

During March, John, Reg and I were laying out a special issue of *Jobs for a Change* on transport. Topics ranged from the GLC's innovation of travel cards and the increased numbers using public transport, to the racism faced by black workers, the terrible conditions of cleaners, called 'fluffers', who cleared the Underground lines in the tunnels at night, along with the stress caused by One Person Operation on bus drivers. We were able to draw on Dave Welsh's knowledge and contacts as well as on the Women's Committee's 'Women Plan London', which stressed the problems of travelling with children in pushchairs and the urgent need for measures to counter violence towards women, especially during the nights.[220] The GLC's differing areas of activity complemented one another.

* * *

Despite being so immersed at the GLC, I had not forgotten the imaginative power gleaned from transformatory glimpses like that convivial free bus ride through Hackney. During March the writer Lisa Appignanesi, who was then working at the Institute of Contemporary Arts, recruited me to speak on 'Utopias and Feminism'.[221] From the 1970s, after reading Ursula le Guin I had moved on to Doris Lessing's *Shikasta* and her *Canopus in Argos* trilogy, then in 1982 Marsha Rowe had introduced me to Naomi Mitchison's *Memoirs of a Spacewoman* (1962) by giving me a signed copy of the paperback for my birthday. This aroused my curiosity about a woman who could imagine sex across other life species in space. I went on to read *The Corn King and the Spring Queen,* republished by Virago in 1983, and marvelled how, in 1930, she had written about women's sexual desires, explored sources of female power while empathetically entering another culture in the distant past.

At the ICA, I zoomed in on two contrasting utopian feminist novels about motherhood: Charlotte Perkins Gilman's *Herland* (1915) and Marge Piercy's *Woman on the Edge of Time* (1976). In *Herland* women's mothering is amplified and extended into a social system, in Piercy's biological differences are dissolved. The two novels went to the crux of a recurring conflict in both feminism and attempts to devise beneficial social reforms for women.

While Gillman's envisioning was insightful, I was aware that the stress on sexual difference could restrict women's scope, I inclined more to Piercy's exploration of an egalitarian utopia. I did admit to feeling uneasy at the red bearded Barbarossa breastfeeding in *Woman on the Edge of Time*, but I supposed that if this were to become customary, I would acclimatize to such intimate sexual blending. Even so, postulating an equality dependent on a utopia which required the physical elimination of all differences between the sexes seemed too deterministic. Like Piercy's heroine Connie, I baulked at the idea of machine-bred children as a solution, declaring that if I ever got to that particular 'Edge of Time', I would 'hang on to my return ticket to the bad old world …'.[222]

The ding-dong recurrence within feminist thought of difference versus equality, indicated to me the need for economic and social changes beyond gender alone. Moreover, it meant examining critically taken-for-granted assumptions. During March I went to hear Mike Cooley and the incisive socialist feminist Veronica Beechey on 'Post Industrial Useful Work' at the ICA and came away pondering how far the definition of 'socially useful' could be stretched.[223] Through March and April the talks at the ICA on utopias were linked to an exhibition, 'William Morris Today'. The accompanying book was partly funded by the GLC and included an interview with Mike Cooley in which he noted that technology, far from being neutral, contained control systems defined by an exceedingly 'narrow concept of rationality'.[224]

On 17 March, at the Ford Workers' Combine party, on a boat sailing down the Thames I watched Ian Saville, the Marxist Magician, pulling things out of hats and grumbling about the difficulty of doing magic while travelling by water.[225] Metaphorically I knew what he meant. Nothing seemed to stay in the same place long enough to think anything through. Left-wing socialists were trying to transcend the society we lived within, while being forced to defend the existing social gains which were under threat.

The GLC had staked out space for doing this on a larger scale and in a more concerted way than I had ever known. I suspect this was why it aroused such vehement Tory ire. Ken Livingstone as the leader of the Council was unusual in being experienced in Labour Party politics, at ease with the left and, as a closet fan of science fantasy novels, open to the counterculture. He combined acumen with a rebel spirit. Michael Ward's great skill was in spotting crevices which could be extended into creative ways through terrain that seemed impenetrable. Robin, Hilary and Mike Cooley all edged their own utopias into economic policy. So, saving existing jobs and services spilled over, shifting the meaning of what constituted 'the economy' by pitting imaginative ingenuity against the jeopardies of daily life.

County Hall and its ramifications attracted and generated a truly remarkable agglomeration of diverse knowledge and know-how. The London Hazards Centre, for example, investigated concerns raised by trade unionists, tenants and community groups. These ranged from varicose veins caused by shop workers standing for long periods, to the lethal effects of asbestos and pesticides.

The GLC's attempts to tackle unhealthy food and the threat to the environment provoked as much derision in the right-wing popular newspapers as our opposition to all forms of discrimination. The Daily Star initiated the term 'loony left' in 1983 and the Daily Express had picked it up by 1984.[226] It became a mind-numbing incantation over the next few years. When a GLC press release revealed evidence on the fat content in sausage meat, a storm of patriotic passion was released by the tabloids in defence of the great British sausage, accompanied by mockery of 'Red Ken's sausage'. Unintentionally, I would contribute to another wave of mockery in an interview I did with Andrew Puddephatt. Andrew, who had become a Labour member of Hackney Council, made an off-hand reference to wind turbines on council flats as a possible means of generating clean energy. This provoked a tirade of scorn because it would make the buildings unstable.

* * *

That March the miners' strike was transmuting into an extraordinary social movement as women, finding that a change in the law meant they were no longer entitled to any benefits, started to get together to work out what to do. Jean McCrindle was teaching trade unionists at Northern College in Yorkshire and so I heard how in Barnsley within a few weeks of the strike being called on 5 March they had formed a women's group and elected Jean as the treasurer.[227] Desperation meant similar groups were sprouting all over the country. When Jean wrote a letter appealing for donations to various friends, I sent some money and passed the letter on to Nigel Fountain, who put it in *City Limits*. Readers responded with spontaneous generosity.

Money and food started arriving in Barnsley from individuals; workplaces and union branches adopted pits and spontaneous support groups sprang up. After the Garston Miners' Support Group in Liverpool collected food on local housing estates, they decided to take it to the Point of Ayr Colliery near Prestatyn, but were unsure precisely how to get there. Two cars set off, with Joan Bohanna and her friend Eileen Turnbull in one and the provisions stashed in the other, but its load was so heavy that the car broke down and had to be fixed by (former naval driver) Joan. Finding a member of the Miners' Welfare Club, they deposited great piles of food at his house. This was his first contact with a support group, and he was flabbergasted that Liverpudlians he had never seen before were delivering gifts to his door. Such deliveries were to become common, and the Garston group developed a long-term connection to miners and their families in Bolsover.[228] These bonds were multiplying throughout Britain.

* * *

Will and I went to Whitby for a short holiday on 17 April and he was reunited with Che Gannarelli and his younger brother, Luke, in Blackburn's Yard. I took the children out for a walk along the beach, pleased to be able to give Laureen and Pete, who had done me many favours, a break.[229] We headed off in the direction of Robin Hood's Bay. Will, who was just seven, and Che, a few months younger, scrambled easily ahead across the rocks and sand, delighting in the space and freedom, but Luke, who was four, took longer, cheerily splashing in rock pools, and he and I fell behind on the way back. I was not particularly worried: jutting cliffs obscured my view and I assumed Will and Che were just ahead until we turned a corner on the beach and empty sand stretched before us. I hustled Luke along as fast as his little legs could go, but there was no sign of the bigger boys. Panic seized me. Had they wandered too close to the incoming tide, had an extra strong wave swept them off their feet?

Chiding myself for not keeping them in sight, I alerted the coastguards and the warning sirens sounded. They were still going when we reached the narrow passageway leading from Church Street into Blackburn's Yard, I entered holding Luke's hand in dread. A second later familiar voices wafted towards us, Luke quickened his steps. And there, in the Yard, playing happily, were Che and Will! Relief swept over me, followed by incredulity that they had moved so quickly down the beach, across the pier and then navigated their way down and across Church Street, a narrow busy road. I was left feeling acutely embarrassed about alerting the coastguards with a false alarm.

Laureen and Pete just took it in their stride. Long afterwards, 'The day Sheila lost the kids' was to be recalled with amusement in Blackburn's Yard. It was perhaps as well for me that my childminding shemozzle never reached the Conservative councillors at the GLC.

* * *

Back in London, John and I were struggling to keep up; the April *Jobs for a Change* on transport was followed by two special issues on race and finance. Fortunately, Gail Lewis prepared the one on London's black workers and Richard Minns provided copy on the social investment of pension funds.[230] We could not have done these without them, especially as we were already working on the June paper ready for the Jobs Festival.

In the early afternoon of Sunday 10 June, I arrived at County Hall carrying a pile of *Jobs for a Change*. The front page carried two arresting photographs by Gina Glover and Angela Phillips of teenagers and young children with the headings, 'Give Us a Job. Give Us a Future. Give Us a London Worth Growing Up In'.[231] A huge crowd had already gathered. It grew larger as the day went on, spreading out across the car park and through Jubilee Gardens, making it very hard to move around, especially if you were short and carrying newspapers.

I particularly wanted to see the material assembled by Kath Falcon and women from the Nursery Campaign in the childcare and domestic labour section of an Industry and Employment exhibition and headed towards the 'Industry Tent', only to be caught in such an overwhelming crush of people I feared I was going to be squashed and smothered.

Though 'Industry Tents', 'Theatre', 'Co-ops', 'Films', 'Trade Unions','Poetry' were all announced on the poster, it was musicians like The Smiths, Aswad, Misty in Roots, Billy Bragg, Hank Wangford, Mari Wilson and The Redskins, who drew the crowds. Ken Livingstone, adept at crossing cultures of dissent, received enormous cheers when he spoke and was photographed in between Morrissey and Mari Wilson, with 'Direct Intervention To Save Jobs' blazoned over his head at the tent. At one point I found myself standing next to Ken in front of County Hall, watching as young men climbed lizard-like up its wall. Terrified that one was going to fall, I looked round to see if he was going to try and stop them, but he was smiling with sublime joy at the anarchical takeover of London's municipal citadel.

John Hoyland describes meeting Anne Scargill, with a group of Yorkshire women from Women Against Pit Closures. Amazed by the 'punk hairdos' and delighted by the steel bands, she told him how inspired she was to meet Connie Hunt, the resourceful tenants' campaigner involved in the docklands Peoples' Plan, 'battling in a man's environment'. Moved by the many black Londoners at the Festival who approached her with messages of support for people in mining communities, she remarked, 'We know what harassment they're getting because we're getting it now'. Anne added, 'It were beyond our comprehension to get all these people together. It were a new world opened up to us.'[232]

I retreated towards the Popular Planning office. It was designated as the performers' green room but seemed to have turned into a first aid centre. A young skinhead with a short blond fringe was seated there and his face was bleeding. Someone looking after him explained he was in the left-wing band the Redskins; about eighty white power skinheads had targeted them when they were playing. I was shaken to see how a relatively small group intent on violence and acting swiftly could terrorize a much larger crowd intent simply on having a good time. Uncompromisingly, the Redskins sang 'Keep on Keeping On'.[233]

So, the festival was eventful and huge – one estimate was 100,000 – but for me, not exactly 'fun'. Indeed, it has been my experience that fun anticipated rarely tallies with actual fun, which is apt to just arise unexpectedly, like bliss out of the blue. Nevertheless, the 1984 Jobs for a Change Festival showed how the radicalism of the GLC could connect to a resounding spirit of rebellion among a new generation of Londoners, who were bursting with an energy and confidence that had not experienced defeat.

* * *

Mass resistance of a different kind was emerging too from within the miners' strike. On 12 May around ten thousand women converged at a rally in Barnsley, surprising the leaders of the National Union of Mineworkers and, indeed, Jean McCrindle and members of the Barnsley Women's Action group. The young women drummers, the majorettes, were given the place of honour at the head of the demonstration, leading them round and round Barnsley in great excitement.[234]

The networks of women's groups in mining communities had discovered one another, initially mobilizing women not for equal rights or liberation on their own behalf, but because they were unable to feed their families. Finding themselves parachuted into a contested political arena, many of them had reached out to communicate with people who were not directly connected to the mines. When I went up to Northern College to speak on 'Working-class Women and Autobiography' that June, I was caught up in the great flurry of support activity.[235]

The following month, 'Women Against Pit Closures' was formally established; Jean became its treasurer. Anne Scargill and Betty Heathfield were ex-officio officers, along with several supporters, one of whom was Shelley Adams from Brent Trades Council and the South-East Region of the TUC (SERTUC). Shelley acted as the link between Women Against Pit Closures and the printers in SOGAT, who not only donated large sums of money but, prodded by Shelley, were to organize an enormous demonstration later in the summer for them in London.[236]

Crushing the miners' strike became imperative for the Conservative government. Police were brought in from other areas. Mounted on horseback, they dealt violently with the pickets, invaded colliery villages and set up roadblocks as if they were occupiers at war with their own people. At the onset of the strike, Labour politics in mining areas had contained intermeshing contradictions. A powerful left memory of community resistance could combine with a deep vein of unquestioning patriotism. Racism and sexism could coexist with a militant trade unionism. But Margaret Thatcher's government and a media that followed her cue, turned striking miners and their families into outcasts and this internal exile led large numbers of them to look outwards to forge new solidarities.

Solidarity with the miners drew people together not only from the left and differing wings of the labour movement, but a much greater host of people. With Will and one of his friends in McDonalds in Hackney, I came across a bewildered cluster of Northern women clutching placards and collecting buckets.

They told me that they had been frightened about coming from their village to London and had been surprised and moved at being surrounded by black people from Hackney wishing them well and donating to the strike. I directed them onto a bus for the station home, remembering the words of a black nurse I had heard speaking at a trade union rally, 'If the miners go down, everybody goes down'.[237]

While some solidarized because they were adversely affected by the government's harsh policies and repressive laws, many others became supporters because they detested the prevailing celebration of greed and gain. Unexpectedly, isolated inhabitants of villages and small towns scattered around the country with a family memory of parents or grandparents who had worked in the mines rallied. As the months went by, the strike led to encounters across national borders. Both miners and women from British mining communities were invited to speak in Europe, North America and beyond.

On 11 August the Women Against Pit Closures march in London saw over twenty thousand protesters walking along in the sun together.[238] The women's tall paper hats, signals of a carnivalesque defiance, caught my eye and so did the SOGAT trade union men sweetly making and serving teas. When the women were getting on buses for home, I met Betty Heathfield for the first time. She was then married to Peter Heathfield, a leading figure in the NUM, and during the strike had emerged as an eloquent public speaker and a formidable organizer. These skills had older roots; Betty had been in the Young Communist League and also active in a women's health and beauty organization, speaking at their huge rallies in London. She had also organized a crèche for the children at the Derbyshire Miners' Holiday Camp at Skegness, where women met and talked with one another. She communicated an arresting mix of charm and wiry strength which fortified my resolve to try and help them by raising more support.

That evening I went to a social organized by a branch of Camden NALGO to raise money for mining families in Bentley,

Yorkshire. I sat watching a young miner dancing through the night with a NALGO member in a wheelchair. They moved together in reciprocal grace. And, through the dim golden light in the hall, I perceived that elusive utopian future of desire, love and delight which sustained my socialism.

* * *

Linda Dove and Bruce Green had invited Will and me to stay with them in Los Angeles that summer. On the first day there Will and I went to the beach; Bruce had warned of rip tides and told me to swim sideways, but when a loud noise from a megaphone was followed by the Americans all heading towards land, I supposed there must be a reason and thought 'Jaws, shark'. In I swam, only to find I stayed in the same place and then mysteriously seemed to be moving back out to sea. I saw an anxious Will running along the beach to the lifeguard; then I was being thrown a rope by an athletic Californian Adonis.

Clutching the handle on the rope, I was overwhelmed by embarrassment at causing this official person trouble through my incompetence and apologized profusely. My dazzling rescuer dismissed my regrets by explaining it could happen to the most experienced of swimmers. He thought I was worried about my inadequate swimming prowess, rather than causing someone extra work! Realizing we were locked in cultural incomprehension, I gave up, and smiled in silent gratitude instead. Still, I learned my lesson – several years later, when caught in a rip tide on the Cape, I calmly swam sideways.

I had arrived with videos of campaigning films about the strike in my bag because the film union, BECTU, had paid for them to be transferred onto Betamax so they could be shown in America. Bruce and Linda assembled a group of friends to watch the videos. Unfortunately, we had not thought about subtitles! Many of the Americans, who were not used to Welsh and northern British accents, listened in polite bemusement to the dialogue. Still, the images on the films spoke for themselves and people gave generously. Bruce passed these campaign videos on to radical distributers, so they were shown all over the country.

He also took me to a large Indian supermarket in LA and bought ingredients for a meal I cooked to raise money. He and Linda lived in a small apartment on Breeze Avenue in Venice near the sea, their kitchen was tiny and no sea breeze penetrated that August. I cooked all day and the thermometer on the wall showed 100 degrees Fahrenheit. A crowd of film technicians arrived paying what seemed to me an astronomical sum of $17, but Bruce insisted this was acceptable. By the time they came, I was limp with exhaustion and filled with admiration for professional cooks. Gratifyingly the technicians were delighted – Indian food was not so usual then in LA – and a man who worked for Jane Fonda arrived with a donation of wine. Thanks to these radical Californians, our two-week holiday yielded around £1,000 for the miners.

We did do some proper tourist things, visiting Disneyland and Universal Studios with Bruce, Linda and their two young daughters. A photo has survived of a mighty me lifting the imitation light-as-a-feather A Team car, and Will was intrigued to discover that the stand-in for Mr T was British and came from Tooting. Most of all I enjoyed just wandering down the Broadwalk by the ocean. Looking at the stalls selling all kinds of unexpected stuff, I noticed, amidst the surf gear and suntan lotion, large beautifully coloured slices of rock crystals in purple, green and amethyst for sale. These rock crystals perplexed a young left-wing refugee from El Salvador who Linda was helping to collect funds. He could not comprehend America at all, confiding in me one day with incredulity, 'You know the Americans will buy anything, they even sell stones to one another here'.

I could understand why people might want to sit looking at the patterns in a rock, but I, too, regarded other aspects of Californian consumption with amazement. People emerged through the vast doors of the local hypermarket pushing trolleys laden with mountains of toilet rolls. Inside a red, gleaming car was parked awaiting a buyer. In a pet shop we visited, mice were displayed in a diverse assortment of fun palace cages, mouse

Disneylands in miniature.

Capitalism in Los Angeles had a surreal glint, but it was brutal too. When Linda asked me where I would like to visit, I opted for a black working-class area like Hackney. She drove me to streets lined with shanty-like huts. Hackney might be poor, but it was nothing like LA. There was racial prejudice in Britain, but not this absolute separation. The only other white people in sight were in a police car and regarding us with incredulity and suspicion.

* * *

That unbounded, deranged faith that societies were best arranged by market forces was edging its way across the Atlantic and overturning many lives. It was not of course a new misapprehension, but under Margaret Thatcher it was being sanctified into a Cause. Its consequences were evident all around me. When I interviewed a factory worker, Joyce Butler from the Caribbean, for *Jobs for a Change* she told me how a woman from Wales had been brought in to sit next to her in the factory watching how she did her job, which was classed as semi-skilled. Shortly afterwards the company had relocated to Wales. Another woman may have gained a job, but she had been made redundant and her livelihood was gone. Like the former dustmen in Tooting, she was left severed from her known existence without recourse.[239]

Even though opposition was mounting, it was not at all clear how to transmute either global economic forces or the government's harsh economic policies. Like Lynne and Hilary, through our efforts to go beyond the fragments, I had come to see that local community activism or strikes in isolation were not sufficient, nor was any single social movement; instead, somehow, we needed to muster a series of combined resistances.

The GLC's significance lay not only in its innovatory new radicalism but in its accumulated public assets and the extent of its services. For instance, in 1983 the Supplies Department's turnover had been a mind-boggling £186 million. Its bulk buying kept the prices of municipal equipment down and its

1,100 workers served not just the GLC and the Inner London Education Authority but every London borough.[240]

Like the buildings Michael Ward had described to Hackney Trades Council, these were social resources stored from the past. Those dusty committee papers chronicled human dramas and vital collective reserves. I read Winifred Holtby's 1936 novel *South Riding* with new eyes. For her, local government was 'the first-line defence thrown up by the community against our common enemies – poverty, sickness, ignorance, isolation, mental derangement and social maladjustment ... based upon recognition of one fundamental truth about human nature – we are not only single individuals, each face to face with eternity and our separate spirits; we are members one of another'.[241]

1984 was the Supplies Department's 75th Anniversary and Michael arranged for Rodney Mace to compile and edit *Taking Stock: A Documentary History of the Greater London Council's Supplies Department* (1984). This was followed by Ellen Leopold's *In the Service of London: Origins and Development of Council Employment from 1889* (1985). The two books chronicled how the GLC's predecessor, the London County Council, had not only delivered cost effective goods needed by public bodies, but had used its considerable purchasing power to press for fair wages in the agreements it made with firms. The LCC had also backed the reform of low pay and bad conditions, particularly in women's employment. I, who had turned up my nose at the Fabians as elitist in the 1960s and 1970s, begrudgingly came to acknowledge what had been accomplished. These reformist socialists in collaboration with social liberals had bequeathed us a protective buffer against vicissitude.

I went to the celebratory exhibition up in Tottenham Hale mainly out of loyalty to friends in Supplies like Reg.[242] None of them were given to gush, but I knew social supplying was a source of deep pride for them. I wandered past the exhibits, half engaged, until I walked into a reconstruction of a London County Council school room, with small, well-worn wooden desks and inbuilt ink wells. And there, in a spasm of surprise,

I froze, momentarily transported back into the early 1950s. It was as if I was sitting at a desk in my first school in Leeds, amidst strange new words, 'Quinquirine of Nineveh' from John Masefield's poetic paeon to trade, 'Cargoes' – my first conscious memory of the excitement of the rhythm of words.

* * *

As an historian, I had charted many times how socialists and anarchists, in struggling against past social ills, had harboured longings for beauty, pleasure and enjoyment. From my twenties I had been particularly drawn to the life of the fun-loving American anarchist Emma Goldman and the nature-loving socialist Edward Carpenter, who had dared to write on homosexual love when it was still illegal.[243]

David Fernbach and Noël Greig had both been influenced by him too, and in September 1984 were about to launch *Edward Carpenter's Selected Writings* which gathered up his essays on love and sex. David, a thorough organizer, must have impressed upon me the necessity of punctilious timing, for I encircled '15-20 mins' in red ink in my diary.[244] This was understandable; my fellow panellists were two consummate stars, Dora Russell, the socialist and feminist who had been campaigning for birth control, sex reform and women's freedom since the 1920s and Fenner Brockway, the legendary Labour leftist, who had been a friend of Carpenter's in the early twentieth century. Despite being aged ninety and nearly ninety-six respectively, they were both accomplished speakers. I listened as Fenner Brockway described with affection how important Carpenter's non-judgmental attitudes to sex had been for him as a young man, while Dora startled the young gay men in the audience with her foghorn frankness about sex, just as she had amazed and entranced me when I had first met her in the 1970s.[245] Several generations mingled in this meeting of memories.

Later in the month I took Will to Dublin when I was invited to contribute to the Irish Labour History Conference. This meant a reunion with a close friend from the 1960s, Theresa Moriarty, who had done extensive research on Irish women's trade union history and her partner, Gerry Doherty, a builder, who was a strategically-minded socialist and a former member of the Official wing of the IRA. He and Theresa appointed an older boy they knew to be Will's minder so I could speak at the conference. Like the Welsh, the Irish labour historians had close links with contemporary trade unions, and in December 1983 Theresa had started working with a group of women from the National Union of Public Employees (NUPE), who had embarked on an oral history project. Initially they had intended to oppose privatization by showing the work they did. But their enquiry had extended in scope and vision to document the broader context of working-class women's health, diet, housing, sexual relationships, childbirth and childcare. In the process the researchers themselves had gained confidence. As Anna McGonigle, a school meals worker from Omagh, explained, 'We want to advance. You cannot really do that unless you know where you have been .... We have settled for too little in the past. We working women are part of history. History is us. We are never going to be invisible again.'[246]

The welcome in Dublin made me feel at home. However, I had no sooner started my talk when the lights went out. After much commotion and technicians rushing around, it transpired that the power supply was not able to run the lights and the microphone simultaneously. I opted for illumination and bellowed, thanking my lucky stars for the school drama teacher who had taught us to throw our voices. An elderly Irish Republican, who I suspected was dubious about hosting an English feminist, chaired the session and I swear I detected a flicker of respect from him at my capacity to boom.

Another wary chairman cropped up in Canada the following month. I had been invited to give a lecture at Dalhousie University which happened to be a Memorial for Dorothy J. Killam, a wealthy donor to the university library. This time it was not my Englishness which was at issue, but the upsetting news that I was a Marxist which led the senior academic in the

chair to give me a decidedly grumpy introduction, ending with
the observation, 'Dorothy Killam was no Marxist'. The audience
reacted by booing and barracking him in my defence.
Things were not beginning well. So, brandishing a broad grin,
I quickly responded with the first thing that came into my head,
'Marx's mother would no doubt have agreed with Dorothy
Killam; she thought it was a pity he did not *make* Capital instead
of just *writing* about it'.[247] Everyone laughed, including the wife
of the chairman and it cleared the air for me to launch into my
lecture with the grand title of, 'What Do Women Want? Woman
Centred Values and the World As It Is'.

I took the term 'woman-centred values' from Hester
Eisenstein's *Contemporary Feminist Thought* (1984) in which
she argued for 'entering the world and attempting to change
it' by putting these 'at the core of feminism'.[248] I agreed on
the combination. However, still worried about freezing some
fixed difference of womankind, which was likely to turn into a
future obstacle, I was uncertain quite how such values were to
be delineated. I wondered too, 'How do you create and assert an
alternative in a world that is not your own?'[249]

I had observed that even while seeking transformation, we
carried the old forms of relating along with us. Of course, we
had to begin with what we knew, but this could lumber us with
misleading signals. Nor did radical movements for change
necessarily share the same starting points, so suppositions
and perspectives could be at variance. In contrast to women's
liberation's emphasis on personal and social freedom, Women
Against Pit Closures had begun by claiming respect as contributors to their communities' well-being. I was convinced both
were needed. Yet I remained unsure how particular realizations
which came from specific struggles might extend beyond them?

Wants were complicated too. I warned that utopian
alternatives were not sitting around 'in neat bundles' to
be picked up. I saw them as dynamically created through
movements of resistance and rebellion, often fractured and
ambivalent, realized, then forgotten, to be reinterpreted by

new generations.[250] My American socialist feminist friend, the historian Temma Kaplan, was more positive. Familiar with women's grass-roots activism in Latin America and Africa, she observed that 'without fetishizing the feminine we ought to be able to appropriate certain values formerly denigrated or idealized as feminine …'[251] I recognized that resources for alternative values were vital, but continued to fear that this appropriation could constrain us.

* * *

Transformatory envisaging seemed a long way indeed from the world as it was in Britain that autumn. In October, Margaret Thatcher had narrowly escaped a bomb attack from the Provisional IRA at the Conservatives' conference in Brighton. She emerged, intent on improving the National Coal Board's public relations and devising ploys to coax and elbow miners back to work. Some miners did return, but the majority held out and that besieged winter I came across a young Yorkshire miner with a collecting bucket outside the GLC. I noticed he had no gloves and his hands were red in the cold. But he spoke animatedly to me, 'They talk about community. But this is community. All these people coming in. We don't go to our Town Hall like here. You could spend a real day out, just coming here.'

He was right, County Hall did buzz with an unpredictable energy. One day you would hear the London fire brigade brass band practising sonorously in a committee room and on another be confronted by an excited group of gondoliers from Venice who were on strike, stuck in the swing doors at the main entrance and protesting animatedly in Italian.

An intimation of freedom, release and possibility emanated through the visual arts, the theatre, the films, the dances for pensioners in the parks, and of course the concerts supported by the GLC's arts policies. The humour was there in the pink and white commemorative cake artists made for the LCC/GLC. It squatted on the Southbank, aptly in front of Phil Vaughan's kinetic light sculpture on the Hayward Gallery which constantly changed colour.

With so many diverse people gathered together, County
Hall hummed with information and ideas, both individually
and collectively. Pete Turner, the gentle, principled anarchist-
syndicalist convenor for the huge GLC Construction branch,
used to tell me about the dangers of asbestos to workers and
residents in between conversations on William Morris and
labour history.[252] There was a moving solemnity too in watching
as serried cohorts of our defenders, public sector workers and
pensioners marched past the windows of the Popular Planning
Unit. It felt as if the GLC had come to represent a symbolic
solidity, Martin Luther's 'safe, stronghold', a secular version of
his 'trusty shield and weapon'.

However, part of our heritage was also the rigidity and
hierarchy which lingered in local government and working in
the PPU made me wonder about the possibility of different
approaches to administration. Occasionally I used to bump into
Damien Welfare, who I had met through the People's Marchers
and their sleeping bags, and we used to chat as we passed one
another in the corridors. Damien was spending more time in
Parliament because of the government's threats of abolition,
and he observed how different it was from local government.
At the GLC decisions acquired a paper trail of meetings and
committees, but to Damien's surprise in the Commons and
the Lords he had noticed that matters were often settled by a
handshake.

When I remarked that administration might take various
forms, Damien averred, 'Sheila, Popular Planning is about
getting people to do what they want; administration is getting
them to do what they don't want'. I deferred to his experience
but was not entirely convinced. While I could see the latter was
likely to be a harder pursuit, I continued to puzzle over how the
structures of implementing change themselves might alter.

The PPU was filling up. A new desk had been added to the
narrow space by the windows because John and I had gained an
assistant, Joy Sable, who wrote for *Jobs for a Change* and greatly
improved our use of images. A tall young Londoner of Nigerian

descent, Kunle Olulode was looking extremely glum, sitting at a desk in front of Trevor's. When I investigated, I discovered he was a bored history graduate with left-wing politics. Before long Kunle was working with Alan Hayling on an Inquiry into Ford's.[253] Rosina Stanford arrived in the office too, and soon became involved in collecting together the London-wide contacts Dave Welsh and Gail Lewis were developing with transport workers in the TGWU, the NUR and ASLEF.[254] Trevor used to sigh as his clerical staff transmogrified into popular planners, but being an enlightened administrator, he approved, even though it left him with more work.

Brought up in Bow, East London, Rosina never adopted the post-hippie clothing common within the PPU, always dressing in suits of a rare and special elegance. When I commented on them once, she smiled and told me that her mother, after emigrating from the Caribbean to London, had gone out to work. An old Jewish tailor in East London, who was a neighbour, used to let Rosina sit in his workshop during school holidays. She would watch him with such intense interest that eventually he taught her how to cut out patterns and to sew. Thus, Rosina learned bespoke tailoring skills for men's suits and adapted them for her own wardrobe.

Working at the GLC had a big impact on Rosina. When I interviewed her in *Jobs for a Change* she told me, 'Since doing this job I've got more aware that problems where I live are not just my individual problems. I see them more collectively now, instead of letting my mum deal with everything.'[255] She identified particularly strongly with the tenants and other groups in Docklands who were resisting the London Docklands' Development Corporation (LDDC), a non-elected government 'quango' (Quasi Autonomous non-Government Organization).[256]

This powerful quango had been created by an Act of Parliament to develop public land and favoured expensive real estate. The LDDC's proposals had met with strong criticism from trade unionists and community groups in East London, as well as challenges from local planners like Bob Colenutt and radical artists such as Loraine Leeson. Hilary, helped by her PA, Lliane Phillips, gave support to the Docklands community activists who began to put together their alternative 'People's Plan' in opposition to the LDDC.

Strengthened by GLC backing, the astute tenants' campaigner Connie Hunt, along with other residents, had set up an organizational centre in order to consult their neighbours. Their large pamphlet, 'Peoples' Plan for the Royal Docks' (1983), produced by Reg in Supplies with colourful illustrations, graphically demonstrated a local economy based on peoples' needs, ranging from jobs, housing and nurseries to a five-a-side football pitch. Peoples' Planners resolutely delivered copies through Newham residents' letter boxes and mounted a campaigning 'People's Armada'. Led by a barge provided by a sympathetic Wapping lighterman, this decorated fleet was watched by thousands lining the shore, as it sailed down the Thames to the pier at Jubilee Gardens, opposite Parliament, to be greeted by Ken Livingstone on behalf of the GLC.[257]

While the right-wing tabloids berated the GLC for 'loony leftism', a small left opposition within the GLC workforce was castigating us as not being left enough. I knew two of the older ones: the porter Terry Barrett, who had made a brave stand on the docks in 1968 against Enoch Powell's racist speech against immigrants, and Don Milligan, who had been a member of several left groups and had written a pioneering pamphlet, published by Pluto Press, 'The Politics of Homosexuality' (1973), which I had helped to fund.

Schismatic and witty, Don once mused ironically that it was pointless denouncing members of Industry and Employment as 'Kautskyites' – opponents of the Bolsheviks – as no one but Sheila would know what he was talking about, and she wouldn't care anyway. He was right. Being denounced had become water off a duck's back. I found the left opposition absolute and intransigent in their views, but our arguments were friendly ones.

A truce developed over the course of the miners' strike and a left oppositionist from Ireland, Conor MacAvinchey, opted to come to the Virago Christmas party.[258] Upon being introduced to the novelist Naomi Mitchison, who was then in her late-eighties, I was star-struck and became lost for words. So, she turned to Conor, who worked in the housing department monitoring the compressed sewage which was carried down the Thames on barges, and enquired what he did. He informed her in resolute tones, with a strong Armagh accent, 'I work in solid waste'. She responded by wishing he could come up to Carradale House in Scotland, 'and sort out our dustbins'.

I smuggled the questions I had been too shy to ask her into an article I did for *Marxism Today* called 'Hopes, Dreams and Dirty Nappies'. Why did utopian fantasy exercise such a fascination? Was it because of a recognition that 'an impasse had been reached' or did it 'transport and transform' our conceptions by dissolving what we could see in the present into a new setting.[259] The answers, I fear, were left hanging.

* * *

Paul came round with a bike for Will on 21 December and then Will and I went to stay with Dorothy and Edward. They had provided me with innumerable ideas and an unstinting refuge for nearly twenty years.[260] I took special gifts with me, pleased to be able to show my gratitude; a pair of sapphire earrings my mother had left me, for Dorothy, and a truly beautiful jumper of blues and greys that matched Edward's colouring. It came from Covent Garden, and he handled it warily, as a strange alien London trendy thing. But it definitely suited him. I also brought copies of *Jobs for a Change* to distribute, gabbling away to them about what we were doing. It felt strange to me to know more about something than they did and to see how they were both listening so intently.

Another visitor was there for Christmas, Shen Han, the first Chinese labour historian I had ever encountered, who was happily copying documents on Chartism to take back with him. I could see that he was extremely curious about many strange aspects of contemporary life he encountered while in

Britain, and frequently had a puzzled look. This turned into complete bafflement when he watched *Raiders of the Lost Ark* on television with Will and me, despite, or perhaps because of, our explanations about the plot. I think it was the tongue in cheek dialogue that perplexed him.

He later visited me in Hackney, and I invited him to the GLC where he settled happily into the staff canteen. But it was not the food that delighted Shen Han so much as the orange squash, which he drank with a sublime expression of happiness. Alerted by members of the GLC's Food Commission on the dire dangers of sugar, I sought to warn my guest about orange squash. Shen Han politely disregarded my doom-ridden tones. But he did not resent my admonitions. When the Thompsons visited Nanking University, they transmitted his greetings to me and Will and reported that Shen Han was encouraging his students to read my book, *Hidden from History*.

Sheila Rowbotham in the kitchen at Powerscroft Road, c1980

Marc Karlin in his office, Berwick Street, Soho. Early 1980s

Lynne Segal and Sheila Rowbotham © Christopher Whitbread

Hilary Wainwright at the GLC

Sheila Rowbotham at the GLC

John Hoyland, mid 1980s © Elizabeth Woodeson

Peoples' Planners preparing their Centre

Newham Out of Work Centre

Members of Brent Black Music (project funded by the GLC)

Workplace Co-operative Nursery (project funded by the GLC)

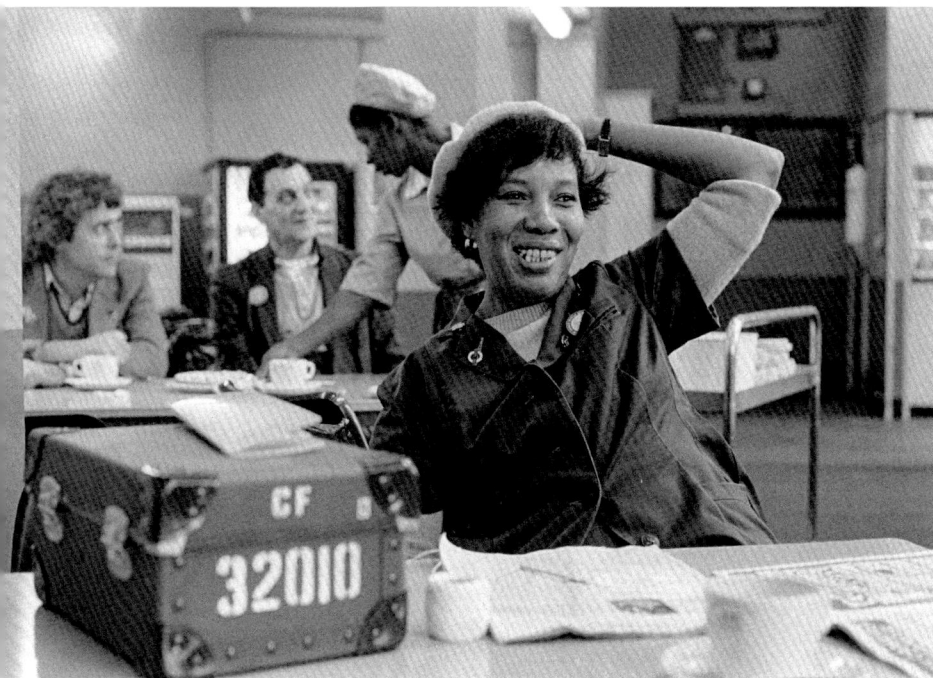

Vivian Bell, bus conductress, Chalk Farm Garage, 1984 © Val Wilmer

Barking NHS Cleaners protesting against privatisation, 1984
© Gina Glover, Photo Co-op

Knottingley banner, 'Miners' Wives' March 1984 © Maggie Ellis

Joan Bohanna at home in Liverpool

John Bohanna with Will Atkinson and a member of the Bolton Whitmanites, drinking from the Loving Cup on the Whitman Walk

Swasti Mitter, Sheila Rowbotham and Marja-Liisa Swantz at WIDER, UNU seminar, late 1980s

Women at WIDER, UNU, late 1980s. Left to right Radha Kumar, not identified, Kumudhini Rosa, three members of 'Les Femmes Mahgreb', Val Moghadam, Fatima Mernissi, Kumari Jayawardena, Swasti Mitter

Miners and their families with Sheila Rowbotham and mining officials at Dhanbad, late 1980s

Women surface workers at Dhanbad, late 1980s

Miners at Dhanbad, late 1980s

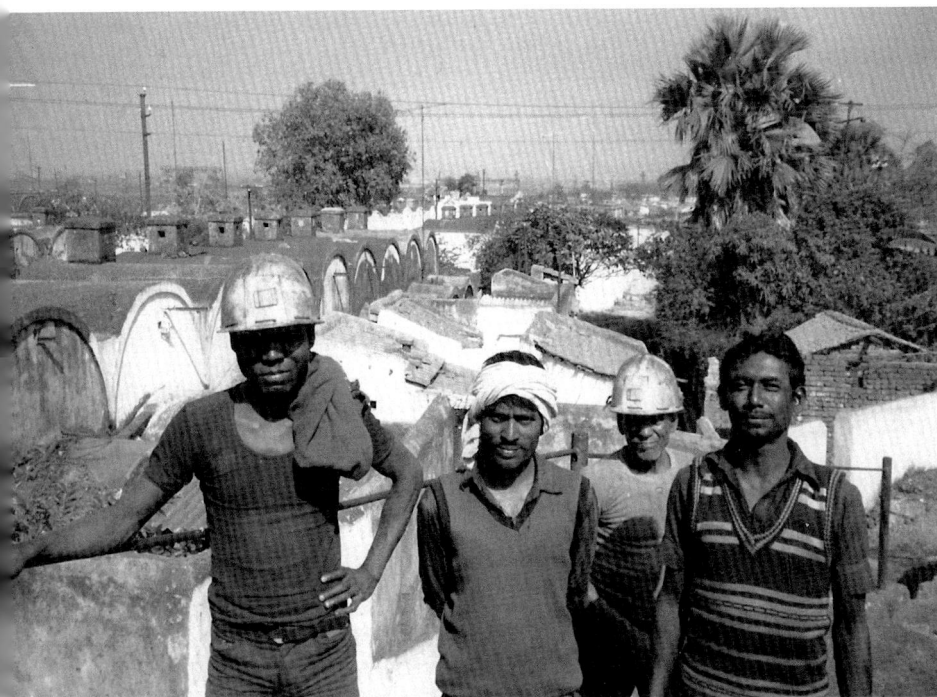

1985

The miners had hung on through the winter. But months of hardship as well as being battered and felled on the picket lines by police on overtime, recruited from around the country, had taken a toll. Hilary came back from the Christmas break resolved to make a big push to raise money for them. Encouraged by Jean McCrindle, we collected a small group of friends to contact well-known people for a Miners' Families Appeal for Women Against Pit Closures and Hilary found an eloquent photograph of a young miner with a child on his shoulders, strapped with the words 'Don't Desert Them Now'.

We began by proposing names we considered to be well known. But, fame being elusive, we found ourselves disagreeing over what constituted celebrity. In the end we agreed to differ and just started phoning. Their responses varied: Spike Milligan was predictably funny, while the entertainer Matthew Kelly sternly told me off because the Appeal was not sufficiently revolutionary. Everyone I rang agreed to sign, apart from a furious Doris Lessing, whose novels I so admired. 'How did you get my number?' she demanded. I ummed and ahhed without revealing that Ursula Owen had given it to me. Fortunately, her response was the exception and we collected a long and eclectic list of signatories which included Dorothy Hodgkin, Tony Garnett, Trevor Huddleston, Miriam Karlin, Pete Townshend and members of the band UB40, along with Bridget and Christopher Hill, Michael Foot and Jill Craigie.[261]

On 21 January Ewan MacColl and Peggy Seeger were performing at the Royal Festival Hall on the South Bank. The concert marked his seventieth birthday, and half the proceeds were to go to the miners.[262] I was a fan. Not only had I listened to their innovative Radio Ballads with Charles Parker, MacColl's singing had introduced me to the music of the American IWW, and the song he wrote for Peggy Seeger, 'The First Time Ever I saw Your Face', reminded me of Christopher Marlowe.[263] A group of us from the GLC gathered with our tickets, but the security men, upon hearing an Irish accent, barred Conor, who had helped with the telephoning for the Miners' Families Appeal, partly out of political conviction and partly because he was entranced by the prospect of speaking to his heroine, Glenda Jackson.

My instinct was to protest vociferously. However, a puckish figure appeared from a corner who I recognized as Norman Buchan, the great encourager of young Glaswegian working-class folk musicians. I knew Norman was an MP, though I was not then aware that he was the Shadow Culture spokesperson and a supporter of the GLC's arts programme. 'Hang about, hang about', he murmured to us. Sure enough the security man moved on, Norman signalled all was clear, and we were able to walk in. Conor had said he was banned by his accent from certain pubs, but this response at the Royal Festival Hall was a surprise. I don't think Conor was particularly interested in folk music, but he admired the IWW and loved occasions. And this was a grand left event. Not only because of the singers but because Arthur Scargill was at the concert and revealed that when he had joined the Young Communist League his first political office had been the 'Ballads and Blues Secretary' of his local branch.[264]

Support for the miners came from far-flung sources. Shortly after the concert I spoke on the phone with Obie Bing, who I had met through Ros in the US.[265] Obie worked at Con Edison in New York as an engineer. A celebrated athlete as a young man, he had quickly learned tennis at Cape Cod, where Will and I would sometimes be his hitching companions. He sent me a message of solidarity from his Local of the Utility Workers of America for the miners.[266] I passed it on to the former Fragment Dave Feickert, who had become a research officer for the NUM miners' union and was struggling to steer Scargill towards arguments for less environmentally destructive ways of extracting and producing coal.

* * *

Being an historian made me worry that things might be forgotten even when they were still going on, so I used to spend many hours disseminating written material on the GLC far and wide. On 29 January I was still correcting the copy for the next *Jobs for a Change* until eleven at night.[267] John and I prioritized articles providing information on policies and projects because we saw that as our brief, but we both hankered after something more. Just occasionally, words of foresight flashed onto the page. When I interviewed Winston Beckford, one of the founders of Brent Black Music, he observed, 'People have to have a way to live that their spirit accepts – not in inequality'. He reflected that otherwise they would just want 'to be on top themselves'.[268]

Early in February, taking a break from the PPU, I walked down the South Bank from County Hall to the opening of 'Exploring Living Memory', an exhibition generated by a group of oral historians connected to the London History Workshop Centre, including Joanna Bornat. Many London pensioners had loaned precious material and the result was an oral and visual cornucopia; I was particularly struck by the photographs of proud, smiling young servicewomen recruited from the Caribbean during World War Two.[269] I went to congratulate Joanna, who was brimming over with happiness, not only because of the memories recorded in the testimonies and objects, but because the Royal Festival Hall was a transformed space, aglow with excited pensioners reminiscing. They made me feel proud yet again of the GLC and at the same time sad about the impending threat to its survival.

I used to make coffee in a blue tin jug with a strainer in a tiny kitchen in the PPU for myself and friends from the GLC. I had extended this to the miners collecting outside County Hall from whom I used to hear what was happening in the strike. Dai Donovan, who was collecting for the South Wales miners at the GLC, happened to be among the coffee drinkers and when I mentioned that I really wanted Will to remember the strike, Dai generously invited us both to visit his home at Ynyswen in the Swansea Valley.

At the end of February, just before our appeal for the miners and their families was due to appear in the *Guardian*, Hilary took me out for a meal to celebrate my birthday.[270] We had barely ordered when she was called to the phone in the restaurant. Hilary is a woman with nerves of steel, but even she looked flustered when she arrived back. It had been the *Guardian* insisting that Liz Taylor's name must be removed.

Richard Burton's brother supported the strike and had urged Hilary to approach Elizabeth Taylor, who was staying at the Dorchester. He was convinced that she would be sympathetic. So Hilary and a miner went to the foyer of the Dorchester with a miner's lamp, flowers and a note about the appeal. Someone came down to collect them, after which Hilary had heard nothing and, with her characteristic optimism and Richard Burton's brother's firm assurances on where Liz Taylor's loyalties lay, took this for assent. What she thought is not clear, but her appalled agent had managed to terrify the newspaper. Her name was removed.

News that the strike had ended came on 3 March. The NUM executive had voted by a narrow majority to return to work. The suffering inflicted upon them, the odds they confronted, and the lack of mass trade union solidarity action had combined to defeat them. The National Coal Board officials, Ian MacGregor and Michael Eaton, were unconciliatory in victory.[271] David Widgery's mother, Margaret, a Christian socialist, who was taking food to the women at Greenham, sent me a card, 'Don't agonise, organise'.[272] Her son, a doctor and writer in the Socialist Workers' Party, had been my love in the early 1970s and I knew he would concur with her. Margaret's resolve gave me hope. So did the amazing response that came from our appeal.[273]

Though the destructive impact of the strike's defeat did gradually seep into our spirits, initially the momentum seemed unstoppable. On 8 March I went to visit Paul's parents in Nottingham, before going on the next day to Chesterfield for an enormous Women Against Pit Closures rally in the football stadium.[274] Joining Jean McCrindle and Ursula Owen on the march to Saltergate Recreation Ground surrounded by a crowd of several thousand working-class women, it felt as if an invincible force had been unleashed.

Perched on wooden seats we cheered the speakers, among them Anne Scargill, who had emerged as a forthright communicator during the strike. Her frankness, tenacity and warmth aroused both respect and affection and she was greeted with fond enthusiasm. Though I noticed that the eyes of the male trade union officials standing by Anne were lowered in distress, watching as her high heels irrevocably pierced the turf of the pitch. But football was relegated that day in Chesterfield; instead, the crisp March air rang loud with applause for Anne, for gays, lesbians, the Greenham peace camp and a woman speaker from the South African mines. Like the tender dance at the NALGO benefit for the miners at Bentley colliery, those bonds of resistance stayed with me. Quite how we were to sustain them I did not know.

* * *

So much was happening that our March issue of *Jobs for a Change* bulged to 16 pages. The headline was 'A New Deal for London' and it included reports on the GLC's inquiry on Ford held during January and February. The inquiry, along with an international conference of shop floor representatives, aimed to make information available to workers and trade unionists in an effort to offset the power of the multinationals.

One of the witnesses, Carole Tongue, a member of the European Parliament, happened to chance upon my desk when she first arrived, lost, clutching her suitcase and in a panic. I trotted her through the maze of GLC corridors. At the Inquiry, along with Professor Hilary Rose, she encouraged the women sewing machinists to air long-standing grievances about the unequal grading system that did not acknowledge their skills. Their militant strike action in 1968 had helped to inspire the women's liberation movement and triggered Barbara Castle's Equal Pay Act. But it was not until their six-week strike in 1984 that Ford had finally agreed to regrade them.

At the Inquiry I recognized Henk Vos the Dutch Labour MP from the occupation at Ford in Amsterdam and I slipped one of Jarti's photographs, taken when we had visited the occupation, into *Jobs for a Change*. We also carried a photograph of Dan Peters, a black shop steward from Ford in South Africa, along with Joe Gordon from Ford Dagenham, the first black convener in the UK, doing a clenched fist salute. The image carried a plethora of histories within histories – colonialism, race, class and a shared hope of challenging the information inequality shop floor workers faced. They were both about to head up to Liverpool for the international conference, partly funded by the GLC.[275]

Alan Hayling had drawn on his involvement in the Ford Combine to develop these active contacts, first within Europe in 1984, and then on a wider international basis at the conference held in Liverpool on the 15 to 17 March 1985.[276] Kunle Olulode worked alongside him with Jane Barker, the socialist feminist researcher from the Centre for Alternative Industrial and Technological Systems (CAITS). Both gatherings fostered vital direct solidarities among shop floor representatives, but not without some hiccups. The women in Liverpool did not hear of the conference until Jane tipped them off; their representative turned up at the last minute, pointedly plonking down the shopping bag she was still carrying.[277]

Robin Murray was aware that alternative international links were also needed among more isolated groups such as small producers and homeworkers. Early in 1985, along with Michael Barratt Brown, the adult educationalist who had founded Northern College, he had set up Twin Trading to encourage fair trade on a co-operative basis.[278] Twin Trading not only disseminated *ideas* of fair trade, actual goods started to arrive in the shop in County Hall. Instead of Masefield's cargoes from Nineveh, we had Nicaraguan coffee in abundance. When I struggled to explain to the sales assistant, an elderly woman from the Caribbean, the economic and political drama behind all these packets piled up around her, she regarded me with incredulity.

She was not alone. The GLC's globalism led Ann Sofer, the Social Democratic Party councillor, to comment sardonically in a committee meeting on 'our foreign policy'. She was mistakenly dismissive. The goods in the GLC shop marked the beginning of a co-operative distribution network which revealed the demand for fair trade. Small independent outlets and students' unions took the goods at first. Then, over the years, first coffee and later Fair Trade chocolate and nuts were slowly to make their way onto supermarket shelves. These visionary Twin Trading links not only survived long after the abolition of the GLC, they had a decisive impact upon poor people in many parts of the world.

* * *

I felt a personal connection to that Nicaraguan coffee. Marc Karlin had been making several films on the Nicaraguan revolution for Channel 4, helped by another close friend, Hermione Harris.[279] She and I had met at university in the early 1960s. Later we were both members of the Arsenal Women's Liberation Workshop group which used to gather at her home in Highbury each week until 1978 when she went to work in Honduras and Nicaragua for a development NGO.[280] Hermione came into contact with the socialist Sandanistas, and, in 1979, she and Marc happened to be visiting Managua when the National Liberation Front (FSLN) overthrew the American-backed dictator, Somoza. Hermione's contacts and research subsequently enabled Marc to return to Nicaragua several times; the result would be five films examining the everyday complexities of the revolution through the eyes of participants.[281]

By 1985 they were back in London with a young son, Alexis (known as Lexi), and a baby, Anna. In March, over dinner cooked by Marc, Hermione and I decided to take the children to Whitby during my Easter break from the GLC.[282] I planned to edit the lengthy introduction on the historical background I had written for the publication of my play *Friends of Alice Wheeldon* by Pluto Press. This had extended beyond suffrage, shop stewards and the peace movement into the less familiar territory of the intelligence agencies which proliferated during World War One.

On 11 April we set off northwards in Hermione's Volkswagen.[283] By the afternoon, we were in South Yorkshire chugging along on the motorway in the rain. Suddenly the windscreen wipers stopped. Hermione managed to get us to a service station, where she went to phone the RAC and change Anna's nappy. Will, Lexi and I waited for what seemed like a very long time. When she and Anna reappeared, we all sat waiting once again. There was no sign of the RAC and dusk had fallen. I was worried. Crossing the Whitby moors in the night with the rain pounding upon us, three children and wonky wipers was not on, but a night in the car park was not a good prospect either.

Then Will leaned forward and experimentally shifted the wind screen wipers whereupon they moved again of their own volition. Miraculously, all they had been waiting for, it seemed was a small eight-year-old hand to reanimate them. Taking heart, I realized that we must be near Doncaster where Ron Rose, who had put on my play about Alice Wheeldon, lived. Another telephone call and we were saved for the night. The next morning, we were awakened by the children early, the skies had cleared and we resumed our unexpectedly lengthy journey.

Accustomed to one child, I discovered that being with three in a cottage made it markedly more difficult to write, I resorted to staying up into the early hours, only to catch conjunctivitis and find myself peering at the paper through pink and bleary eyes. Going home at the end of the week began to look like a rest.

Alice Wheeldon plus the GLC had made me try to be ruthless

in refusing talks. But on Saturday 11 May I did go to honour the rebel Leveller soldiers who had been shot in the churchyard at Burford in Oxfordshire because they supported a mutiny over arrears of pay and lack of democracy in Oliver Cromwell's army. My topic, 'The Roots of Socialism', was familiar.[284] However, I was not confident about speaking in the open air and was touched when the former trade union leader Jack Jones, now an active pensioner, encouraged me. Luckily, he had forgotten the onslaughts mounted against the inertia of the Transport and General Workers' Union in the early 1970s when we women's liberation members had been campaigning with the night cleaners.[285]

But the most nerve-racking gig ever was reading from the personal account I had written about growing up in suburban Leeds during the 1950s. 'Revolt in Roundhay' appeared in the Virago collection of feminist reminiscences edited by Liz Heron, *Truth, Dare or Promise*.[286] There was no way out, for Liz was now sitting at a desk between me and Gail Lewis in the PPU, working on a campaigning newspaper about abolition.

Before we were due to start, I was rigid with terror at the prospect of revealing my youthful naivety and gormless encounters with boys. Alison Fell, poet and the novelist that she was, and thus accustomed to such events, came up with the solution. Her advice was to drink two vodkas beforehand, but no more as I would go slurry. Two vodkas later, I expanded with confidence. After the first laugh from the audience, it began to be enjoyable. Not only did their good humour bounce back and encourage me, such is the communicative power of vodka and mirth that as we went out, two men who had gate-crashed left shaking their heads and declaring they would never believe anyone again who said feminists didn't have a sense of humour.

Will and I departed on a big adventure during his half term at the end of May to Ancient Cottage, Ynyswen in South Wales. Dai Donovan collected us at the station, telling Will about his two young sons and relating what had been happening since the end of the strike. Dai was so genial and at ease, it made me

wonder how he had preserved such ebullience and equanimity
through that desperate year of swings, roundabouts and reverses.
When I came to know him a little better, I decided that he really
liked relating with people and possessed a profound faith in the
importance of direct human to human communication. The
same conviction was deeply engrained in me too.

Margaret Donovan, the willowy dark-haired woman waiting
for us at Ancient Cottage, was less immediately outgoing. She
observed and sussed you out before connecting, and then
slowly reached out strongly and surely. We had young sons in
common, but also politics, for Margaret was a socialist active
in the Labour Party and CND who had gone to Greenham and
was involved in the South Wales Women's Support Group. She
proudly held out the poetry women had written about the strike
and joked that never before had they been so fashionably dressed
in the village thanks to all the clothes donated by supportive
local government workers in Camden NALGO.

Seven young men were staying too from the Gays and
Lesbians of London group who had rallied to support the
miners' strike. I later learned that Dai had played a crucial part
in forging links with them. A neighbour dropped in, looked
around at us all and teased Margaret about being surrounded
by so many men. An embarrassed Margaret, protective of our
moral reputations, hustled her into the kitchen, shushing and
whispering, 'They're gay'. There was no such sotto voce for the
neighbour. Unabashed she declared loudly she didn't care what
they were and announced she liked 'the one with the earring'.
Margaret and I wryly smiled.

I was grateful to the gay men for their offer to stay with
the children while we went to the Miners' Social Club, where
I was introduced to a fellow historian, Hywel Francis, whose
book on the South Wales miners I had read. Deeply committed
to working-class education, Hywel was intent on keeping
memories of what had happened in the strike alive and had
organized an archive.

I spent that evening sitting at a table with an elderly man and woman who poured out memories of their lives and told me of their heartfelt affection and admiration for the gays and lesbians who had been such loyal supporters. When a young black Londoner from Broadwater Farm council estate stood up and made a rousing speech of solidarity, proffering an invitation to his listeners to spend their holidays on the estate in Haringey, I witnessed another barrier of fear and distrust being overcome. Surreptitiously, I did wonder if exchanging the subtle medley of greens in the Welsh countryside for the Brutalist-style architecture of Broadwater Farm would suit everyone. But I was clearly in a minority, as everybody vigorously applauded.

The following day a group of us travelled on a bus to the Powys home of Richard George William Pitt Booth, the eccentric bookseller and friend of Arthur Scargill, who supported the miners. He lived in Hay-on-Wye, which he had helped to turn into a town packed full of second-hand books. Dai loved these shops, and I wandered happily in them too, coming out clutching *Jane at War,* a wonderful collection of 1940s cartoons. Jane had been an early source of inspiration aged six because a kindly waiter in a Whitby hotel had taught me to read from the cartoons in the *Daily Mirror.* I remembered admiring Jane's resourceful pluck and wondering vaguely why she so often wore only frilly underclothes.

We all sat on the grass with a ruined Norman castle looming over us. Evidently our host, Richard Booth, had lived in the castle before it had caught fire. His hope was to bring about harmony between the miners and local hippies. This did not quite gel. Several toddlers were crawling happily in the grass with nothing on. This could have been construed as infants enjoying nature on a warm and sunny day, but the consensus among the women was that it was not right and showed negligence. I have never felt too confident on motherly matters and my loyalties were divided, so I tried to mumble reassurance and slunk off to the tarot reader.

In the 1960s and 1970s I used to go to fortune tellers in the hope that they would illuminate my love life. Instead, they invariably left my erotic fate dangling. Indeed, one in a tent in Blackpool, after hearing my complex woes, advised me to concentrate on my writing. Although this Welsh hippy one was far into the cider, he seemed to have blown my cover and spotted a socialist feminist bureaucrat, for he saw a large building in the cards and much creativity being sacrificed. This disturbed me, but I perceived it was not going to be possible to explain to such a dazed prophet about Winifred Holtby or the human dramas embedded in the GLC's London Industrial Strategy.

Margaret was politely tolerant towards the hippies, but a forceful and eloquent friend of hers, Siân James, who was involved in both the Labour Party and the Campaign for Nuclear Disarmament, was totally unphased. Siân was ready to meet and take on all kinds of people. The violent policing in the strike had convinced her that the miners and their families were being targeted by the government, becoming 'next in line after lesbians and gays, black men, black women'.[287]

We were seated near an old, broad-trunked tree, and Siân began to describe to Will the lives of little beings who inhabit tree-roots. She had a way with words, and I noticed that Will, despite his London kid scepticism, was listening intently. After one glass of cider I, too, was believing they might peep out at any moment. Siân's dynamism took her to university and eventually to become a Labour MP.

That weekend, filled with thoughts, feelings and fellowship, remained with me; but it was the Donovans' playful collie dogs running free in the countryside and nuzzling craftily towards his plate of egg and chips that imprinted themselves on Will's memory.

* * *

I returned to the GLC to find Robin Murray pounding out his introduction to the London Industrial Strategy (LIS). Written section by section by researchers in the Economic Policy Group, it detailed the conditions of work and labour relations in twenty-three major areas of Londoners' employment, from health care to construction, from software to the docks. Robin was surrounded not only by these contemporary sectoral reports but by Charles Booth's monumental volumes on London's life and labour during the late nineteenth century and the 1940s optimism of Patrick Abercrombie's Greater London Plan.

The Conference at County Hall on 4 June when Neil Kinnock and Tony Benn were due to speak on the LIS was drawing closer.[288] John and I were becoming apprehensive about how we were to do an issue of *Jobs for a Change* on a document that did not yet exist. Yet Robin's typewriter still could be heard clattering away in his office and rumours reached us in Popular Planning that he was sleeping in his office overnight.[289] Charles Foster, the Publications Coordinator, was seriously worried. In between copy-editing, he was scuttling between Robin and Reg up in Supplies who was assembling the sections on his paste board. The introduction kept being revised; Robin delivered his sixty-four pages only at the eleventh hour.

It was little wonder he had taken so long. He was surveying a London scarred with wastelands where factories once had been, looking down 'roads of corrugated iron and guard dogs'.[290] Not only was he documenting rapid and destructive deindustrialization, with peaks of unemployment in some years of up to 50 per cent among young black Londoners, he was annotating its dismal concomitant, the decline in the power of trade unions to protect their members.

Critical of both the government's monetarism and of the Keynesian emphasis on economic growth as a panacea, Robin stressed an economics based on peoples' needs, sustained by combining differing kinds of human resources and driven by social values. He described how the Greater London Enterprise Board (GLEB) had countered the prevailing bias towards short term criteria by investing with a perspective which took account of the broader consequences for society over the long term.

Robin proposed extending the public economy and linking various forms of co-operative ownership to improve their provision of goods and services. But unlike the top-down nationalization introduced by the Labour Party in the past, he argued for greater control by workers and users over the state's activities, as well as the extension of opportunities for equality for all groups who faced discrimination.

He stressed how closer combinations on the ground, for instance between trade unionists and people in local communities, strengthened the possibility of making changes, and cited the People's Plan for the Docks and Coin Street, a democratic, co-operative project with housing, a market and small business units that had held property developers at bay with help from the GLC.

Responding to the pressure for childcare, Robin extended the Lucas workers' insights on socially useful work to the reproduction of daily life, without diminishing the human value of caring. He recognized both the realities of domestic labour and the need to respect and safeguard those aspects of home life that nourished loving personal emotions. The LIS was unusual in encompassing domestic activity rather than detaching it from 'the economy'.

His synthesizing task was complicated. The GLC might be a large and well-resourced body but it remained part of local government, within a capitalist society competing in a global world gouged by the imperatives of profit. This was a calculation that GLEB too had to confront in making decisions, for they were investing money from the public.

The selection of key themes was complex too because Robin's sources were disparate. While the LIS sectoral reports spun on the axle of an economics geared to the interests of labour rather than finance capital, their emphases varied. Some analysed the *existing* context and prospects within economic sectors, others, like food, health, domestic labour and childcare, along with the cultural industries, explicitly drew out transformatory possibilities.

'The Food Industry' is there right at the beginning of the LIS and drew on the work of the London Food Commission headed by Tim Lang.[291] It focused on jobs and the economy, but also on nutrition and the cultural significance of food. When researchers from the Food Commission arrived to do a special edition of *Jobs for a Change*, they had pulled out an array of packaged food, explaining to John, Reg and me the meanings of the unintelligible 'E' signs that indicated processing. Forever more, I would squint to read the tiny print of those food labels – coded prophecies of doom.

Similarly, the section on 'health' was not simply about defending the National Health Service from cuts and the implications of privatization; it challenged the top-down administrative structures of the NHS. The LIS also linked 'health' to other sectors, such as food and cleaning, noting the occupational hazards faced by workers in transport and in offices and embraced preventative projects that could enhance wellbeing, including a popular group in Hackney which encouraged pensioners with arthritis to exercise their hands by kneading dough.

* * *

In a short foreword to the LIS, Michael Ward observed that 'restructuring industry in the interests of labour' had become an actuality by people doing it.[292] Witnessing this 'doing' was educative and the GLC led me into many unfamiliar zones, from new technology to the environmental protection of toads.

In the late 1960s I had become friendly with Ben Birnbaum, a left trade unionist in the East End clothing industry. Ben had started work as a tailor and cutter in 1941 and could remember how they would defend tenants against the bailiffs who were trying to evict them. The clothing industry was in difficulties by the 1980s and Ben was working with the Hackney Fashion Centre, which the GLC helped to fund. By making new technology available to small local businesses on a co-operative basis, jobs had been saved in the clothing industry.[293] Like Mike Cooley, Ben was a firm believer both in the tacit knowledge associated with skill and in the social uses of technology.

I was not the most obvious technological campaigner, however I did ride the pioneering hybrid pedal and electric 'Pedelec' bicycle on a trial run. Its development had been supported by one of GLEB's Technology Networks, the London Energy and Employment Network (LEEN) and its inventor, one of many who had approached GLEB, proudly gave me a little yellow card inscribed with his name, Felice Campopiano. After the GLC's abolition, his innovatory model was finalized in Europe, proving popular there and in China rather than the UK.

Contact with LEEN, now headed by Susie Parsons, the socialist feminist whose organizational skills had helped to set up the Westway co-operative laundry, made me wonder if LEEN could technologize scrubbing. So, I started nobbling two young men from LEEN whenever I saw them in County Hall. It took a little time, but on 30 May they did come with Michael Ward to Westway where he was photographed putting clothes in one of the machines.[294] I smiled to myself as the young technologists stared in disbelief at the women scrubbing away, as they washed clothes by hand on wooden boards. LEEN did not manage to mechanize scrubbing, but they did devise a means of applying Combined Heat and Power (now called Cogeneration) which reduced the amount of energy used by the dryers. Subsequently adopted by large local authorities, in 1985 it was innovatory.

Our social economics extended to the environment. Ken Livingstone's enthusiasm for reptiles and amphibians from his zookeeping past had stimulated awareness of the dangers of exterminating rare species. So, when Balfour Beatty Construction were building a new road, the GLC insisted they had to protect the natterjack toads' breeding grounds and *Jobs for a Change* pleaded the toads' cause.[295] Subsequently firms such as Balfour Beatty might boast of saving animals and the environment, but in the mid-80s this was still widely regarded as outlandish.

Environmental issues could be divisive. Upon hearing about the dangers of lead in petrol, some Hackney parents formed a supportive lobby for the GLC's lorry ban. The lorry drivers, however, were not happy. When John and I met a group of their ferocious representatives, we were confronted with a volley of abuse. I blinked queasily as strong arms bristling with large and menacing cuff links and fists studded with gold rings, waved rather too close for comfort in our direction. I might be all for participation, but I was secretly grateful there were some desks between us and them.

In *Jobs for a Change* that summer, we struggled to summarize the critical implications of the wide-ranging ideas and policies which had emerged from the Economic Policy Group's research and the projects backed by the Industry and Employment Committee. This was difficult, for it entailed conveying complexity clearly and making the implicit evident without distorting either. The headline I came up with was, 'Who needs a new economics?' Simple things can be the hardest to write and I spent much labour on a few words.

> Most people are not particularly interested in economics.
> And to be quite frank most economics is not particularly interested in them.
> It is concerned about profitability and competitiveness – from which a minority gain the most benefit.
> Increasingly large numbers of people are being written off by economists.
> People, it seems, are uneconomic.[296]

The accompanying photograph by Val Wilmer communicated the tacit understandings bundled up in Mike Cooley's 'Things We Know But Cannot Tell'.[297] Her picture of Vivian Bell an Afro-Caribbean bus conductress, caught in a moment of spontaneous energy and joy during her break at Chalk Farm Bus Garage, expressed a resistance to human exploitation and confinement, all the more poignant because she was facing imminent redundancy because of One Person Operation (OPO). Val, who had started 'Format', the first all-woman photo agency, with Maggie Murray in 1983, is one of the truly great photographers.

* * *

1985 had been designated as 'Jobs Year' and Dick Muskett, in Industry and Employment's Project Development Unit, was organizing our second Jobs for a Change Festival.[298] Dick had acquired considerable experience through the PDU's involvement with local events put on by tenants, youth groups and trades unionists, as well as the larger 'Concerts for the Unemployed', and had two imperatives for success – plenty of space and a wide range of music. Discovering that Battersea Park was already booked by Wandsworth and Battersea Trades Council, he combined forces with them. Tony Hollingsworth and the musicians ensured diversity in the bands.

Before working at the GLC, Dick had been in the army and then the fire brigade. He used to assume a tough nitty gritty you-can-keep-your-utopias demeanour, calling the Popular Planning Unit 'California', because he claimed we were always smiling, sunny side up and hippie-like. But there was a twinkle under the gruffness, and John Hoyland and I saw him as our ally. We believed that like us, deep down and if at all possible, Dick wanted socialism to be about creative expression and fun.

The sun really was shining on 7 July when I went by bus from Hackney via the Angel, Islington. A large crowd had already congregated at the stop down to South London. As I scrambled on, I realized with amazement that the entire bus load was heading to Battersea Park. I arrived to find comedians, inflatables, clowns, donkey rides, discussions on the London Industrial Strategy and poetry readings by women from mining communities. *Jobs for a Change* and a joyous John Hoyland were there too, along with five stages and musicians ranging from Ravi Shankar and Thomas Mapfumo to the Pogues and Billy Bragg.[299] The *Evening Standard* estimated a crowd of 500,000 but, unlike the previous year, I could wander freely, examining the stalls stocked with food from London's many ethnic groups and T-shirts for every left cause imaginable.

The Local Government Act abolishing the GLC was passed that July. Yet despite the scorn of the right-wing media and the political power Margaret Thatcher was mustering from across

the river against her opponents, that large banner reminding
her of the numbers of people unemployed continued to billow
in the wind. To many ornery Londoners, Ken Livingstone and
the GLC had become emblematic of cocking a snook at the Tory
government and a resilient fondness towards it persisted in
London's numerous radical crannies. Moreover, regardless of
party politics, the advantages of having a London-wide authority
were evident well beyond the left. Some had benefited from its
job saving and redistributive policies, others from its opposition
to prejudice or from its support for invention, the environment,
childcare, education, healthy food and the creative arts.[300]

* * *

When I visited Ros Baxandall at the Cape that August and
climbed the steep old winding staircase to her bedroom-cum-
study, as usual, I discovered new women's history books on
her shelves. I seized on Paula Giddings' *When and Where I
Enter* (1984), an invaluable overview of the differing forms the
resistance of black American women to racism and sexism has
taken, and an exciting collection edited by the young historical
sociologist Ruth Milkman, *Women Work and Protest* (1985).
Ruth's own contribution examined the influence of feminism
on American women workers from the late 1960s, while noting
their alienation from the emphasis on individual advancement
currently being pushed in the US media.[301]

Ros and Liz Ewen were working together on a study of the
lives and thoughts of women in the New York suburbs and
Liz had just written a book, *Immigrant Women in the Land of
Dollars* (1985), about the history of Italian and Jewish women
on the Lower East Side, published by *Monthly Review*'s Feminist
Library. Like other American socialist feminists, they were both
researching against the mainstream.

In their tribute to the New Left founders of *Monthly Review*,
Harry Magdoff and Paul Sweezy, Ros and Liz reflected on the
submergence of the radical edge of women's liberation. They
described having seen the 'autonomous women's movement'
as creating space for women to define specific grievances and

develop strategies for 'the transformation of society', but were now both troubled by the narrowing of the feminist movement in the States.[302] Instead of an outgoing collectivity and sisterhood, they detected enclosure and a 'circumscribed' preoccupation with a 'self' of careers and cash.[303] The British media also was inclined to present feminism in terms of individual success, though in a more muted form, partly, I think, because the co-operative values of socialism had not been assailed as ruthlessly as they had in America.

The conversations with Liz and Ros were in my mind when I flew from Boston to Toronto where, on 16 August, I gave the introductory talk at the international 'Issues for the Next Generation Conference'.[304] I encouraged the young audience not to confine themselves to a feminism that only expressed privileged women's predicaments, nor to be content with the older liberal-radical tradition of individual rights because it overlooked the social and economic needs of many women. Reflecting on the women's liberation movement, I summed up two knots we had tussled to unravel: how to change our lives and perceptions of ourselves within a male-defined culture, while challenging the external structures that perpetuated domination.

I argued it was important to seek alliances, for men, as well as women, could contribute to uncovering the sources of male power. Describing the women from British mining communities in the Chesterfield football stadium cheering trade union supporters from South Africa, lesbian women and the protesters at Greenham, I asserted how strength accrued when movements from below connected and combined.

I ended by stressing that looking back at history did not mean being weighed down uncritically by what had gone before. I had been reading *The Russian Enigma* by the left oppositionist imprisoned by the Bolsheviks, Ante Ciliga, and quoted his counsel. 'The authority of Marx and Lenin permitted the economizing of strength and prevented the necessity of battering down open doors; but too often it caused entirely new phenomena to be overlooked.' Then, adapting from Goethe, Ciliga added, 'All theory is hoary, but the tree of life is eternally green'.[305] I ended by urging 'the Next Generation' not to waste energy battering down open doors, but never to disregard new phenomena and that tree of life.

I was feeling lonely and was grateful when Skye Stollmeyer, a Canadian of Caribbean descent, and a young man from the South African Black Consciousness Movement, who had been sitting together at the front grinning encouragement, came up to greet me after the lecture. A youthful David Miliband, who I knew slightly through his parents Ralph and Marion, was also at the 'Issues for the Next Generation Conference' and we happened to go to the same workshop. David was sitting next to a miner from Britain at the back of the room, when a slick enthusiast put a deterministic case for technological modernization and capitalism Inc. I turned around hoping they would argue back. Both were frowning anxiously but neither of them spoke, so I stuck my hand up.

It was a rash intervention, for while I recognized the value of socially useful technologies theoretically, and had accrued experience through dryers, LEEN and that Pedelec bicycle, personally I did, and still do, resist learning how to work new things. But with Mike Cooley's calm and incisive voice echoing across the Atlantic, I contested the assumption of neutrality in how technology was designed and applied. Though I was brushed aside with condescension, I felt relieved to have cast dissent into the bland celebration of technology as the means of making capitalism the best of all possible worlds.

* * *

In October the *New Socialist* printed my review of Raymond Williams' essays *Towards 2000*. I had been reading his work on cultural history since I was at school and respected him as a member of the new left of the 1950s and 1960s who had critiqued technological fatalism. I had been puzzled, though, that in the early days of women's liberation, despite arguing for a Marxism which spanned the material activities and social relationships

of human beings, Williams had resisted feminists' critiques of
male perspectives in culture.

Nevertheless, much in these probing essays resonated. For
instance, he examined how socialism needed to establish a
central power strong enough to resist reaction, while enabling
new co-operative forms to flourish and also posited the mix of
representative and participatory democracy which the GLC had
been practising.[306]

Because the GLC covered a city with a population the size of
some small countries, it had seemed inconceivable that it could
be simply annihilated. But, by the autumn of 1985, it felt as if
hope hung by increasingly fragile threads. I was apprehensive
about the future and adhered to Williams' resolute insistence
that we must 'safeguard and nurture our resources'.[307]

The restrictions placed by the Conservative government
upon the GLC meant John and I could no longer produce
Jobs for a Change each month. However, the government had
not thought to ban *talking* with people. An interview catches
a particular moment like a snapshot, but on being multiplied
these can testify to a wider process. When combined with
written records, for greater accuracy, oral accounts offer a
means of comprehending more deeply what happened and
what was understood at the time.

I decided to assemble a record of accounts from trade
unionists and community activists on the impact of the GLC
upon their work, projects and campaigns. I encouraged others
in the PPU to do the same because I knew that these were the
kind of understandings that tended to dissolve as memory fades,
leaving only the stripped-down structures of officialese. I hoped
they might help to prevent wasting energy in battering down
doors that had already been opened.[308]

I was aware that Ernie Scarborough, who was working
in the GLC's Industrial Development Unit, had played an
important role in developing the Lucas workers' alternative
plan. I interviewed him in his office, where he was helping trade
unionists to spot the early warning signs of redundancies or

closures – a left-wing version of 'Be Prepared'.

When I enquired how he became a socialist, Ernie went back to his traumatic time in the navy during the war when as a young sailor he had been involved in resisting an order they had been given. His gaunt face crumpled as he recalled how the officers had staged a fake trial of the men accused, blindfolded them and lined them up for summary execution. Ernie had stood with the others expecting to be shot.

I listened in sober shock, aware that no one had ever been able to exercise such cruel and impersonal power over me. I think if they had that I would have either become deranged or been consumed by hatred. And yet Ernie had survived as a caring human being and had risked his own job security at Lucas Aerospace because he wanted to help children with disabilities rather than bringing death to unseen people in distant lands.

My diary in the autumn of 1985 and early 1986 notes interviews with some of the people I had met through doing *Jobs for a Change*. Several were at Ford and included convenors and shop stewards Joe Gordon, Steve Riley, Dora Challingsworth, a sewing machinist from the 1968 equal pay strike and Bernie Passingham, the steward who had supported their claim.

I focused particularly on health because Jeannette Mitchell, who had brought transformatory Politics of Health ideas into the PPU, was seriously ill with cancer. So, it fell to me to interview researchers and campaigners and to write up their testimonies for the collection *A Taste of Power: The Politics of Local Economics* that Hilary was planning with Maureen Mackintosh. It was difficult to do justice to the material I uncovered.

The London Black Women's Health Action Project, aware of the lack of research into their health needs, had made the case for specific measures for black and ethnic minority women. With support from the Women's Committee, Shamis Dirir, a women's health adviser in Tower Hamlets, told me how she visited women at home to learn about their needs and strengthen trust among them.[309] It was evident to her that the Somali and Arab women with whom she was in touch had to contend with racism on top of the widespread deprivation in the borough.

Defensive resistance and the recognition that more fundamental changes were needed, appeared in differing contexts.
Margery Bane, who had taken part in the 1981 occupation of
Hayes Cottage Hospital, recalled how workers had continued to
relate directly to patients and their relatives while also assuming
responsibility for their own areas of activity.[310] Lily Cook, a
veteran Hackney Labour Party member, who could remember
how her teacher had led the children in her school on a march
in support of the 1926 General Strike, had quickly assimilated
the holistic approach, kneading dough in the health group for
pensioners funded by the GLC. She declared, 'You don't want
to be packed off with pills'.[311] Her friend, another Labour Party
member in her eighties, told me how her racist assumptions had
changed because of the women she met through the group.

When I interviewed the Hackney Health Emergency workers Myra Garrett, Jane Foot and Lucy de Groot, all three
explained how they wanted immediate improvements in the
National Health Service, while also trying to initiate longer
term alternatives.[312] But they were conscious too how pressure
was mounting against such a combination. In Lucy de Groot's
words, it was 'a difficult dynamic'.[313] Even while I was collecting
the interviews, I could see it was getting harder.

* * *

I was in the midst of doing these interviews and checking the
transcripts when I learned that a group of tenants from Belfast's
Divis flats were coming to London. On 26 November I met
members of the Divis Residents' Association at the Town and
Country Planning Association's exhibition of photographs
which revealed the flats' grim and inhospitable architecture.[314]
The tenants explained that the poverty and violence rife in the
flats had convinced them an alternative was needed. Having
heard how the GLC had assisted tenants in Waterloo at
Coin Street, they wanted to discuss their campaign with Ken
Livingstone. He had agreed with Hilary to meet them for lunch
in the PPU.

Lunch. What lunch? I was bothered about what they would eat. The canteen was not practical because there were 16 Divi tenants coming, plus PPU members and Ken Livingstone. I was not familiar with the details of the social and political dangers in their estate, but I could guess enough about their schedule in London to be sure they needed proper food rather than tea and biscuits. So somehow, I became responsible for provisions.

Marks and Spencer's had recently opened a food store in Clapton. It was not universally welcomed. 'And why would I be needing pickled artichokes,' one irritated elderly woman had exclaimed, jabbing her finger angrily at a glass pot. But I regarded it as a great asset. Fortunately, two friends of Will's were visiting on 27 November, so the four of us scoured the shop for treats, carrying them home between us, with me pushing the plastic wheely bag. I had to get a mini cab to take the provisions in next day, tottering laden into the PPU. Our assistant, Joy Sable, had arranged for fresh loaves from the GLC shop.

The Divis tenants arrived a little early. They had been marching around London meeting tenants' groups. I could see they were weary and famished, but no Joy and no loaves were in sight. The visitors, obviously pleased about the food, were not put out by the lack of bread and started to eat. Ken Livingstone arrived, sat down chatting amicably with them, and he too munched contentedly away. I watched as the insides for the sandwiches; paté, ham, chicken, tomatoes all vanished well before a flustered Joy appeared at the door with a great armful of loaves.

If Dick Muskett had been there, he would have had a few quips about 'Popular Planning'. But as everyone else seemed to be happily oblivious, I relaxed enough to watch Ken slip with consummate ease from genial socializing to making a speech. What a skill, I thought to myself. I always found moving through that invisible boundary forced and difficult. I might be passionate about politics, but by temperament, I was an observer and a writer rather than a politician.

* * *

Christopher Pollitt, who was then lecturing in government at
the Open University, sent a panicky, last-minute request to
write on 'Feminism and Democracy' for a book he was editing
with the Marxist theorist David Held, *New Forms of Democracy*.
My deadline was a crazy two weeks. It was a roller coaster.
Embedding concepts of rights, needs, wants and equality
in the complexity that surrounds them circumstantially, I
zoomed through American Civil Rights, the early women's
liberation movements, working-class women's trade union
and community resistance. I argued that personal life and
prefigurative politics needed to be linked to democracy and
asserted that peoples' creative participation was not an optional
extra, for nothing would last that was not actively desired and
tended. I wrote 'Feminism and Democracy' by hand in ten days.
An heroic team of women typed it up, muttering about how
only women and donkeys could produce under such stringent
conditions. Together we did it and the book was published in
1986.[315]

I had also been asked to select the non-fiction prize winners
for the Feminist Fortnight Award. The ceremony was early in
December. One of the books that I had chosen was Kumari
Jayawardena's *Feminism and Nationalism in the Third World*
and there she was in person, a small, slight woman who beamed
out an inner energy as she spoke.[316] She had travelled all the
way from Sri Lanka and her first words to me were, 'You're
interested in Robert Weare'. I was amazed. I was, indeed,
extremely interested in the Bristol nineteenth-century working-
class socialist who had been friendly with Edward Carpenter and
had supported the 'new women' who joined the Bristol Socialist
Society. But he was hardly a household name in Britain, and I
was mystified to discover that he was internationally renowned.

I did not then know anything about his granddaughter, Doreen
Wickremasinghe, a progressive teacher and anti-imperialist, married
to the leftist doctor and politician S.A. Wickremasinghe. In 1948 she
had formed Sri Lanka's first socialist feminist group and exerted a
deep and lasting influence upon Kumari.[317] And, though I did not

know it, Kumari was to have a significant impact on my own life.

* * *

By December it was impossible for me to ignore that the GLC was coming to an end. Only a few months were left. My time working there had been so meaningful and fulfilling that I had been wrapped in an enormous survival bolster. The realization of the GLC's demise released those feelings of personal and political unhappiness that I had buried under my busyness. However much I tried to keep depression at bay, it would suddenly coil around me. I must have given vent to a sense of not being able to accomplish enough and to an inner despair, because a letter of reassurance came from Sally Alexander. Composed on a Saturday night at 2 a.m., it included a Sally-like reflection that was perceptive and wise:

> I know what is happening to us living in the '80s with dreams and desires shaped in the late fifties and 60s. And we are not young anymore. Just vulnerable still. We don't live 'proper' lives … But then we don't want to !!'[318]

She returned me to precious continuities – the strong friendships which had sprung up amidst those dreams, desires and strenuous efforts to dump capitalism, along with all forms of domination. On 23 December in green ink Nigel Fountain wrote in my diary, 'Nigel is coming to dinner avec pudding Noël'. The memory of dinner and pudding is gone but I am sure both were good. Despite those old altercations with my former communal house friend over food buying rotas, I loved his company and his cooking. And so did Will.

8

1986

In the space and silence that opened between Christmas and New Year, I wrote an introduction for Emma Goldman's autobiography, *Living My Life* (1931), which Pluto Press were reissuing. I had first learned about her when I was a student through Richard Drinnon's inspiring biography, *Rebel in Paradise* (1961), and her aspiration as an anarchist woman for 'freedom, the right to self-expression. everybody's right to beautiful radiant things,' retained its appeal.[319] By the mid-1980s I was intrigued too by the mesh of radical survival networks that had surrounded her along with the dexterity with which she embodied opposing values through stories about the people she met.

From January I was encompassed by the maelstrom of the GLC's last few months. John and I were doing a final issue of *Jobs for a Change,* I was interviewing people about Ford Dagenham and health, going to talk on the GLC at a comprehensive school in Eltham, writing a summary for the London boroughs on Popular Planning, while collecting material together for an archive. I was still officially on half a job, but it sometimes extended into the early mornings. I had regarded my work as a political and social calling rather than just a job and felt fortunate to be doing it. But now unemployment loomed, I forced myself to keep systematic records of my hours in my diary, totting up my overtime claims.

Hilary and I did a long interview with Ken Livingstone that January. Because I had been so immersed in the women's movement during the 1970s, rather than the Labour Party, it had taken me a while to comprehend how innovatory and controversial his recognition of the significance of all the social movements had been in the context of mainstream Labour politics. Ken was adept in facing off his opponents with a South London twang of humour, but underneath the politicking, he stubbornly held on to a vision of what could be. At the end of our interview, he confronted abolition with equanimity, telling us he was sure that young people in the future would remember what had been achieved.[320] Though I hoped most fervently this was true, as an historian I knew all too well how the memory of dissidence could be summarily wafted away.

I used to make frantic forays from the PPU downstairs to the basement of County Hall, coming up with armfuls of archival treasures. But even as I struggled to salvage newsletters, pamphlets and magazines, they were in danger of being taken away to be shredded. The shredders were impatient about appeals to posterity, and I began to feel like Mickey Mouse hopelessly bailing water in Walt Disney's *The Sorcerer's Apprentice*.

Luckily the porter in our building believed in preserving historical records and would pop his head through the door to warn, 'The shredders are out'. He would then give me a hand salvaging publications and depositing them into the PPU office on his trolley. Rodney Mace, who was also rescuing material on Industry and Employment, was another ally, and so were the school inspectors from the Inner London Education Authority, who met up with me and departed with numerous copies of *Jobs for a Change* to use in the classrooms.

Abolition aroused powerful emotions among many public sector workers linked to the GLC, who took great pride in what they did. At an exhibition, mounted to demonstrate their skills, some engineers surprised me by displaying what seemed like a magical telephone box containing a phone that could transmit your image as you spoke. They knew better than I how ahead of its time this was and were happy to talk about it. They were baffled by the waste of municipal expertise and shaken by the prospect of losing an institution they knew was a force for so much that was good.

Early in February I found myself pronouncing to a group of students from San Diego State University on 'What I have learned about politics in the last twenty years'. This was the daunting question set by their resolute politics teacher, Kathleen Jones. I had tried to wriggle out when she phoned, but she had stressed how important it would be for them and I had agreed because Kathy, an Irish-Welsh New Yorker, sounded like a fellow spirit.

She and her class arrived at County Hall on 10 February and I related my political life story written in a non-stop burst on eight sides of foolscap. In contrast to my frazzled self, the students looked bright eyed and bushy tailed, if somewhat bewildered. Optimistically imagining them establishing mini GLC's throughout Southern California in the decades to come, I explained how the Economic Policy Group had linked 'the rebellion against the denial of human resourcefulness and a demand for a more equitable access to the resources accumulated by human labour'.[321] Whatever they made of the talk, I could see from their faces that the emotional perception of dissolution had registered. The enormous bustling political institution they were visiting was soon to be gone forever.

That February a large van appeared outside our house in Hackney. Blazoned on its sides in large lettering was the announcement that it had been presented to the Dulais Valley Women's Support Group by the Gays and Lesbians of London. Margaret Donovan, with her sons, Llinos and Owain, were visiting for a Women Against Pit Closures meeting.[322] Will and I piled in to accompany them on an outing to see the sights and I chuckled in delight at the baffled looks from passers-by as we sailed through the streets in our valiant vector of memory.

Towards the end of the month I was truly exhausted and when, one weekend, Hilary pressed me to come to speak at a meeting of the Socialist Society, I knew I should have said no. But it sounded very important to her, so I said yes. By the time I arrived I was distraught and incapable of coherence. Standing by the registration desk, I could not stop weeping. A concerned miner put his hand on my arm, 'I got like this in the strike,' he told me. Whereupon I wept all the more at our shared misfortunes.

Hilary too was tired yet possessed a resilient capacity to keep going. She was looking somewhat exasperated at all this unhelpful emotion gushing about and I could see she was quickly trying to work out how to reorganize the meeting. I would often groan about her indomitable resolve, but another part of me admired her ability to keep on track. I took a deep breath, retired to the lavatory, sat on the toilet seat and, creating a metaphorical eiderdown around me, I emerged to start off the workshop.

It felt as if there was no choice but to keep on. From 24 January nearly 6,000 printers in the National Graphical Association (NGA) and the Society of Graphical and Allied Trades (SOGAT) had gone on strike to save their jobs. The newspaper owner Rupert Murdoch proposed to reduce the workforce and curb union rights through the introduction of new technology in the plant at Wapping. The pickets were being charged by riot police on horseback and the company was bussing in electricians who were scabbing.[323]

On 8 March, International Women's Day, feminists joined trade union women and members of women's support groups from both the colliery areas and the print industry on the Wapping picket.[324] I was grateful when Mary Rosser, who ran the Marx Memorial Library, offered me a lift from Hackney to Wapping, for road blocks and the presence of large numbers of police had placed the whole neighbourhood under occupation. I liked Mary, a tough and feisty Communist, though after she had shown me her bust of Joseph Stalin tucked away in the library's cupboard waiting for his glorious rehabilitation, I avoided discussing politics and stuck to conversing on their archives.

Mary, along with Mike Hicks from SOGAT, guarded me with excessive zeal, steering me around like a china doll. But I managed to hail Siân James from the South Wales Women's Support Group. Familiar with mass picketing, their contingent was dressed in sensible demonstrating clothes, the kind of outfits the Marxist historian Eric Hobsbawm called 'struggle gear'. In contrast, some of the women supporting the London printers had donned their own version of 'struggle gear', high heels and fur coats. True, it was cold on the picket, but the stilettos did not seem practical. I decided the glamour signalled their own species of defiant self-esteem against the police, Murdoch and indeed the government, for this had quickly become a politicized strike.

My own contribution to the Wapping struggle I confess was strictly on the sidelines. I listened in amazement to Mike Hicks rebuking police through the window of their van and was moved when a poetic printer greeted me on the picket with the words, 'That smile will warm me up all night'. Sadly, no dangerous liaison ensued, for Mary swiftly whisked me away home. The printers picketed for a year, only to be defeated.

* * *

That March the BBC finally showed Marc Karlin's 1982 film, For Memory, which portrayed the past being both forgotten and retrieved.[325] Memories folded into memories as I watched Edward Thompson, on the screen, speaking in the early 1980s at one of the annual gatherings at Burford to remember the stand taken by the Leveller soldiers who had mutinied in 1649. Edward had taken Will and I with him and we can be briefly glimpsed on the film, leaving the churchyard where the three leaders had been executed.[326]

For Memory records Edward speaking with conviction against past and present Leviathans.

The Levellers felt they were in a spiritual contest with the beast. And they had an extraordinary sense of the autonomy of their own judgment and spiritual faith. Each member of the army felt that if he came to a conviction of faith on a matter, then he must act as a witness.[327]

He continued, oblivious, as a bluish green banner slipped down behind him; an undesigned but appropriate symbol for

Marc's film which was about both the underground resilience and the fragility of radical remembering. Marc described Edward as 'The king of the tribe of the Great Reminders'.[328]

As an historian, Edward did, indeed, remind people, while also bearing a contemporary witness politically, in print and in person. Burford had been his second speaking engagement; in the morning Will and I had joined a huge crowd of demonstrators at a nearby American military base, listening as he warned of the dangers from nuclear missiles. His shock of anarchical hair was grey and turning white; he kept trying to contain these unruly locks by sweeping his hand through his hair, but invariably they would escape.

As we were winding our way along the bumpy track that surrounded the base, Will had become tired and I was grateful when a young man carried him on his shoulders. When some demonstrators behind us started a chorus of 'Yanks Out. Yanks Out', Edward, who was half American, turned back to challenge them with the ironic query, 'Where's your class analysis?' Amidst smiles, the nationalist chant subsided.

By 1986 Marc had embarked on a new film, *Utopia*s – a contrary topic when radical hope was beginning to disintegrate in Britain. Noting that socialists had been so intent on analysing crises in capitalism that they had evaded the cracks and cavities opening within socialism itself, Marc went to six people with differing experiences and perspectives for their comments. Apart from me, the others were Jack Jones, the trade unionist and campaigner for pensioners who had fought against fascism in Spain, Marsha Marshall from Women Against Pit Closures, David Widgery, East End doctor and writer, a loyal dissenter within the Socialist Workers' Party, Bob Rowthorn, the Cambridge economist, concerned about the ability of big finance companies in the City to thwart Labour Party policies and Ambalavaner Sivanandan, the editor of *Race and Class*. After coming to Britain from Sri Lanka and witnessing the racist riots of the late 1950s, he had exposed the impact of colonial rule and imperialism in shaping not simply attitudes, but the structures of state institutions.[329] In the film he stressed the interconnections of race and class.[330]

At the end of March, when Marc and the crew from Lusia films resolutely arrived in the PPU office to film me for *Utopias*, they caught me well-nigh buried among boxes and papers on wooden trays. Their film captures the fleeting chaos of the GLC disintegrating. Anxious to preserve as much as possible, in the last desperate days before abolition, I had requisitioned Kunle and another young revolutionary oppositionist working in the Economic Policy Group, Martin Durkin, who had studied classics and ancient history, on the grounds that they were fellow historians and, being in their twenties, were likely to be good at climbing on tables to take posters off the wall. I aimed to complement the GLC archive with the oral interviews and transcripts as well as the posters announcing all the varied events. I knew images and objects would communicate in ways that words alone could not.[331]

Despondency came to predominate in our last few weeks, and I felt apprehensive about the future. It was particularly hard for workers on low pay who had begun to experience some improvements in their conditions. The cleaner in our building, who was from the Caribbean, ended up embracing me as we talked about the politics behind abolition – there was nothing that either of us could do.

There was also personal sadness within the PPU – not only was Jeannette Mitchell suffering from cancer, but Frank Campbell, a former Direct Labour Organisation building worker, had recently died. Frank, who was from Glasgow, had been an early member of the International Socialist group and he liked to chat about politics over one of my PPU coffees from the blue enamel jug. At his funeral on 18 March, we had remembered the Swedish-American labour organizer Frank admired by singing, 'I dreamed I saw Joe Hill last night'.[332]

An excited Rosina Stanford cheered me up. She had been to see a performance by the Talawa Theatre Company of *The Black Jacobins*, directed by Yvonne Brewster and based on the book by

CLR James. Remembering how that kindly Haitian cab driver in New York had told me of his history teacher, I proceeded to hold forth in the PPU office on the various political tendencies active in the French Revolution. Rosina's face fell and she exclaimed in disbelief, 'You mean there were white Jacobins!'

Though the GLC had partially funded *The Black Jacobins*, it was now too late to back a proposal from a group of women pensioners from South London. Following the example of the Westway women they were campaigning to save their public wash house where they had always met one another. I had to explain the harsh consequences of abolition when we met in County Hall.

I had, however, booked two of the GLC limousines to give them a lift home after our talk. These used to be reserved for councillors and big wigs, but this had been democratized during Ken's regime. It was cold and the cars were still there. Those pensioners, who had worked all their lives with little acknowledgement and had contributed towards the rates over several decades, deserved a lift home in style. Miraculously I was able to use the redistributive power that still remained. Ensconced in elegance, with a grinning driver, they departed in a joyous flurry, whooping and waving out of the windows. I waved back until they vanished into the night.

The final committee meeting proved to be unexpectedly moving. Robin spoke with his customary skill and curiously the Conservative members, rudely sidelined by their adamant Prime Minister, expressed their regrets not only about abolition, but about being parted from us. One remarked with perplexed awe that he had never seen people work so hard.

Our Assistant Director of Finance Chris Duffield's comment afterwards was less starry eyed. He said he had never worked with such nice people and such bad managers.[333] I mulled this over afterwards and reckoned that he was assuming managing was about following an established formula of command, rather than considering how the context, and indeed the purposes, of managing varied. We worked so intensely at the GLC because we believed in what we did and were able to use our initiative. Indeed, such was the faith in strategizing a better future for London that two substantial studies, *The London Labour Plan* and the *London Financial Strategy,* appeared in those last few months.

I was so weary by the time of the 'Goodbye' party on 31 March that I drifted through it in a dream. I can vaguely recall the crowds and music playing and Hilary ingeniously declaring to a security guard that I was her husband in order to get me through some gates. Needless to say, I bore no resemblance to her real husband, the philosopher Roy Bhaskar, who was over six foot.

I found myself standing next to the elderly lawyer John Fitzpatrick, who I had lectured on the sacked Wandsworth dustbin men. He had postponed his retirement to help fight abolition. When I told him rather weakly that now I did not know what else to do but to tell people the story of what had been done, he looked at me with firm conviction and replied with the utmost solemnity, 'You must never stop telling people the story'.

An image of the GLC flag crumpling into the night as it was slowly lowered remains imprinted in my mind. When it finally went down I, who had never felt patriotic towards countries or institutions (apart from Market Nursery) cried because the end had come. Regret turned to helpless rage just after midnight when we were confronted by imported security men threatening us with Alsatian dogs in the building where we had worked. It was Margaret Thatcher and her associates' bailiwick now. County Hall was to be sold as an entertainment venue that eventually housed Shrek, sharks and karaoke.

Along with Hilary, I had decided not to stay on and join friends who carried on working in the new London Strategic Policy Unit, partially funded by nine London Labour boroughs. Others had put their names in a computer to be reallocated to jobs in the boroughs. Kunle went to Camden where he worked in equal opportunities and was later to organize Black History

Month. Robin Jenkins, who had worked on the food policy with Tim Lang, and had been responsible for healthier school dinners, seemed to puzzle the computer. After clicking and clocking away to itself, it redeployed him to managing women who made school dinners. Rising to the occasion, he secured their participation in devising ways of improving their conditions. Migrants from the GLC thus took some aspects of our work with them into differing contexts, while radical ideas about politics and economics percolated through to left organizations in other countries, like the Brazilian Workers' Party.

Many vitally needed projects were forced to close down, but the Workers' Beer Company, the Food Commission and Twin Trading were among the ingenious offshoots that survived. The latter had begun by buying and selling rocking chairs and cigars from co-operatives in poor countries, moving on to Fair Trade chocolate and coffee which eventually was to be sold in supermarkets.

When the GLC was destroyed it was extremely hard to think through and sum up what had been done. Hilary demonstrated her usual tenacity and persisted regardless of abolition. She had spent a year in intensive discussions with a group of workers from the furniture industry and the resulting pamphlet, *Beneath the Veneer*, appeared in June 1986, *after* abolition, with the backing of the Furniture, Timber and Allied Trades Union and members of the Labour Party – John Prescott, Margaret Hodge and Michael Ward.[334] The workers' in-depth understanding of what was happening in their industrial sector exposed details a top-down analysis could not have reached.

Hilary also edited a collection with Maureen Mackintosh, *A Taste of Power: The Politics of Local Economics* (1987), passing on knowledge collected through the Economic Policy Group's work. Chapters ranged from working conditions in transport and construction, to those of people in the creative industries.[335] Entangled within all these were intimations of a co-operative economy, voiced by members of community organizations like the docklands Peoples' Plan or workers and parents involved in childcare projects. Their words echoed aspirations from long ago, summed up in the old American slogan, 'Bread and Roses'.[336]

John Hoyland's essay 'Reggae on the Rates' quoted Ken Livingstone reflecting on how music festivals undermined strands within the politics of both the right and the left that strove 'to achieve, to control, to dominate'. He thought this 'inability to come to terms with yourself physically and emotionally' drove people to turn inwards, and close up psychologically. In contrast, his 'alternative world, a co-operative one' would be 'enjoyable' and allow people to 'relate easier to each other', coming 'to terms with themselves, their own bodies, their sexuality'.[337] When I read this, I decided the nature-loving left-wing Swindon councillor Reuben George was surely among Ken's political forebears. As Mayor of Swindon in 1922, he had startled onlookers by launching a new wooden diving board at an open-air pool by leaping into the water.[338]

* * *

Living resistance in practice could be rather more prosaic; Hilary, busy with Maureen editing *A Taste of Power*, while at the same time finishing writing her own book, *Labour: A Tale of Two Parties*, remarked, 'My life is very worthy at the moment. I'm beginning to feel like Beatrice Webb. All effort & brain & no fun … I should not complain though because it's all self-imposed.'[339] Marc Karlin, ostensibly so different from Hilary, understood her obdurate adherence to unpopular causes and used to refer to her affectionately as, 'Our alternative government in waiting'. But there was no denying the waiting time had lengthened.

Cut adrift from the friendships and that precious sense of collective purpose I had experienced at the GLC, yet still driven by John Fitzpatrick's admonition to keep on telling the story of what had been done, I travelled around the country trying to do just that. During April, I was invited by John Fairley, who had moved from the GLC to a job at Edinburgh Council on economic planning, to go up to speak.[340] The content of what was formally discussed that day has faded from my memory, but by chance I happened to be sitting next to John Smith, who was then the Labour Shadow Minister for Trade and Industry, and we began chatting about the shop stewards' movement in early twentieth century Glasgow. His direct friendliness and interest in labour history surprised me. There was no trace of self-importance as a politician, just a comradely civility. Like Jack Jones, he encouraged me when I stood up to go and speak despite the obvious difference in our politics.

In May I was at the trade union adult education centre, Northern College, near Barnsley, where Jean McCrindle taught.[341] We sat with a group of working-class women students watching Margaret Thatcher speaking about politics on the television. We all loathed what she was saying, but nevertheless could observe how cannily she moved between the 'men's' public sphere of politics and the domestic realm. One minute she was to be seen perching in her tank draped in white kit, appearing the next on film as the immaculate housewife, ironing shirts and washing up.

I continued to be convinced of the importance of economic alternatives. But I was pulled back towards women's and labour history when my play about Alice Wheeldon, an opponent of the First World War, imprisoned on the evidence of police informants of plotting to assassinate Lloyd George, was published by Pluto on 29 May.[342] Writing the long introduction to the book had enabled me to think historically about the converse faces of the British state.

At the end of May I went to talk on Local Economic Strategy in Birkenhead and stayed with John and Joan Bohanna.[343] Utopians and history came to claim me once again when Paul Salveson invited me to join the Bolton Socialist Club's yearly convivial and comradely walk on 31 May. They had revived an old tradition. Through my research on Edward Carpenter, I had learned of Walt Whitman's friendship with a group of his Bolton late nineteenth-century socialist followers. Whitman had given them a cherished gift of his 'Loving Cup'. This large round vessel had been deposited in the library but used to be released each year for the walk and we drank from it as we climbed uphill.[344] John Bohanna warily accompanied me to Bolton. He made a gallant effort, but I could tell he thought it was a rum kind of trek.

I had £500 redundancy money and some savings from the GLC so I resolved to get that long deferred book on the women's liberation movement in Britain done.

* * *

A small, furry diversion intervened. Walking back from Gayhurst School to Clapton with Will one sunny day in June, I acted on a wild and spontaneous impulse. Curiously, the remains of a farm had survived in Hackney. It was not one of the alternative community farms that had begun to appear in the 1970s to bring city kids closer to nature. This one had somehow resisted the growth of buildings around it and was run by two old men who still wore the white scarves tucked into their waistcoats that I had noticed when I first moved to East London in 1964. They were standing by a hand-pulled cart containing three puppies, one of which had gingery fur and floppy ears. It was love at first sight. 'A fiver,' barked one of the old men, spotting a sale. I nodded in mute assent and handed him the cash.

I carried the tiny quivering creature in my arms to the pet shop where a disapproving woman viewed us sourly and told me to go to the vet. Off we went to discover all was well, our puppy was just nervous. Will and I called her 'Scarlett' after the equal opportunities woman in his GI Joe action force to help boost her courage. So, Will and I became dog owners and, de facto, so did an appalled Dave Phillips, when he returned home from work that day. Dave was inclined to think further ahead than either Will or I and was not impressed by my assertion that I had not *intended* to buy a dog. Nor did he think much to my explanation that this foolhardy action might have been affected by the fact that Marc Karlin had come round to film *Utopias* that morning. Dave did not connect puppies with Utopias, especially not little mongrel ones resembling the kind of Cockney dogs Henry Mayhew documented in the nineteenth century who were trained to jump through hoops.

Dog-owning did contain unexpected perils. Will took Scarlett for a walk on Hackney Marshes by the River Lea and somehow she slipped into the water. Fortunately, a man was passing and he held Will by his ankles so he could rescue her. After that Will's unaccompanied dog-walking was deferred. As he grew older and more sussed, he came to realize that a small ginger mongrel with floppy ears did not enhance your Hackney street cred. So I, who had no street cred anyway, became dog owner in-chief.

* * *

By 1986 there was no longer any national organization for women's liberation in Britain, though there was a militant and multifaceted activism, a growth in international women's movements and vigorous debates, not simply between differing groups of feminists, but among socialist feminists too.

Feminist Review that summer included articles on race, class, the miners' strike, Greenham, the Labour Party and Republican women prisoners in Ireland. It also carried reports on two very different international meetings of women held in 1985: the European Forum of Socialist-Feminists and a gathering of 14,000 women in Nairobi to mark the end of the United Nations Women's Decade, which raised a debate that was new to me. Should 'black' be used to denote only women of African descent or more broadly to signify a political affiliation that comprised all women of colour?[345]

I read one *Feminist Review* article by Susan Ardill and Sue O'Sullivan, 'Upsetting the Applecart: Difference, Desire and Lesbian Sadomasochism', over and over again. It had arisen out of conflicts among women at the London Lesbian and Gay Centre over 'defining, discussing and organizing around sexuality as lesbians'.[346] The arrival of pro SM lesbians had been opposed by a group called Lesbians Against Sado Masochism, which included members of the separatist Revolutionary Feminist group. Neither were given to compromise.

By broaching an alternative approach to these absolute

positions of political correctness in relation to sexual desire, difference and identity and by taking a critical look at several received understandings, Susan Ardill and Sue O'Sullivan overturned more than one applecart. While asserting the importance of empathy with opposing feminist views, they resolutely challenged the tendency to acquire moral power in naming oneself as the most oppressed, pointing out how it could transmogrify into an inverted hierarchy. They also noted that the 'problem with taking subjective experience as the main key to political action is that people have differing experiences'.[347] Their article showed how feminist political assumptions should not be assumed as somehow exempt from scrutiny,

I too had become conscious of theoretical lacunae, including obvious ambiguities in the slogan the 'personal is political', but I, like them, did not want just to veer back to a left politics that stressed only strategic considerations, or the ends justifying the means. 'Upsetting the Applecart' opened new dimensions for what Audrey Wise had called 'generalizing feminism and feminizing the general'. It was all the more powerful for having been 'written at a time of depression and lack of confidence in feminist and left-wing politics'.[348]

Its two authors had to contend with their predicament of relative isolation as socialist feminist lesbians engaged in women's grassroots politics as so many socialist feminists had withdrawn and were focusing on left politics. I took heart from the manner in which they presented their ideas and their article helped to crystallize issues milling about in my head. Most of all I was grateful to them both for making a space in which intimate feelings could be aired without resorting to destructive recriminations. They had broken through an oppressive silence in declaring that sexual pleasure could be manifold and varied. Nonetheless I remained personally perplexed about the interlacing of sex and politics. In my forties I no longer possessed the certainties I had assumed in my twenties.

Dora Russell had died in May and her daughter, Harriet Ward, asked me to speak at the Memorial meeting on 8 July. I found it sobering that so many of the causes Dora had embraced – socialism, feminism, sexual freedom and world peace – were on the defensive still in Britain. Her book, *The Right To Be Happy*, published in 1927, had put forward such a simple claim, yet its implications were far-reaching.[349] Fenner Brockway, who had shared her struggles on the left and was, moreover, a staunch anti-imperialist, had been a close and loving friend and his sorrow was evident as he spoke. As I listened, I felt connected to him, both through my friendship with Dora and because I knew he had been deeply influenced by Edward Carpenter as a young man.

Harriet, like her husband, the innovative anarchist Colin, was quietly imposing. Her tribute to Dora was an adroit mix of fondness and irony. To me the bohemian, intellectual upbringing she described sounded wonderful, but Harriet intimated that this was not quite the case, for when she was young she had often longed for a 'normal' family with orderly domestic routines. While I knew from my own childhood that 'normal' was not necessarily as it might seem on the surface, Harriet's reflections set me thinking nonetheless.

* * *

When Will's school holidays began we flew to Madison, Wisconsin, where we were reunited with Linda Gordon, Allen Hunter and their daughter Rosie. I had been invited by the Marxist academic Erik Olin Wright, a theorist of class and the state at the University of Wisconsin. I gave lectures and held seminars on 'The Origins of the Welfare State in Britain', 'The Contemporary Women's Movement and the State', along with 'The Greater London Council and Extending Democracy'. I suspected that my approach was too historical and not sufficiently analytical for Erik and I observed that he would wiggle noticeably in his seat when I was speaking. I commented on this to the graduate students, who smiled and explained that Erik always wiggled while listening to lectures.

Outside the university, Erik was jovial and friendly. He took me canvassing with him for the Democratic candidate and I remember a wonderful sunny outing with his family in which Erik sang 'My gal's a corker, she's a New Yorker' at full volume as he drove. We were heading to a large swimming pool with a very high diving board from which Will jumped. The weather was warm in Madison and there was more swimming with Linda, Allen and Rosie in the lake-like 'ponds' and evening meals with their hospitable friends.

We went then to visit Ros Baxandall at the Cape for two weeks where I could flop and read. Stuart and Liz Ewen's two sons had grown up and Stuart took Will under his wing on long swims around a big pond. These expeditions became a holiday ritual. Rosie meanwhile built municipal towns in the sand with me and read *Anne of Green Gables,* just as I had. I worried Will did not show much interest in reading. 'Neither did Phinny,' observed Ros philosophically and proceeded to ply him with comics. Sure enough, Will did read them.

* * *

When I returned that autumn, I concentrated on writing those long overdue chapters for my book on the British women's liberation movement. But inevitably there were interruptions, including a trip to the Labour Party conference in Blackpool, where I spoke on 'Alice Wheeldon and the State in World War One', sharing a platform with a friend, the historian of women and the peace movement Jill Liddington.[350] To me as a child Blackpool had seemed so glitzy – a candy-floss town illuminated by Mickey Mouse – but in 1986 it looked sadly seedy and neglected.

When the St Albans Communist Party branch asked me to talk on the sweeping topic of 'One World: Whose World?' I was initially daunted.[351] I am not sure what they expected, but their invitation led me to connect several stray strands. Through early articles by Americans Rachael Grossman, Barbara Ehrenreich and Annette Fuentes in the late 1970s and early 1980s, I had learned how women in poor countries were being employed in global factories. In Britain I had met Kate Young and Diane Elson who, from the mid-1970s, had been in discussions with socialist feminist anthropologists, economists and sociologists about 'Women and Development'. They were part of a loose international network of feminists who had started to ask 'development for whom?' Diane was involved in Women Working Worldwide, a group set up in April 1983 after a conference at County Hall of women from the labour, trade union and feminist movements in countries ranging from Holland to the Philippines and Scotland to Sri Lanka. The impetus for it had come from women in the radical charity War on Want and the Archway Development Education Centre.[352]

I was aware too that a National Steering group on homeworkers had been formed and the Homeworkers' Charter drawn up at a conference on homeworking in 1984, supported by the GLC.[353] Annie Ralph, who had written about homeworking for the GLC's London Industrial Strategy (LIS), cited the Charter and observed with foresight, 'Homeworking, especially in the new technology industries, both in manufacturing and the provision of services, is on the increase; it is now being promoted as the way of working in the future even by multinational concerns'.[354]

When I read Swasti Mitter's *Common Fate, Common Bond: Women in the Global Economy*, which Pluto Press published in 1986, the global ramifications became glaringly obvious. Swasti had interviewed Bangladeshi and Cypriot homeworkers in East London and showed how their labour complemented the goods produced by multinationals.[355] Her book revealed the growth of 'free trade' global production, interconnecting with a proliferation of new forms of the old kinds of sweated labour in Britain.

Clearly condensing the work of economic and social researchers, she showed how invisible homeworkers in clothing, footwear and toys, many of whom were immigrant workers, could be part of an elongated chain that involved the most modern forms of exploitative production in the Free Trade Zones. Distribution too was dominated by large retailers who would then 'boast of selling British'.[356] She described it as 'The Third World in the midst of the first'.[357]

In *Common Fate, Common Bond,* Swasti also included a list of networks which exposed what was happening and offered support to workers, in factories and at home. Among these were Women Working Worldwide in London and the National Group on Homeworking in Leicester, Industrial Restructuring and Educational Network (IRENE) and the Transnational Information Exchange Europe (TIE), both based in Holland.[358] Though I knew of Swasti, who worked in Business Management at Brighton Polytechnic, we had yet to meet. *Common Fate Common Bond* prompted me to seek her out.

Radha Kumar, a historian friend from the Indian women's movement, was visiting London that autumn and when we met she described the horrors of the Bhopal toxic gas leak at Union Carbide in December 1984.[359] Along with other activists she had gone to support the workers and their families, only to be arrested and imprisoned for their efforts. A long campaign for justice had ensued. Radha's first-hand accounts made me comprehend what had happened to individuals in Bhopal and alerted me to a movement that spanned work and community as the miners' strike had done in Britain. Talking with Radha, who, like me, was interested in women's participation in differing kinds of social movements, enabled me to step back and situate women's liberation in Britain in a much wider context.

Through Radha I was to encounter Gita Sahgal, who had come to live in London during the early 1980s. She had been agitating on behalf of the many thousands injured in Bhopal and worked on the Bandung File with Tariq Ali and Darcus Howe, making films for Channel 4 that scrutinized race, ethnicity, class and gender. Gita was also involved with Pragna Patel in Southall Black Sisters (SBS). Formed in the late 1970s, SBS had been supporting and defending women in Southall who were resisting forced marriages and domestic violence. Members of the group were equally vociferous in opposing racist and sexist prejudices entrenched in British immigration laws, while resolutely challenging blinkered assumptions in the labour movement which equated workplace resistance exclusively with white men.

Working at the GLC had projected me into one vast city and its abolition had cast me down into the dumps. But now a plethora of new insights began to form as I started following these diverse but globally interconnected aspects of women's circumstances, some of which were contributing to a series of rebellious movements. They tumbled me into a quest to learn more which would consume me for several years.

* * *

In November I went on a short expedition to Ontario, mixing politics with earning money through lectures in universities. I received the same welcome as before from the impressively organized Canadian socialist feminists, many of whom had close links to trade unions and community campaigns as well as the universities. I had an intensive schedule. On 25 November, my diary records '2 talks Hamilton'. Over the following two days, I was in Kingston for two lectures and two meetings, relaxing briefly during the evening of the 27th by going to hear the British art historian Griselda Pollock on 'Women and Art'. Not only was I interested in the topic, it felt sublimely pleasant not to be responsible for delivering.[360]

I spoke twice in Peterborough, followed by two more over the weekend in Toronto at the Marxist Institute, where I met the political scientist Leo Panitch. A thoughtful, rigorous Marxist, Leo was also a caring and encouraging human being who could engage with people of all kinds. He had a gift for a democratic and empathetic kind of leadership which animated others to think and to write. As I finished talking about the GLC, sadness overcame me and I said limply, 'We failed', whereupon an elderly man in the audience intervened, shaking a head of shaggy grey hair, 'You didn't fail; you were defeated. That's different.' I saw Leo sitting on the sidelines smiling confidently in assent. His eyes communicated both comprehension and solidarity, for Leo, who was from a Jewish working-class, Canadian family, possessed an exhaustive knowledge of British labour politics.[361]

There was much debate in Toronto over the Ontario New Democratic Party (NDP), which had social movement and labour union supporters but was viewed with suspicion by many in the Marxist left. I was asked by some of its members for a fifteen-minute summary of our work at the GLC. This was *far* more challenging than speaking in universities or Marxist institutes. How to do justice to three years of non-stop innovating in fifteen minutes!

At the Ontario Institute for Studies in Education (OISE) I was happily reunited with a vivacious Skye Stollmeyer, who was involved in Canada's first black women's newspaper, *Our Lives*. Then I was off again to London, Ontario to lecture on 'Women and the State'. I returned to Hackney on 3 December, just in time for Will's Open day at school. I had two articles to write and deliver.[362] Not having a job was proving hard work.

* * *

On 12 December I joined thousands of parents, schoolteachers, caretakers, cleaners and children on a massive lobby in defence of the Inner London Education Authority (ILEA).[363] There was a powerful feeling of solidarity as we assembled at Will's primary school, Gayhurst. After abolishing the GLC Margaret Thatcher now had ILEA within her sights; she argued it was high spending and did not achieve good exam results and berated its '"child-centred" teaching techniques, the emphasis on imaginative engagement'.[364] Instead, Conservative Party educational 'reforms' favoured involving businesses more closely in running schools. It felt as if Charles Dickens' bugbears, the capitalist Mr Gradgrind and educationalists like Mr M'Choakumchild, were rising again in triumph.

It proved harder to get rid of ILEA than the GLC, for though Conservative MPs tended to dislike ILEA's anti-racism and defence of homosexuality and lesbianism, they wavered on abolition, partly because the advantages of a London-wide educational authority were so evident. Also, though the Conservatives' emphasis on discipline, competition and a narrow job-oriented syllabus did gain adherents, many London parents wanted ILEA to continue. Along with teachers and manual workers in the schools, they were aware of the assets and resources ILEA provided, especially for inner city children. Some (myself included) also approved the efforts in schools to offset Tory policies that accentuated prejudices and inequality.

An elderly speaker from one of the manual trade unions at the rally that day turned the idea of 'equal opportunities' around to demand 'opportunities for equality'. He did not deny that 'equal opportunities' were needed, but showed how the meritocratic thinking behind the slogan wrongly assumed that pushing individuals upwards constituted the solution to social ills. It paid no heed to those people left behind by the narrow ladders of individual celebrity and success. He put my doubts in a nutshell, and I clapped and cheered with the crowd. We needed more, much more, than equality for a few.

After the lobby I went to visit Westway Laundry, one of the projects which had been reprieved by funding from the local council, to see how their new combined heat and power dryers were doing. We got talking about the GLC and one of the women said, 'I've got one of the books on it'. She used an old pram to bring in her washing and, lifting its plastic mattress, she uncovered an Industry and Employment pamphlet with the photograph of a beaming Michael Ward putting washing into one of the Westway machines on the cover. Strapped across it in large black lettering were the words 'There is an Alternative'.

I stared at it in disbelief and wonder, overwhelmed by an Areopagitican moment. A sardonic Milton was spot on: repressive authorities were well advised to keep their eyes peeled on 'how books demean themselves' for they 'do contain a potency of life in them'.[365] I set off home to Hackney musing on how Margaret Thatcher might have been able to abolish the mighty institution of the Greater London Council, but she had missed how subversive messages could be lurking under washing in old prams.

Heading down Powerscroft Road that evening, still infused with my cheery socialist 'There-is-an-Alternative' endorphins, I felt a sudden tug on my arm. The next second my handbag was being carried at speed by a young man running ahead of me. I registered a white, short-haired, stocky figure vanishing not just with my money, but with the basic organization of my existence. In fury, I set off in pursuit, hurling extraneous insults about his cowardice as I ran. Before long I faltered, not only was I puffed, it occurred to me what would I do if I caught up with him? Sullenly I slouched home.

Luckily that Christmas, because Will was with me, we were off to the Thompsons. I found solace in playing the lion, the witch and the wardrobe in charades at Wick Episcopi.

9

1987

By January, after years of prevarication and innumerable diversions, the chapter churning finally ceased. I had, at last, managed to complete the manuscript about ideas that had arisen within the women's liberation movement in Britain. It was a tremendous relief to hand it in to my editor, Geraldine Cook, because so many years had gone by since I had received the advance from Penguin books in the mid-1970s.

Acknowledging the passage of time, I decided its title would be *The Past is Before Us*. The words were borrowed from a talk the Hungarian dissident Marxist Nicolas Krasso had given to our Young Socialist group in Hackney Labour Party in the mid-1960s, when he had added, 'The future's behind us'. The 'backwards-way-round' phrase made sense and stayed with me: you can see the past, albeit darkly, but the unhappened future is not visible.[366]

I never got to know Nicolas well, and after he died in 1986, an obituary by Robin Blackburn in the *New Left Review* led me to ponder on how people can glide in and out of your life leaving you with flickers of memory and only a sketchy understanding of the circumstances which had formed them. Born in Hungary in 1930, Nicolas had joined the Communist Party in 1945. As a young philosophy student he, and his friend Istvan Meszaros, had translated works by Georg Lukacs on literature from German into Hungarian. In 1956, at the time of the Hungarian uprising, Nicolas had participated actively in the chaotic and spontaneous district and factory councils and had initiated a move to create a coordinating Central Workers' Council. He had been forced to flee Hungary when the Soviet Union crushed the rebellion.[367]

From the early 1960s when I first became a socialist, I was all too aware of the contradictions between communism as an ideal and as a lived experience. But by the late 1980s I had come to fear that in Britain the onslaught of the new monetarist right was marginalizing *all* forms of socialism. This was not, however, the case in Spain where the Spanish Socialist Workers' Party (PSOE) had been in power since 1982. It was invigorating to be invited to speak at a conference that January in Madrid on 'Women and the State' organized by the Institute of Women at the socialist Fundación Pablo Iglesias.[368]

I had read the English translation of the exhaustive history by its director, Fernando Claudin, *The Communist Movement: From Comintern To Cominform*. Its 644 pages of text, followed by a further 100 pages of endnotes detailed the Soviet Union's relations with Communists internationally.[369] In laying bare the creation of the myth around Stalin, Claudin had produced at once an epic, affirming thought against dogma, and a truly tragic testimony of so much faith splattered in vain. Upon reading it I had wondered that a man who had given his life to Communism could nevertheless write a Marxist political history without giving vent to venom or despair, in which individuals believed, spoke and acted, enmeshed in duplicity, with their backs against the wall.

And there he was, sitting on my right, a small man in his seventies, having a drink. He looked worried and remained silent. I was in awe of him and aware that my touristic Spanish was not equipped for discourse on the history of the CP. Observing stasis, the Belgian political theorist Chantal Mouffe intervened by recounting how, in the late 1970s, she had taken some Italian socialist women to visit me in Hackney because they wanted to talk about *Beyond the Fragments*. I was looking after Will and another toddler that day and my room was in disarray. Chantal chuckled how the enquiring visitors had been so horrified by Hackney, the communal house and the unruly small children, that they had gone away convinced it was better to stick with Leninism. Chantal, a delightful and witty raconteur, who could move between languages, broke the ice and made us all laugh.[370] She later revealed that Fernando Claudin had been reluctant to come owing to his terror of British and American feminists. This was hard for me to fathom. How could a veteran of the Spanish Civil War, an underground resister of Franco's fascism, who had worked for the Communist Party in several countries and had been an influential left force in Eurocommunism, be frightened by me?

In Britain, even salvaging basic social reforms was proving a challenge. 1980s style capitalism disdained human needs and worsened conditions in innumerable nasty ways. Nevertheless, some campaigns had survived. That January I went to give a short talk at the National Child Care Conference in Wandsworth. Not only was childcare desperately needed, it had found a remarkable national organizer in the calm, efficient and steadfast Helen Penn.[371]

Understandings lingered too. While at the GLC I had become friendly with two left-wing bus drivers, Brian Collins and Steve Johnson, who would toot the horn of the 253 bus if he spotted me in Hackney. They had confirmed everything Dave Feickert and Marina Lewycka had told me about the impact of One Person Operation (OPO). But achieving positive changes seemed increasingly remote.

On 23 February I was invited to speak to OPO drivers in an adult education class in Leeds. The drivers, who were mainly men, with one woman among them, spelled out the stress caused by having to drive, collect fares and deal with aggressive incidents on the buses. This was compounded by the privatization of bus services; drivers from different companies were forced to race one another to get to stops first. This application of free competition to bus transport resulted in relentless battles for passengers.[372]

Some of these tensions burst out in the meeting. When we reassembled after a short break, a man from the group walked in holding the *Sun* newspaper. Not only was it notoriously anti-trade union, it carried topless pin-ups. As he stuffed the paper nonchalantly into his pocket, the woman driver erupted in rage about the pin-ups and fled the room in tears. Her work had become a nightmare, and she did not know what to do about it. Isolated, she felt betrayed by a man who was her workmate and should have been her comrade. She could not cope with struggling on so many fronts.

I sensed trade unionists, feminists and socialists were all on the defensive, yet I was unable to see any means of overturning what was happening. Acrimonies I had no means of assuaging seemed pervasive that spring. On Friday 13 March I went up to Manchester to see Alan Hayling, who since the abolition of the GLC had been concentrating on setting up a socialist newspaper, *News on Sunday*.[373] It sounded like a dream, but it wasn't. I winced at some bright spark's advertising slogan aimed at the *Sun* pin-ups, 'No tits but a lot of balls', ironically accompanied by 'The paper that bites back'. Conflicts had broken out, not just between the editor and the journalists, but between men and women on the staff and between Alan and people in the supporters' group.

I was friendly with Alan through the PPU, with two socialist feminists on the paper, Anna Coote and Polly Patullo, as well as with members of the supporters' group which included Steve Riley, the shop steward from Ford Dagenham, who I had interviewed, as well as my close friends, John and Joan Bohanna. Now they were all at odds. The paper proved not to be economically viable, despite generous donations from trade unions. It folded that autumn leaving deep wounds.

* * *

Despite being chuffed because I had a regular column in *New Society*, I could see my savings from the GLC dwindling and my attempts to live from freelance writing were not yielding enough money. When I visited the historian Gareth Stedman Jones, a friend from my student days in Cambridge, he rebuked me for being so slow in registering reality and put me in contact with his literary agent, Margaret Hanbury.

Then Kathy Jones came up with a proposition. The Women's Studies department at San Diego State University had received lottery money that year. They suggested that I should come and do some classes and seminars over several weeks rather than doing the customary bumper lottery lecture. Because of the Easter holidays this meant being away from Will for five and a half weeks. He would be with Paul, but we had never been parted for such a long period. Still, I had little choice, and left for San Diego on 25 March, the day after Will's birthday.

The San Diego State campus was like being on a vast film set – sun, white buildings, green grass. The students attended their lottery money classes and lectures politely and diligently in T-shirts and shorts and I transplanted fragile shoots of subversion from far away: 'Early Nineteenth Century Radicalism', 'Socialism and Suffrage', 'Sexual Politics and the Labour Movement', holding forth respectively on Mary Wollstonecraft, Sylvia Pankhurst and Stella Browne.[374] I garnered contemporary themes from *The Past Is Before Us* – 'The Women's Movement', 'New Forms of Democracy' and 'The Welfare State'. But the session I enjoyed doing most was on the GLC, delivered unpaid to a class of sixth formers in a working-class part of town who asked me searching questions about local economic policies.

I went up to Los Angeles to stay with Bruce Green and Linda Dove and their two young daughters on Saturday 11 April. Word got round and Jane Jaquette, who taught Politics and International Relations at Occidental College, asked me to give a seminar on 'Women's Liberation and the State' on the Monday afternoon and talk about the GLC to her class in the morning. This sounded pretty easy, but something got lost in translation. A class to me was about fifteen to thirty students in a small room, so I went in with about half a page of notes. Once through the door, I entered an enormous lecture hall containing more than a thousand students. I walked down the aisle to the podium on jelly legs, spotting Jane near the front beaming encouragement.

Normally I need time to prepare for being spontaneous,

but there I was, pinioned in this giant 'class', surveying tiers of expectancy. Somehow, I floated over them in a metaphorical air balloon and delivered on the GLC for about forty minutes, mopping my brow at the end. There was an unexpected recompense. Subsequent conversations with Jane introduced me to broader contours through her own field of study, democracy and participation in Latin America.[375] The parallels with what we had been doing at the GLC were evident.

Dee Dee Halleck from the alternative film group Paper Tiger, also sought me out in LA. Paper Tiger wanted to subvert the slick, mainstream media, by countering it with a consciously unworked format and hand-held cameras. Dee Dee was a fount of supreme confidence, enabling me to hold forth, albeit with an excessive amount of 'ums', on royals, recipes and celebrities. Hence, I am preserved online, 'deconstructing' the tittle tattle in *The Star,* a magazine sold in supermarkets and owned by Rupert Murdoch.[376] Despite the encouragement of the brave film-makers, I cannot say that I constituted any threat at all to the mainstream popular media.

It was sunny in San Diego, vivid red and yellow spring flowers wafted luxuriance, and my stay with Kathy was interesting and fun. In the evenings, when her likeable young soccer-playing son, Ari, had gone to bed, she and I settled down to watch rented videos of *My Beautiful Laundrette* and *Blue Velvet* in her home. I knew about videos through visually advanced friends like James Swinson and Stuart Ewen, and, of course, through the campaign films I had taken to California during the miners' strike. But these videos of films from rental stores were new to me and seemed the epitome of a modern hedonistic lifestyle. Kathy, Ari, the videos and a lilac dress I bought in San Diego restored my spirits.

* * *

I went canvassing in May and June, but when Labour lost again, I could see no hope of ousting the Conservative government. I sat down with a concentrated intensity and wrote an article, 'Commanding the Heart', about Edward Carpenter and his

circle for *History Today*.[377] I poured into it the strong affinity I
felt towards Carpenter's expansive and inclusive radical vision
which had embraced rebellious new women and gay men,
workers and the colonized. 'Commanding the Heart' served
as a shield against the gloom of defeats and division. It helped
me to cleave to the possibility of creating a human-centred
socialism.[378]

Peering into the past had been with me from childhood. I
remain unsure how it arose, perhaps from my mothers' stories
of King Alfred burning the cakes or Robert Bruce on the
run learning from the spider in the cave to try, try, try again.
Somehow, I became a time bandit, forever circumnavigating a
multitude of concentric circles, moment to moment, era to era,
searching for clues of forgotten pasts.

Yet this diving backwards to hobnob with ghosts has always
coincided with an enthusiasm for embracing the new in the
now. So, I have hovered between polarities. I was wrapped in the
immediacy of a sunny day when Marc Karlin came and filmed
Will, Scarlett and me for *Utopias*. He caught us meandering
along from Gayhurst School through London Fields with Will's
friends Joe Pipal and Juliet Ash's son, Jesse.

Marc grumbled because I had a new hairstyle – 'You've ruined
the continuity', he remonstrated. I felt privately grumpy about
this. How could I keep the same hairstyle for years on end just
because Marc spent so long making his films? I knew it would be
impossible to explain to my other-worldly creative film-maker
friend how new hair was a vital defiance against feeling down
about the state of the world.

My hairdresser, a young gay Asian man, forced to leave
Uganda, had examined my rather tired curly perm and
announced I needed 'to look more clear-cut'. He had chopped
away at the sides, leaving a shock of hair on the top so I
resembled a belated teddy boy. This clarity did give me a certain
bounce and I was pleased with my new look, apart from just one
lingering doubt – my ears were visible.

When I was a child, my mother used to tell me they were

large because they were peasant ears, inherited from my father, the son of a tenant farmer. In her opinion peasants had acquired big ears because they were always listening to the earth. As I grew older vanity scored higher than earth-listening and to be on the safe side I had concealed them in hair.

The routines of collecting Will from Gayhurst allowed me space to be at once fanciful and purposeless. I retain a clutch of memories from his primary school. One is of the headmaster, a bearded member of the Socialist Workers' Party, playing his guitar in Assembly, another of Gayhurst pupils standing in a large circle and singing, instead of Christmas carols, John Lennon and Yoko Ono's 'Give Peace a Chance', their Cockney voices turning it into 'Charnce'.

The school attracted some inspired teachers. One day when Will forgot his lunch box, I arrived at the door of his classroom to be struck by a paper dart. The experimental young teacher was demonstrating wind currents. A teacher also came on an exchange from the Caribbean and told the children to search for British historical figures of African descent. I rose in the esteem of a group of Will's friends by introducing them to William Cuffay, the black Chartist tailor who, on the evidence of police spies, was deported to Tasmania for life in 1848 after a huge demonstration for political rights.

When I shopped or swam in Hackney, children's voices would make me feel rooted by hailing me as 'Will's mum', but there was much I was unable to fathom about their world. I had expanded with motherly pride in the audience at the National Theatre when London schools provided rotating casts in the poet Adrian Mitchell's 'Pied Piper' and Will played a rat and a child. But he and his friends remained unconcerned, as if the stage of the Olivier Theatre was no big deal.

While the teachers were concerned to offset the pressures and dangers of life in Hackney, the children were more fearful of the unknown. On a bus heading off to our yearly seaside outing I found myself attempting to reassure Will's classmates that the unfamiliar large houses we passed with lawns and bushes were not to be feared as 'spooky' or 'scary'.

Now that Will was ten, sport, especially football, had become serious. Joe Pipal's stepfather, Mick Hugo, a keen footballer, patiently trained Joe, Jesse and Will until they all excelled at it, particularly Joe. This was a boy-world I could not grasp. But Mick did, and in giving them his time, he handed them a vital patrimony. Football proved to be vital for survival and esteem in Hackney. But for me sport remained incomprehensively esoteric, apart from a momentary surge of triumph when I confounded younger fathers at Gayhurst by being the first to reach the post in the hula hoop race. My secret weapon was being the only contestant old enough to have learned how to keep the hoop around my waist as a child during the 1950s.

Will was revealing some puzzling decisive responses. In early July we went to a party to celebrate the wedding of Raphael Samuel and Alison Light at Raphael's home at Elder Street, in Spitalfields.[379] It was a real historian's abode, built in the eighteenth century, narrow, with wooden stairs climbing upwards and an outside toilet in the garden. The street had been due for demolition and the area deserted except for squatters when Raphael had moved in. The old houses had been saved as historic treasures by campaigners and were spruced up, though the bricks did not change. They were still red, grey and dark brown in random patterns, collected from here and there, rather like Raphael's overflowing, exploratory essays.

I always liked visiting Elder Street, fantasizing about French refugee Huguenots fleeing persecution, weaving memories into their silk, but Will took an instant and emphatic dislike to the house, announcing he liked modern places. On a visit to Jean McCrindle at Northern College near Barnsley, we had stayed in one of the new rooms for the trade union students who lived on site. These flats became Will's ideal of the good life.

* * *

Shortly after I came back from California, I had received a peculiar phone call inviting me to come as a consultant on women to the United Nations University's World Institute for

Development Economic Research. I would be paid a fee plus a daily allowance which was enough to last Will and me for several months. I was dumbfounded and tried to explain to the man on the line that I was not an economist. Next a resolute Kumari Jayawardena rang. She said her husband, Lal, was the Director of UNU WIDER and they needed someone to introduce a general perspective on women. Could I come to Helsinki for a month? We had a mutual interest in the history of socialism and feminism, plus that surprising link to Edward Carpenter, through Kumari's friend and mentor in Sri Lanka, Doreen Wickremasinghe. Moreover Kumari, a quietly compelling woman, was difficult to refuse.

Upon arriving in Helsinki, I was to learn that in real terms the prosperity proffered by WIDER constituted somewhat less than I had imagined because a meal in Finland cost three times the amount I would pay in Britain. Like other British hotel guests, I smuggled out food from my breakfasts for the first two days before giving in and buying my first meal.

My work was puzzling. No one appeared to know why I was there at all. Lal Jayawardena was away and so too was Kumari; violence had broken out in Sri Lanka between the Tamils and Sinhalese and India had become involved in the Peace Accord that was signed on 29 July. Unmoored in my WIDER office, I decided to start by finding out about the Institute, so I went along to the library, where I learned that WIDER had arisen because of pressure within the United Nations to focus on poverty and inequality; the Finns had offered to host it and it had opened in 1985. As I cast my eyes over the library shelves no books on women and the global economy were to be seen. I asked the young Finnish librarian for their whereabouts, explaining I was initiating WIDER's 'women's programme'. Baffled, he shook his head and replied aloofly, 'But this is an Economics Institute'. I realized then what I was up against. Things were obviously at a rather basic stage. So, I compiled a list of books for the library to buy.

As it made sense for a gender perspective to be congruent

with the existing research projects at WIDER, I resolved to find out what the economists at WIDER wrote about. Discovering a room filled with shelves of duplicated copies of papers which had been presented at WIDER seminars and conferences by visiting academics. I read these, but again could find nothing about women. Still, all this scholarly knowledge seemed to be wasted just sitting there, so, when the British Press and Communications officer came into the room, I suggested it would be good to disseminate them and do summaries for the Finnish press. I told him about the GLC's London Industrial Strategy and *Jobs for a Change*. He had worked for international financial institutions and our politics were poles apart, but he became very animated about how good it would be to communicate the work more broadly.

Then I toured every office asking the distinguished visiting economists, all of whom were male and mostly from South Asia, what they were working on. They were surprised, but happy to tell me. Fortunately, I was able to follow most of what they were saying because, assuming that I was *utterly* ignorant, they explained at length. I began to suspect that they were perhaps a little lonely closeted in their rooms studying. Unlike the Popular Planning Unit no one chatted much.

The overall gist appeared to be the pursuit of economic development in combination with a more equitable distribution of wealth. But the approach was somewhat abstract and directed towards UN institutions, elite universities and national policy makers. I ended up with another pile of notes but could not see precisely how to connect what I was learning to issues relating to women. A further complication was that fresh from Popular Planning, I was not only committed to reorientating the content of development research, I rejected an exclusively top-down exchange of knowledge.

Amidst these travels around the offices, I discovered the Finnish anthropologist Marja-Liisa Swantz. When I met her, she was sixty-one with grey cropped hair, mischievous eyes and an expansive smile. She was a senior researcher at WIDER, greatly respected in Finland and Tanzania, where she had studied, but without any airs of self-importance. An exponent of democratizing knowledge and active participation in devising policies, she had written on *Ritual and Symbol in Transitional Tanzanian Society* (1970) by consulting participants. A devout Lutheran and a Christian socialist, she was surprised that I shared her appreciation of tacit understanding and knowledge from below, as she did not associate these with Marxists.

Marja-Liisa seemed to know the whole of Helsinki. Through her I made contact with a large number of Finns from feminist groups and more traditional organisations of country women, as well as from trade unions and co-operatives. I visited social democratic and Communist Party politicians, concerned adult educationalists and liberally-minded journalists, all of whom were keen on WIDER having a women's programme. Finnish names were hard for me, so I hoarded the cards they gave me or asked them to write them down.

I was intrigued to see how Marja-Liisa operated a kind of personal ecological economy within the UNU. Not only did she collect all the discarded paper and pencils left over from the seminars and conferences, she kept all the little packets of sugar and dried milk powder from her airline flights. When I remarked on this store of packets in her cupboard, she explained it was a habit she had acquired while doing field work in Tanzania because they had been light to carry.

A conference was due to begin on Monday 27 July on poverty, undernutrition and living standards. Who should turn up for this but my former PhD supervisor, Eric Hobsbawm, along with his wife Marlene, who was in a state of consternation. They had arrived at their flat to discover crucial absences such as blankets. Marja-Liisa lent them her own, along with an electric toaster, and I passed them sachets of soap and shampoo from my hotel, musing on the bizarre irony of this disconnect between academic debate and the details of provisioning. Eric, who was a McDonnell Douglas Visiting Scholar at WIDER, appeared to soar above such insignificant matters, but I suspected this was because he relied on Marlene to focus on them for him.[380]

The conference pivoted around the research of the economist Amartya Sen, who had studied with Lal Jayawardena at Cambridge, and was closely involved with WIDER.[381] Concerned to challenge global inequality, he was aware that famines can occur not simply because of a *lack* of food, but because the poor were unable to obtain it when prices rose. He was convinced that establishing greater precision in analysing famines was vital if their causes were to be overcome.[382]

The mathematical input from the econometricians who contributed was lost on me, but the broader debates on how to define and measure poverty were not completely unfamiliar. Indeed, Eric had played a key role in these as an historian in relation to British early economic development, rather than in a global context. I attended a lecture by Roderick Floud, who I remembered from the Oxford Labour Club, on using height and weight to measure poverty, an anthropometric approach which caused much furore. While there was little specific mention of women, the Oxford economist Barbara Harriss-White, who was interested in rural workers outside the formal economy, did speak on 'The intra family distribution of hunger in South Asia'.[383] When it was over, I joined Marja-Liisa in rescuing all the paper and pencils for her store.

Coinciding with Marlene and Eric in Helsinki enabled me to get to know them much better. I had only met Marlene a few times and my connections to Eric had been somewhat stormy. As an undergraduate I had been enthused by both his *Primitive Rebels* and *The Age of Revolution*. Subsequently Eric had been a stimulating PhD supervisor, though he had reduced me to tears by instructing me to cut out my painstaking individual biographies of adult working-class students. In all fairness, he had a point, my uncompleted thesis was three times too long.

From the 1970s we were to be at odds because he adamantly denied the need for women's history. This did not diminish during the 1980s. Indeed, on one occasion, when he and Kumari coincided in Helsinki, she and I combined against him.

Furiously, I had waved a scribbled a list of books on women's history which had broken new ground, in front of him. But to my exasperation Eric wafted this away with the remark that these authors would have produced them anyway. Still a liking existed between us, despite our differences.

This was strengthened by our time in Helsinki, where I also bonded with Marlene. One weekend Eric led us both on an outing to Hvitträsk, the studio and home of three late nineteenth-century architects, one of whom, Eliel Saarinen, had later designed Helsinki's railway station. Hvitträsk is by Lake Vitträsk, and thus outside the city, but Eric could read Finnish railway timetables with an uncanny aplomb, while discoursing intriguingly on historic interactions between Viennese and Finnish architecture. Even more unexpected was his ability to identify Finnish birds, a skill that derived from his boyhood.

When Marja-Liisa invited me to dinner I met her husband Lloyd, a Lutheran pastor who, like herself, had worked in Tanzania as an anthropologist and missionary. Seated opposite me in an armchair was another former missionary to Africa, a Swede in his late seventies with white hair and a face deeply lined by the sun. Marja-Liisa requested that we should all tell something about our lives and asked him, as the eldest, to begin. Whereupon Bengt Sundkler related how, on going to Southern Africa as a young man, he had come across independent African churches. He began talking to their members and writing down what they told him, and his fascination grew into the book he was still writing on their histories.[384]

The topic resonated with me partly because his rendering was at once meticulous and charismatic and because it evoked Hermione Harris's descriptions of her research into an African church in Hackney.[385] When I mentioned hearing Bengt Sundkler to Eric, who knew his work, he groaned in regret not to have met him. I later learned that this enquiring missionary had been Marja-Liisa's supervisor when she had done her thesis at the University of Uppsala on ritual and symbols in Tanzania.

Right at the end of my stay Lal arrived back and when we met

on 20 August it was agreed that I should go on a fact-finding trip
to India and report on new forms of organizing among women
around work, helped by Radha Kumar, who was researching
the history of women in Bombay's (now Mumbai's) textile
industry.[386]

* * *

My trip to WIDER and long conversations with Marja-Liisa
confirmed my excitement about Swasti Mitter's *Common Fate,
Common Bond*. When Swasti and I corresponded and spoke on
the phone, it became evident how we had covered some similar
tracks, not only had Swasti worked with the GLC, she, too, had
encountered Peter Waterman from the International Institute
of Social Studies at The Hague, and was aware of his efforts to
stimulate grassroots contact between women internationally.

Regardless of the prevailing mood of confusion and
demoralization on the left, Hilary Wainwright was involved
through the Socialist Society in planning a conference in
Chesterfield with the Campaign Group of Labour MPs and the
Conference of Socialist Economists.[387] I had agreed to coordinate
a workshop with Jean McCrindle on 'Women, international links
and the labour movement'. When I asked Swasti to speak at this,
she responded with enthusiasm: 'I feel somehow that I know you
(and Hilary) already through your writings, but still it will be
wonderful to see you and exchange our ideas in person ... I shall
get in touch with some of the grassroots organisations of black
women workers here in case they want to participate.'[388]

I went with Lynne Segal and two radical philosophers,
Peter Osborne and Gregory Elliott, to Chesterfield on 24 and
25 October for the Socialist Conference.[389] Two thousand
people arrived including a wonderful women's band, socialist
pensioners, trade unionists and prominent figures in the
Labour Party left, including Tony Benn, Jeremy Corbyn and
Ken Livingstone. Hilary's focus was, as ever, on grassroots
organizing, but I thought this tended to get submerged in the
rousing general sessions. I noted a lack of women speakers in
these and a small core of sectarian men from left groups who,

considering themselves to be all knowing, muscled noisily in, making discussion difficult. I had gambled on our workshop being regarded as insignificant by such bossy types, and so it proved.

Jean McCrindle and I had invited Barbara Dinham, Gita Sahgal and Anne Scargill to start off the discussion with Swasti. I could only intuit that they would be on the same wavelength and, though we had corresponded and spoken on the phone, it was the first time I had met Swasti. I must have looked worried because the smile with which she greeted me radiated reassurance.

She summarized her research on 'The International Division of Labour: The Experience of Women' with clarity and was followed by Barbara Dinham who had been developing direct international links between workers in multinational cocoa factories and was now trying to do this among cleaners through a research group that had been funded by the GLC, called the Transnational Information Centre (TICL). Gita Sahgal spoke on the Bhopal disaster and the impact it had had on 'black groups, trades unionists and Trade Union Resource Centres' in Britain. She described too how Southall Black Sisters had tried to support the striking miners and the printers but had met with indifference and hostility from some trade unionists and labour organisations. Anne Scargill emphasized the international awareness and personal links that women in mining communities had developed through the strike. Several women, including Lynne Segal, had been to the European Socialist Feminist Conference and Lynne reported how marked differences in labour laws had been noted there.[390]

Thirty-five women and three men from a wide variety of causes and groups came to the workshop. Along with Southall Black Sisters, TICL, the European Socialist Feminist Conference and Women Against Pit Closures, there were members of Anti-Apartheid, Brent Asian Women's Centre, the Centre for Local Economic Strategies, the EEC Women's Network, *Feminist Review*, the Green Party, the International

Conference of Councillors for a Nuclear Free Zone, Labour
Action for Peace, Twin Trading, Women for Nicaragua and the
Workers' Educational Association development peace group in
Norwich.[391] We might no longer have a women's movement but
diverse groups of women were intensely active.

Our workshop was searching and open, making links rather
than laying down lessons. But, as I had feared, this was not
the case in the conference as a whole. Two thousand excited,
argumentative leftists buoyed the spirits and spilled out into
the pubs in the evenings, but they sure could disagree. On the
Saturday evening around 10 o'clock I was relieved to find myself
walking away from the conference in the calm company of Bruce
Kent from the Campaign for Nuclear Disarmament, when we
bumped into crowds of young men and women laughing and
yelling at one another as they circulated in groups around the
town. I realized we had hit the 'monkey parade' that I had read
about with envy at school in H. G. Wells' *Kipps*. The sexual
banter was frank and I glanced at Bruce Kent, but he sailed right
through Chesterfield's courtship rituals undisturbed. I figured
being a former Catholic priest must prepare you for all human
life. I allowed myself a moment of utopian wonder – would
the day come when monkey paraders would roister into the
Chesterfield conferences?

The following weekend I went to the National Abortion
Campaign Conference because a new threat to abortion had
arisen.[392] There I joined a workshop on campaigning with a
group of young women dressed in black leather jackets with
enormous boots and rings through their noses. They looked
formidable but were docilely listening to an older, experienced
abortion campaigner from the pre-1970s lobbying days
instructing them on how to leaflet for abortion rights. When
she explained that they must take care to dress in a neutral and
uncontroversial manner in order to blend in as a member of
the public, I smiled inwardly, remembering Bernard Shaw's
admonition to women supporters of radical causes to always
propagandise in a very nice hat indeed. In 1987 this was going to

involve a major reconstruction job. Transmogrify they did and our abortion rights were saved.

On 27 November I was awarded an honorary degree by North London Polytechnic (later London Metropolitan University) and addressed the students and parents on 'Women and Local Government'. They made a video of this occasion which I watched with curiosity, for I had never seen myself speak before. I might not have any nose rings but still did not look like a serene and learned honorary doctor, for those peasant ears resisted a scholar's hat, protruding instead on either side.

* * *

After a brief trip to WIDER, more discussions with Swasti, a visit to see Dorothy and Edward, where we talked about India and an informative meeting with Pauline Tiffen at Twin Trading about global grass-roots links, I set off with Will for New Delhi on 17 December. We arrived at Radha's grandparents' home the morning of the following day.[393] Will was lively and pleased to be reunited with Radha, but I had not slept all night and my head was swimming from the malaria pills prescribed by my friend and GP, Dr Leibson. As I unpacked, I brought out a stash of pills for every conceivable traveller's ailment. Radha raised her eyebrows in incredulity, 'You think we have no pharmacies in Delhi?' She took a dim view of our malaria pills too which she said were ridiculously old fashioned. It was true that Michael Leibson had become a GP in Bethnal Green after being in the army during the war and may not have been always exactly up to the minute. Her response to the cheddar cheese and marmite which she had instructed me to bring was far more positive. So was Will's; his diet at that time consisted mainly of baked potatoes with cheese and bread and marmite. Radha's grandparents' cook used to solemnly cook him a baked potato each day.

I awoke the following morning to voices and the curious sound of many small jangly bells. Then I remembered how those bells on the cows moving through the streets had figured in my mother's many stories of her life in India, where my father had worked as a mining engineer during the 1920s and early 1930s. I had not bargained for the intensity of these childhood memories of her voice and of the objects from India that had surrounded me at home in Leeds – buddhas, shrines, shells, elephants, embroidered pictures of birds.

My older brother, Peter, had been born in India and my mother used to talk of the 'ayah' who had cared for him before he was sent to school in England. My parents had left in 1933 after my father had refused to sign an order to reduce the miners' wages. He argued they were already on starvation rates, whereupon the company had sacked him. I used to puzzle over an old photograph of the bungalow where my parents had lived with the word 'Sendra' written on it.

My first few days in Delhi were disorienting, I was not sure whether I was being slothful or overcome by the echoes of my mother's reminiscences or whether it was the relaxed rhythms in Radha's grandparents' home or perhaps something about the vast antiquity of India's culture, but I just could not somehow manage to do anything in a straight line. Will, in contrast, was happy. He and grandmother, a lively eighty-year-old, shared a liking for Bollywood and grandfather's chauffeur, Hukam Singh, took us to rent videos. Will returned triumphantly with James Bond movies and *Grease,* introducing grandmother to these and to his twangy Walkman. They formed such a bond that she began to talk about visiting us in London.

Through Radha I was introduced to members of the strong feminist movement in Delhi who were confronting many forms of violence against women in campaigns against rape, dowry deaths and widow immolation (sati), an old practice that was being recast to accommodate familial male power and local economic gain. That September Roop Kanwar had been drugged, dressed in her bridal clothes and burned on a pyre in a village in Rajasthan.[394]

Radha's knowledge of women's conditions and movements of resistance historically and in contemporary times was extensive. She described how Indian feminists had supported

women workers' strikes, community protests against price rises
and environmental destruction. There were numerous women's
co-operatives too, providing a basic livelihood and alternative
social forms of employment, and Radha arranged for the writer
and activist against violence against women Subhadra Butalia to
take me to visit a tailoresses' co-operative, where a woman she
had counselled, Gurbachen, was working. Subhadra's daughter,
Urvashi, was one of the founders of the path-breaking Indian
feminist publishing house Kali for Women.[395]

Both the women and the left-wing men assumed I was in
India to give lectures on feminism and seemed perplexed when
I tried to explain I wanted to find out about contemporary
women's projects organizing around work. I have never found
it easy to negotiate other peoples' expectations of me, while
hanging on to my own pursuits. In India this proved especially
difficult. However, I managed to focus by reading all the articles
on work in the feminist magazine *Manushi*.

I was excited to discover how Indian feminists were challenging
male historical bias. As well as the studies of women's industrial
work and participation in trade unions, I heard that a group called
Stree Shakti Sanghatana were doing oral interviews with women
who, in 1948-50, had taken part in a sharecroppers' rebellion in
Telengana.[396]

Their work felt very recognizable. Nevertheless, there were
significant contextual differences, for the legacy of British
colonialism had left difficult knots. While the older radical
generation who had come of age just after independence had
broadly endorsed 'progressive' measures and 'modernising'
policies, when I visited India some aspects of these were
beginning to be equated with colonialism by sections of both the
left and the right. The tension presented itself in a particularly
acute form for the Indian women's movement. I was on a steep
learning curve for, like Radha, they were far better informed
about Britain than I was about India.

We left for Calcutta (now Kolkata) by train at six in the
morning on the 23rd, laden with fruit, water and bread along

with the cheese and marmite from Britain. It was a long journey
of over a day and a night and Radha and Will fell asleep. But
I was too excited and kept peeping out of the window at the
brown and green landscape divided into small squares, the
children on the platform dangerously close to the train, the red-
coated porters.

Contrasts in wealth were visible and extreme. I was about
to throw away a small plastic phial of vitamin pills which was
empty, when the cleaner politely enquired if he could have it.
He bore it off as if it was a prize. Nothing I had ever seen or
known had prepared me for the long wait at the station when
Radha went off to find a taxi. Will and I were besieged by
beggars, among them children without legs moving on sledges
with wheels.

We were put up by some friends of Radha's on the floor for
the night. It was Christmas Eve and I had managed to buy Will
a pair of Russian red and cream binoculars from a stall in the
road, filling two stockings with little things. He awoke in the
night and discovered them. The following day we found a room
in a hotel with furnishings and décor that went back to the Raj
and waiters who called me 'Sir', where I managed to write my
column for New Society. I had no idea how I was going to post it
until an empathetic Maitreyi Chatterjee arrived to interview me
for a Bengali paper. She understood about deadlines and bore it
off with her, promising to send it. I was moved by her kindness
to a nervous stranger.

I was unsure what was usual and what was odd in social
interactions. When Radha took us to call on an old, distinguished
bohemian woman and an oddly abstracted young man who was
a distant relative, living high up in a large, but leaking, house
surrounded by an encampment in the grounds of several poor
families, I asked Radha if this was customary. She replied that
it was not, but the squatters acted as informal guards. Then
Radha and some friends with children organized an outing
for Will in two cars to a Safari Park. We were nonplussed on
discovering that it was closed, so someone suggested boating,

but it seemed I was the only person who had ever rowed a boat and I was uncomfortably aware of my lack of expertise. After much conferring, to my relief, we carried on to an Industrial Exhibition. There the two little girls gleefully went on the big wheel and Will, honour-bound, followed, to descend white-faced with terror. He preferred the motorbikes on display, including a particularly old model that was still being produced. I pored over the jute exhibition feeling perplexed and wondering how to write my WIDER report.

* * *

After the weekend Radha took us to Ranjan and Lindsay in Bally. We found them down a narrow street in an old house Ranjan said had been in his family for many generations. Its rooms surrounded a communal courtyard with a water pump and their walls were covered in a dark distemper, which complemented the sombre grey stone of the floors. The welcome from Ranjan's family shone amicably through the gloom. I was cooked an omelette and potato curry and Will a fried egg; one brother kept a shop attached to the house and presented us with mango juice for our journey to Dhanbad, while a tall, grey-haired cousin appeared out of a room lined with Moscow editions of Marx's writings, keen for discussions. Ranjan's sister, too, wanted to talk, telling me how she was working as a teacher on a low salary having decided not to accept an arranged marriage. I was confused how this squared with the family's Marxism – yet another contradictory facet of India.

At 4.30 the following morning we trekked through the streets and took a local train to Howrah station in Kolkata. It was filled with tiny, confident market-women with enormous bundles of wares who squashed up to give me and Will a seat. At Howrah we took the train to Dhanbad, travelling second class on three wooden seats. En route a man got on, sang a haunting song and then stepped off at the next station without collecting any money. 'What was he singing about?' I asked. 'He was singing about the meaning of life,' Ranjan replied, as if this was an everyday occurrence.

Dhanbad had a Wild West feel. As we walked towards a jeep which served as a kind of bus, Lindsay, in matter-of-fact Lancashire tones, told me it was a good job I could not understand the men's remarks. She was adamant it was not safe for Will and me to stay in a hotel. With remarkable ingenuity, she buttonholed a man at the School of Mines and put it to him that he should let us stay there because she was studying the Indian mines and my father had been an engineer at Sendra in the 1920s and 1930s. These seemed dubious grounds to me, but miraculously Lindsay's appeal worked.

On the next day the four of us wandered around near the Sendra mine looking for the bungalow. People passed us onto friends and after what seemed like a very long time we arrived at the palatial Hindustani guest house where a tall and courtly gentleman dressed in a long grey tunic summonsed tea, eggs and bread and butter for us. Incredibly he knew the names of the colliery managers my mother had mentioned in her stories. Upon looking at my old photo, to my delight he also knew where the bungalow was. When we at last reached the gate, I stood there, peering into the interior, trying in vain to imagine my mother sitting in one of the rooms.

Lindsay led us to the mine she was studying and while Ranjan looked after Will, she took me to meet Girija, the union organizer of the women who loaded the coal on to carts. They did not want to be photographed in their work clothes, which were dusty from the coal, but word spread quickly and a flock of women arrived dressed up in their best saris to pose for Lindsay's camera. Their supervisor too wanted his photo taken.

The miners' earnings were good in the context of Indian working-class wage rates; moreover the militant Marxist MP A.K. Roy had defended the women workers, who received equal pay. However, though the woman shop steward's home contained a large television set showing the cricket, which Will watched with her son, the available housing was basic and rat-infested. Lindsay told me that she had found some high rates of infant mortality among her interviewees. More generally the pollution in the mining area must have affected peoples' health; corruption was rife, and a local mafia countered the power of the union.

We eventually got to meet A.K Roy, sitting at his wooden desk in a small office. Initially the revolutionary leader's regard was dour and his tone prickly. Only when I presented him with a pamphlet by Arthur Scargill castigating the new realism propounded by some leaders in the British TUC, who wanted to confine union resistance to formally negotiated wage claims, did he become a little less stern.

As we were returning to Ranjan and Will, a young miner with a crew cut, walking across the black grime and dust of the coalfield, recognized Lindsay and raising his fist in salute hailed us with 'Lal Salam'. 'He's wishing us revolutionary greetings', explained Lindsay. He looked the epitome of a proletarian hero in some mythical Marxist epic. He was not impressed when I dithered, searching for an appropriate response, and he observed to Lindsay that while she was now 'pucca', having been with them for some time, I was still 'kutcha' - raw, mushy and makeshift. It was up to Lindsay to teach me. I was further enmeshed in kutcha-style class collaboration in the office of the Sikh welfare officer, who took a shine to me and gallantly presented me with a flower, amidst giggles from the women.

That visit to Dhanbad was hard to assimilate, though emotionally consequential. I had glimpsed both the women workers' conditions and traces of the economic and social landscape behind my mother's stories from the 1920s and 1930s. But those few days of walking in the dust over the coalfields left me physically exhausted. It was incredible to me how people managed to live and do heavy work there.

Back in Kolkata I interviewed a woman running an industrial training project and spoke at a meeting on international links between women workers. Among the feminists and socialists I met was the imposing economist Nirmala Bannerjee, who knew Swasti, and made me aware how much I needed to learn. As December came to an end, I was anxious for us to move on.

10

1988

Our departure at the beginning of January proved complicated. We misread the time and missed our plane. I despaired and assumed we would have to pay again, but Radha, showing no signs of panic, pushed me and Will forward muttering about how English visitors aroused pride in airport officials. Sure enough, the young man towering above us behind his computer, concentrated hard and proceeded to impassively rechart our journey across India to Bombay (now Mumbai). We travelled in a series of hops and were accompanied part of the way by members of the Indian cricket team, to Radha's great delight. She was endeavouring to encourage Will's interest in the game.

I cheered up in Bombay. A couple of Radha's friends helped to entertain Will and prepared a curry of lamb chops with fresh mint and coriander which I tried hard to memorize and make ever afterwards, but only ever approximated.[397] Two intense conversations with Sujata Gothoskar, an insightful researcher on trade unions and women's work, reassured me of the importance of looking at the diverse forms of organizing among women workers. Prema Purao, the organizer of an ingenious co-operative called 'Annapurna Mahila Mandal', was similarly encouraging. Founded in 1975 to provide secure employment for women textile workers after the factories closed, 'Annapurna' took its name from the goddess of food. Prema explained the co-operative provided economical but wholesome meals for migrant men from the countryside. These low-paid men worked shifts and rented spaces on the floors of lodging-houses but could not afford food in restaurants. By producing food on a large scale, Annapurna was able to keep costs low. Not only did it provide a vital service for the migrant workers, it aimed to protect and empower the women through the security and mutuality of the co-operative.

On 5 January we took a few days break in Goa. By this time Radha, Will and I had merged into a consonant little band rambling through the vast country. This was just as well for things did not quite go according to plan. Radha knew some Indian hippies who had started a restaurant and hotel. Unfortunately, the power supply had failed in the hotel, so they kindly put us up in a row on their floor. Radha and Will slept soundly, but I was old enough to find that floor exceedingly hard. Still, the food at their restaurant was wonderful and swimming in the balmy waves of the Indian Ocean was heaven.

I was exposed as a thorough westerner in Goa, worried when Radha mentioned snakes on our walk to the restaurant in the evening, alarmed by hearing the pigs chomping away behind the outdoor lavatory and appalled one day on the beach alone when a man seized me by the ear, inserted a steel implement and extracted a blob of grey wax which he waved triumphantly. I bellowed in rage, 'Go away'. Radha explained patiently that while her ears had never been dewaxed, the men were very skilled! I thought to myself that this was one tacit skill I could do without.[398]

Our next stop was the Gujarati city of Ahmedabad. Apart from the camels valiantly pulling and carrying goods amidst lorries and cars, the old industrial centre was reminiscent of Northern English mill towns. When we reached the unassuming headquarters of the Self-Employed Women's Association (SEWA), we were greeted by Renana Jhabvala. My first impression upon meeting her was of a straight-backed woman with a compelling oval face and laughing eyes, who contrived to be busy and efficient while possessing a deep well of serenity. I later learned that Renana, who was then directing SEWA's union wing, had known Radha from childhood.

Remarkably, SEWA had developed effective ways of organizing poor women on a large scale through grassroots networks, combining protests and resistance with co-operatives, support services and a strong morale of personal and collective sisterhood. Their members included small-scale vendors selling food and basic household goods, home-based producers making garments, pottery or bidis (local cigarettes), as well as contract workers in construction, washing clothes or cleaning.

In 1972 SEWA had grown out of the Textile Labour Association (TLA). The TLA's early twentieth century founder, Anasuya Sarabhai, had been influenced by the movement for women's suffrage and the British Fabian socialists and was closely associated with Mahatma Gandhi. She became a mentor for a young lawyer, Ela Bhatt, who was to take over the work with the TLA. In 1981 SEWA broke away from the TLA's Women's Wing and developed a form of organizing poor women which combined co-operatives, militant trade unionism and supportive services, including a bank. Ela Bhatt proved a responsive and resolute organizer and SEWA had grown to include thousands of women: small-scale vendors selling items of food or clothing, home-based producers such as bidi makers and service providers like cleaners and cooks. A bidi worker was its president and a quilt maker one of its vice presidents.[399]

When Ela Bhatt had been elected, despite her reluctance, as an MP in New Delhi to present the demands of poor women as the chairperson of the Commission for the Self-Employed, Renana had taken her place in Ahmedabad. I was surprised to see two familiar documents on Renana's desk. In the 1970s some groups of homeworkers in Britain had formed local links with trade unions and contributed to the Trades Union Congress (TUC) Statement on Homeworking. There it was along with the Homeworkers' Charter from the June 1984 conference funded by the GLC.[400] Incredibly the fruits of British homeworkers' experiences and Annie Ralph's labour had landed in Ahmedabad.

Renana explained how the combined mobilization through

the union and co-operatives drew on the individual strength of the women workers, while fostering this through collective action. Their capacity for trade union resistance was sustained by the security provided by co-operatives, by the practical help of craft and technological training, educational and health services and by their own bank, which could provide credit on fair terms to micro borrowers. As SEWA had come across obstacles they had innovated. Each small step had slowly accumulated into expanding projects which helped practically, while bringing both fulfilment and empowerment.[401]

Radha looked after Will while I went to see some of these. I visited printing-block and basket-making co-ops and watched videos that a young American student from Stuart Ewen's film course at Hunter College in New York had helped SEWA members to make about their bank, the co-operatives, homebased garment work and street selling. I learned how the vendors' struggle for space in the city had extended into a questioning of laws that had survived from the British Empire and of the discriminatory assumptions still rooted in urban planning. Their placard, 'Dignity and Daily Bread', pithily summed up how SEWA balanced transforming and sustaining.

Both Ela Bhatt and Renana Jhabvala regarded organizing the apparently unorganizable as an ongoing strategic process. In Renana's words, it involved 'a series of ups and downs'. While there were unexpected breakthroughs, any success was 'rarely absolute'. Instead, she affirmed resolutely that you just had to keep on keeping on keeping on. The two women possessed that rare mix, a crucial grasp of minutia, combined with a global reach. I saw how SEWA stretched what could be possible when Renana startled me by saying an international campaign on homeworking was needed.[402]

Thursday 14 January was our last day in India. Just before Will and I were due to fly home we went shopping for presents and Will bought Indian shirts for two school-friends whose father was a Hackney bus driver from South Asia. I muttered to him that I had never seen them in Indian shirts, but Will swept this aside. We also met Radha's parents for a meal. Her father, Lovraj, a senior civil servant, was politely interested in our journey to the mines; her mother, Dharma, was a distinguished economic historian, a beautiful and striking figure. I was uneasily aware of being between the two generations in age, for Radha and her mother were at variance, in contrast to the close, loving relationship between Radha and her grandmother.

Our flight was delayed for thirteen hours. Our wait seemed even longer because I had changed my money ready for take-off, so we were without provisions, until eventually the airport issued us with some water and a sandwich. When we finally boarded, we were surrounded by American oil rig workers who had drunk the bar dry during their long confinement. One man from Mississippi was overtly racist and responded in startled amazement when an elegant and confident young woman of Indian descent turned to him and remarked in a New York accent, 'What have I done to be sitting next to a schmuck like you!' It was unlikely that he could speak Yiddish, but he crumpled at her contempt.

Even the London tube proved eventful. As I slumped exhausted in my seat, I heard two French punkish-looking types debating on whether to steal our luggage.[403] The woman was for mercy, but the man was unsentimental about mother and child. Seizing the bags by their handles I told Will we were getting off and glared at them as the doors shut behind us. After the train left carrying our would-be robbers, I explained what I had heard. 'See why it's good to learn other languages,' I declared. Will looked up at me, unconvinced.

* * *

We reached Hackney at midnight and I slept until three in the afternoon.[404] The following week I went to have the curls on the top of my head restored by a perm, felt ill and then noticed I had a hacking cough.[405] By the end of January I had lost my voice. 'Feeling depressed,' I scribbled in my diary.[406] Term had begun at Kent University and so I was back on my route through Faversham and Chatham to Canterbury. My report for

WIDER was a priority, but I was still preoccupied with *The Past is Before Us* and had deadlines for articles as well as classes to prepare. Also, because North London Polytechnic had given me an honorary doctorate, I had decided to organize a conference there on 'Women and the Economy'. Any one of these would have been intrinsically interesting, but because I was weary and low spirited the pile of paper on my desk was discouraging. 'Tasks stretch ahead', I gloomed to myself in my journal.[407]

My glum mood did not only derive from a bad cold. Despite the snatched spasms of passion which had been my sexual destiny over the last few years, I was bereft of loving companionship. In Finland I had been attracted to an Italian man who was staying in the hotel. Our friendship became flirtatious and then desirous, but he was married. 'You must find a man who can be with you,' he had said. Part of me was in agreement, but when I looked back at the years with Paul, I had to admit that I had often been miserable as well as happy. How did passion and long-term connecting combine? Could this ever really be possible? Meanwhile I walked around feeling desperate for sex, just sex. It was so blatant this wanting to be wanted that I suspected it must show.

Conservatism felt culturally smothering after I returned from India. Margaret Thatcher, secure after her election victory in June 1987, had her sights on the 'reform' of education which she envisaged as more tests and a core curriculum informed by 'a duty' to rescue children from 'the propaganda ... coming from left-wing local authorities, teachers and pressure groups'.[408] Despite determined rebellion from gays and lesbians, the Conservative government's congealed prejudices were soon to become law in Section 28 of the Local Government Act of 1988. This banned the sympathetic presentation of homosexuality in schools, further stigmatizing gay men who had suffered so much from Aids over the course of the decade.[409] The danger of Aids had contributed to a resurgence of negative fears around sexuality. This was enhanced by the right-wing tabloids, which flourished on titillation, tempered by hypocritical tut tutting. It was depressing to watch the gradual erosion of efforts to bring knowledge and understanding to bear on sexual relationships.

I was restored by Lynne Segal, whose book *Is the Future Female?* published by Virago grappled with the rise and fall of socialist feminism, the complexities of sexual pleasure, psychoanalytic theory, masculinity, violence against women and the impact of wars.[410] She and I resumed our swimming and saunas, relaxing while we went over politics, controversies and gossip.[411] It was impossible to remain discouraged for long in the company of such an irreverent and indefatigable fighter of a friend.

A trip to see Swasti in Brighton also raised my morale. Not only were we both so committed to our WIDER project, Swasti combined a searching intellect with a generous power to encourage. She and her husband, Partha, a distinguished art historian at Sussex University, greeted me with a joyous hospitality and the bracing winds of Brighton did the rest.[412]

When I visited Liz Waugh, who had walked the city streets in the evenings with me in the 1970s trying to unionize night cleaners, I rebuked myself for moping. Liz had become very ill with multiple sclerosis while I was at the GLC. We had hoped that Liz's illness might stabilize, instead it was becoming obvious it was intensifying and former members of our women's liberation group used to stay with her overnight to allow her mother Lucy, now in her eighties, a break.

Liz could not move easily and needed help writing letters, including ones in French, which she had studied at university.[413] She dictated these to me, but my grammar and spelling were rusty. I was not a reliable scribe and my clumsy French exasperated her. It was frustrating for Liz, who had so many abilities, yet could no longer make use of them. Sitting by her bedside I ruefully reflected that Liz had far more reason to be despairing than I did. Instead, she focused the energy she still possessed on finding alternative remedies, discovering and trying new diets which were meant to help. Tragically none of them proved particularly effective.

* * *

In February I was surprised when Stanley Aronowitz, the American academic and activist who had written on class and social movements, telephoned from Paris. I hardly knew him and thus was unaware he was involved in an exchange programme, teaching University students at Paris VIII about 'American and British Civilization'. He wanted me to come and replace a teacher who had fallen ill. It would mean more travelling and teaching three new courses on top of the MA at the University of Kent.

The prospect was daunting, but there were important inducements. I could meet up with a close friend from the French women's liberation movement, Françoise Barret-Ducrocq. We had met in the late 1960s. Françoise was a social historian who had been influenced by Raphael Samuel and the Ruskin History Workshops. During the late 1980s, she was teaching at Paris VII and doing pioneering research about the sexual relationships of the London Victorian poor. Her university, along with Paris VIII, became seedbeds for women's studies in France.[414] Luckily for me at that time the French estimated lecturers through publications, so they classified me as a professor and paid me accordingly.[415]

My new routine thus became Hackney to Canterbury on Wednesday, followed by an early-morning flight to Paris on Thursday to teach one class on nineteenth-century American women active in radical movements and another on the new left in Britain and the US from the 1950s. Afterwards I made my way to Françoise's home near the metro stop at Tolbiac in the south of the city. On Friday I left early in the morning for the university and travelled north to do a class on American and British nineteenth century radical ideas and movements, returning to London in the afternoon.

My first visit to Paris VIII was discouraging. I was confronted by a great lump of grey concrete covered in layers of rebel graffiti. Initially an experimental college at Vincennes, created partly in response to the 1968 student uprising, in 1980 it had moved to the old working-class area of Saint Denis. When I took Will, he surveyed Paris VIII with Hackney eyes and shook his head, 'Mum you told me it was bad, but not *this* bad'. He was right, the buildings *were* bad in 1988, before being spruced up in the 1990s.

Some opponents of bourgeois individualism had removed Paris VIII's lavatory doors. To my relief these had been restored in the staff toilets. Two harassed women administrators handled the angst of a great host of students, and thus enquiring anything of them seemed akin to a violation. Nor were my colleagues forthcoming. We lecturers huddled uncomfortably in a tiny room like strangers awaiting a dental appointment. Conversation was rare and thus I never explained that I was commuting from London each week.

But my students, who were from Egypt, Martinique, Nigeria, North Africa and Portugal, as well as France, were responsive and interested, especially on topics relating to race and to women. They told me that the history I taught reminded them of the American historian Howard Zinn; I was duly honoured to be associated with the passionate exponent of peoples' power, but of course my knowledge of American history had really been accumulated by symbiosis through friends, particularly Ros Baxandall.

At Paris VIII, I met the political and social theorist Alisa Del Re from Italy, who had been influenced by the Marxism of Mario Tronti and Toni Negri, which stressed the creation of new forms of organizing through workers' militant action. This focus on workers and the workplace had cut out many aspects of everyday life that were crucial in women's lives, including the time and energy women expended in domestic labour and caring for others. She was trying, in a non-sectarian way, to reassess the negative and repressive aspects of the state, alongside the need for new forms of social provision. I felt a close affinity with Alisa's approach to theorizing which was closely integrated with learning through doing.

Martine Spensky, an historian who specialized in the British suffrage movement and the development of social policy, was also teaching at the university. Like me, she was interested in the more recent past and I was able to send her material from the 1970s on women's liberation campaigns around maternity and childcare provision.

Most of all though I would look forward to seeing Françoise on Thursday nights after the long journey on the metro from Saint Denis. The initial bond between us had been forged through our interest in history and socialist feminist politics, but as time went by we had acquired shared memories of friends, loves and children and could relate in many dimensions. I remember laughing away watching *GI Jane* together on the television with French subtitles and gasping at a series staging competitive striptease conducted with a craft eroticism which would have been inconceivable on British TV. Some of these women were taking an overt pride in their bodies, displaying and controlling their power of sexual allure in front of an audience and on screen. They were unimaginably brave, and they discombobulated my assumptions. France was so close geographically, and yet so different in its sexual sensibilities.

My work in Paris was rewarding but the weekly travel combined with teaching at Canterbury, checking the proofs of *The Past is Before Us,* examining at Northern College with the sociologist Huw Beynon, plus writing reviews and articles, on top of my commitments to WIDER, was exhausting. The years of insecurity had created an ingrained habit of taking on work until I became like a railway station with too many lines open. In late March when I spoke in Conway Hall at the memorial for Raymond Williams, a newspaper photograph shocked me by revealing deep contours of exhaustion on my face.[416]

Though we kept on protesting we were repeatedly defeated. Will's school, Gayhurst, was demonstrating again, because Margaret Thatcher's government intended to abolish the Inner London Education Authority. Parents and workers in the schools put up a bitter resistance on behalf of our own and others' children. We delayed it but could not stop the law going through.[417] ILEA went in March 1990.

I was cantankerous and prickly at a Historical Materialism Colloquium in Birmingham on 30 April. Two historians I admired, Eric Hobsbawm and Rodney Hilton, were there, but the terms of reference were enclosed and it was as if the political and social impact of the women's movement had never happened. I erupted in anger, which only resulted in making them wrap themselves more tightly within the familiar contours of their 'historical materialism'.[418]

I diagnosed myself as suffering from an affliction called 'meetingitis', caused by a surfeit of meetings. Beside my list of things to do in April, I scrawled in my SEWA diary, 'Memo. STOP ACCEPTING MORE THINGS'. Yet I never did.

* * *

On 2 May, Marc Karlin arrived at Powerscroft Road with Jonathan Bloom, his cinematographer and friend. Marc's probing of socialism had gathered an accretion of flickering memories and transient histories redrawing the everyday, and, after several years work, they were finally close to finishing *Utopias*.

I had spent years talking with Marc about left politics and was familiar with his films. I was aware how he often expressed concepts in ways that made them seem abstract. From a Jewish family in Russia, with a Polish mother and a Latvian father who had fled from the Russian Revolution, Marc had spent his first two years in a Swiss refugee camp and then lived in France as a child with his grandmother before being sent to an English public school. Sometimes, it felt as if he was thinking in French and translating as he spoke.

Despite being so accustomed to communicating with Marc, on this occasion I was paralysed by his expectations. It seemed as if he wanted me to reach within some buried cavity of consciousness and resurface with illumination. But I could not fathom exactly what it was that he was seeking. The more I wrestled the worse it became. I felt as if someone had stuck a gag down my throat. The words just would not come out of me.

Marc and Jonathan went down to film in my basement study, which had a brown wooden partition. They proceeded to adorn the room with photographs of Edward Carpenter, a Gayhust school picture of Will looking proud in his shell suit, images of Lenin and young majorettes from Fritz Lang's *Metropolis*, conjuring them into a long dreamy compilation on Utopia.

Marc did not give up easily. Back he came the next day, this time with Hermione Harris, Jonathan Bloom and the grip, Glyn Fielding, accompanied by a hired crane. Hermione and I had been close friends since 1961, and looking across at her thoughtfully enquiring face finally overcame my nerves about speaking in front of a camera. I stated that an obvious weakness in modern socialism was that it did not encourage people to imagine what might be. In contrast to the Labour Party which honed its policies 'to try and fit in with what people already accept', I argued that that the GLC had sought 'to develop through concrete examples of what was needed, the capacity for people to imagine how a whole society could be different'.[419]

Jonathan and Glyn had the camera on a crane outside my bedroom window.[420] Up it went, recording me sitting in the luxurious Parker Knoll chair bought with my redundancy money from the GLC, an investment against mysterious aches and pains which had begun to appear. Then they raised it into the beyond, way up over the top of the roof to film the Hackney skyline from an angle I had never, ever seen before.

* * *

The Women and the Economy Conference on Saturday 7 May brought together a remarkable bevy of women.[421] Anne Phillips' opening survey of employment policies indicated just how difficult it was to ensure that women's circumstances and needs were considered within them. Speakers looked at both specific issues and their wider ramifications: Sue Himmelweit argued for significant changes in hours at work so that women and men could share child-rearing; Jean Gardiner tackled the 'Economics of Child Care'; Pat Masters and Hilary Wainwright led a discussion on working time and what was being produced.

Ursula Huws noted that socially useful production was only part of the answer and emphasized improving public services. Jenny Morris spoke on housing policy and Lesley Doyal on women and health care. Marj Mayo looked at the public sector as an employer, Marina Lewycka reflected on linking workplaces with communities and Betty Heathfield reported from Women Against Pit Closures.

Swasti, along with Angela Dale and Naila Kabeer from the Institute of Development Studies (IDS), analyzed the implications of race, class and gender in the new conditions of global work. Haleh Afshar described strategies for dealing with racism at work among three generations of Chinese and Pakistani women. Penny Kemp, from the Green Party, dissected the Third World debt crisis, while Hermione Harris spoke on the economic problems encountered in Nicaragua.

The conference lifted my spirits, by reassuring me that socialist feminists were still engaging with the broad economic and social issues affecting women and reminding me how much investigative thinking had accumulated. When I wrote the article 'Woman's place is in another economy' for the *Guardian*, I outlined how current economic and social policies were accentuating inequalities among women, not simply in Britain, but globally. I also aired the arguments of socialist feminists against male bias in both mainstream and left economics, taking inspiration from Swasti and from Audrey Wise's grounded vision of working-class women wanting 'another economy'.[422]

New vistas opened too. Indirectly, through the conference, I met Delia Jarrett-Macauley, a young writer whose family had originally come from Sierra Leone. Delia was interested in black women's cultural history in Britain, and also thinking through race, gender and class. Through Delia I learned about Una Marson, the pioneering writer and broadcaster from the Caribbean. Moreover, my teaching on the MA in Kent introduced me to several young feminists who were decisively rejecting the negative guilt-tripping about sexuality that had surfaced in the late 1970s. One essay on 'Identity' was so thoughtful I passed it on to *Feminist Review,* who decided to publish it. Mary Louise Adams showed how the concept had enhanced the solidarity of sisterhood and the recognition of groups who were implicitly excluded. Then, drawing on her own experiences as a young lesbian feminist and on the writings of Bell Hooks, Cherie Moraga, Sue O'Sullivan, Bernice Reagon and Alice Walker, she went on to argue that dwelling exclusively *within* a specific identity was restrictive, 'We effectively obscure the interconnectedness of oppressions when we see their solutions as atomized personal efforts'.[423]

* * *

The Chesterfield Socialist Conference on 11 June was invigorating, argumentative and great fun. Once again it defied the simplistic polarities of 'hard' and 'soft' left, attracting variegated socialists, feminists, trade unionists, left Labour MPs, Greens, opponents of Section 28, peace and environmental campaigners.[424] Hilary, whose optimism remained indestructible, was open to resisting the Tories from differing standpoints, in movements and in radical parties. Like me, she wanted a left that could cross boundaries.

Needless to say, not everyone agreed. I told Ros Baxandall that I went to a workshop on the 'flexibility of labour', consisting mainly of left-wing manual workers. They polarized sharply between those who argued for backing Labour Party policies and others insisting on socialist revolution. I bemoaned the eradication of alternative strategies and how 'the GLC has been wiped from memory'.[425]

I had lamented on similar lines to Ken Livingstone when we bumped into one another at the Conference. Ken listened politely, then cheerily remarked on the good time we had all had at the meal two years ago when Hilary and I had interviewed him, and suggested we should all go off and get drunk again.[426] In public at least, Ken was not given to revealing gloom. In the face of adversity, he popped back up like an irrepressible dandelion, face turned to the sun.

A few days later I went up to speak at Northern College where I gave two lectures on women in French Revolutionary movements in the 19th Century.[427] I felt the same delight in researching and writing about them that I had experienced the previous year upon returning to Edward Carpenter and his circle. Eventually I would scrutinize them in greater depth in an article about women clothing workers in the 1848 revolution.[428]

But unexpected commitments kept arising. The National Union of Seamen (NUS) had called a strike in January 1988; it had proved instantly effective, however rulings against them in the High Court had allowed ferry companies to sue the NUS and seize their assets. Nonetheless the rank and file were still resolved to continue resisting cuts in wages, reduced numbers of workers and bad, sometimes dangerous, conditions on the ships. I knew about their predicament because a friend, Roger Kline, then a researcher at the Birmingham Trade Union Resource Centre, had documented the recent P&O ferry disaster in his pamphlet, *Heroes Then, Sacked Now*.

So, when a group of striking seafarers made contact with me because they knew I had helped to organize the appeal for the miners, I agreed to assist them. Marc Karlin offered them space in Berwick Street and they seemed keen. But then silence fell until early August, when I suddenly heard that the Transport and General Workers' office in South London was to be our base.

I had just three days to set them up with lists of names and telephone numbers before Will and I were due to go and stay with Ros at the Cape. Three men arrived; two were completely confused about what to do, but one older man had been an army sergeant. Quickly adapting his administrative skills, he related to me as a kind of junior officer. The sergeant and I assumed command and began telephoning 'celebrities'. He had been trained to always take two copies of written statements, but I managed to reassure him that if the people we rang said 'yes', we could take that as consent. I was anxious about how the men would fare when I went away and was grateful when my old friend Nigel Fountain stepped in to help them.

* * *

Holidays at the Cape were never *totally* calm. This time I
ignorantly swam against the tide in the mouth of the Pamet
River. Amazed by the strength of the current I kept moving my
legs and arms, but the river seemed resolved to return me to the
sea. Momentarily I began to wonder whether I would ever make
the relatively short distance to the shore. I was surrounded by
better informed Americans in small boats, but absurdly I was
too embarrassed to ask for help, so I just battled on, trying to
conceal my relief when I eventually stepped on to dry land.

Stuart Ewen was again leading a blithely untroubled Will on
the long swims around one of the lakes. Will and I made friends
that year with two African Americans who were staying with
Liz and Stuart, Elaine and Harry Scott. Elaine, who taught at
Old Westbury with Liz and Ros, was shy and sensitive and loved
discussing literature, while Harry combined a rooted awareness
of both race and class with a subtle political irony. Through
his trade union he had become interested in law and would
eventually do a degree in it. They both used to laugh a lot with
Will and were intrigued by his accounts of life in Hackney.

Will had become the youngster, as Ros's son Phineas and his
friends had grown up and were at university. Phinny's friend
Marc Perry was visiting and along with Steve Nelson, one of the
veteran leftists who had settled at the Cape, we all packed into
Ros' car to see Chris Menges' film about Ruth First, *A World
Apart*, which was showing in Provincetown. The script was
written by her daughter Shawn Slovo.

The film awakened overwhelming memories of Ruth, who I
had met during the 1970s. On the way home Marc was dismissive
because it dwelt on a white opponent of apartheid. As an African
American he identified strongly with Africa and Africans, and
was aware how they were under-represented in the dominant
culture of remembering. But I argued with him vehemently, for
Ruth's contribution to the anti-apartheid movement had made
her a target for assassination. I insisted that her life and work
deserved to be remembered.

Our clash aroused painful recollections for Steve Nelson of

his arrest and imprisonment during the1950s on a charge of sedition. Steve was a tall, powerful man in his eighties, but his voice cracked as he described, with tears in his eyes, how they had kept him in irons even when his children had visited him. I was sitting next to him in the back of the car and was shaken by his account of how his case had dragged on from 1950 until 1956, when the Supreme Court overturned his twenty-year sentence. That decision proved to be a significant step in the fight against Senator McCarthy's crusade against the left in America.

Over the years I learned more about Steve's life. Born in 1903 in Croatia, he had emigrated to the US as a young teenager, working in a slaughterhouse and later in car plants. Influenced by his workmates, he became a Communist and went to fight fascism in Spain during the Civil War, where he was a political commissar in the left-wing Abraham Lincoln Brigade. After being shot in the neck and face, he was made responsible for escorting visiting celebrities like Dorothy Parker and Ernest Hemingway around the war zone.

After a long fight within the Communist Party because of the Hungarian Uprising, he eventually left it, moving to Truro where he built a house. He would continue to be a committed socialist, excitedly discovering Rosa Luxemburg and ardently hoping for a reformed Soviet Union from Mikhail Gorbachev's 'Perestroika', regardless of being in what Ros used to call 'older age'.

Ros had several other 'older-age' visitors for dinner while Will and I were there. They included the Nobel-Prize-winning scientist George Wald and his wife, Ruth Hubbard, an equally eminent biochemist, with striking long white hair. The couple had fallen in love while researching sight and vitamin A. The gifted lawyer Leonard Boudin and his wife, the poet Jean Roisman, came too. When I met all four of them I was moved that they had driven so far to visit and drawn to their charm and calm modesty.[429] Needless to say their lives had not been so calm; the Boudins' daughter, Kathy, had been involved in one of the groups of young white Americans who responded

to police violence against black Americans with direct action
against property. Tragically, a death occurred, and they were
imprisoned for many years.

As ever, long discussions took place on the beach. Despite
differing contexts, the American left's dilemmas resonated
with ours in Britain and I listened with recognition as they
debated Jesse Jackson's second bid for the presidency backed
by the 'Rainbow Coalition'. It was heartening to hear how, in
July, white gays had joined trade unionists, African Americans,
Hispanics and members of Puerto Rican communities at a
huge Rainbow meeting in Harlem. Obie Bing was sceptical
about changing the Democratic Party, but hopeful that a
combination of local oppositional initiatives from below to
the devastating deindustrialization in American cities might
present an alternative. An uneasy Elaine Scott thought the
Rainbow Coalition's assumption that people could be summed
up through single identities was an oversimplification and
everyone was dubious about the cult of personality surrounding
Jackson. Nevertheless, Jackson's saying, 'Just because it rains,
you don't have to drown', made me smile ruefully.[430] It was an
appropriate maxim for the times!

* * *

Back in London, the seafarers had done a remarkable job with
their strike appeal and greeted me with triumph. With Nigel
Fountain's help they had made a huge chart with pins on the
names of assenting celebrities. These included academics,
actors, singers, musicians, journalists, novelists, film-makers, art
workers, designers and the football manager Brian Clough. The
Labour Party figures were notably wide-ranging and included
Neil and Glenys Kinnock, John Prescott, Michael Foot and Jill
Craigie, Norman and Janey Buchan, Kim Howells, Ann Clwyd,
Michael Meacher, Tony Benn and Ken Livingstone.

The sergeant ceremoniously took me to the pub and
presented me with my reward, a blue and white china thimble,
which he explained was usually given to gay seamen. I was duly
honoured. A printers' strike meant we lost the appeal's slot in

the *Guardian,* but it appeared in many trade union and left papers, raising support and money.

Theresa Moriarty, my friend in the Irish Labour History Society, had invited me and Sally Alexander to a weekend conference on 23 to 25 September with women in the National Union of Public Employees (NUPE).[431] Their oral history project on women's health, drawing on the memories of working-class members in Northern Ireland, had taken off. The initial organizing group, who I had met through Theresa in South Wales at *Llafur,* had gained a formidable supporter in the socialist feminist Inez McCormack, the Divisional Officer for NUPE in Northern Ireland. Inez, whose family had been Protestants, supported Catholic civil rights and resolutely crossed boundaries of religion, class and culture. Many of the women participating had lost their jobs through privatization or the lack of childcare and Inez remarked that despite the 'responsibility' they had shown for others, they had been written out of history.[432]

Established initially to defend the NHS against privatization, by 1988 their project had evolved into a comprehensive study not simply of work, but of childhood, sexuality and childbirth, documenting food, diet and housing. At the evening workshop on sex, I was appalled to hear even women my age describing it as still ineradicably associated with fear when they were growing up. They said they had been ignorant of periods, contraception, abortion and pregnancy. I too had not received much information; however, when I was a student at Oxford in the early sixties, my then boyfriend, Bob Rowthorn, found out that there was a Fabian woman doctor in London, willing to fit diaphragms for girls who were unmarried.[433] As I related how I had gone to her for a diaphragm, there was a stunned silence, then gasps of disbelief. Finally, one of the NUPE women, shook her head in incredulity, observing, 'Another country'.

Sally and I glimpsed a disturbing facet of this 'other' country when the taxi we were sharing with the official from NUPE was halted and rigorously searched by the police. Without

any explanation, the police took aside the cab driver, who had
picked us up at a hotel. Goodness knows what they told him,
for, when Sally later enquired if it was usual for women in a
taxi to be stopped, his response was a tight lipped, 'Three dodgy
women'. After this conversation stopper, we continued our
journey in silence, mystified as to why a women's oral history
meeting should pose such a threat to state security.

Early in October I went briefly up to Blackpool to speak
at the Labour Party Conference on a panel organized by the
Fabians on 'consumption', with Jack Straw in the chair. I had
met him once briefly in 1968 at a meeting with the police, when
we were both involved in organizing a festival in support of the
Vietnamese who were opposing American intervention. I was
there representing 'Agitprop', the radical cultural network John
Hoyland and I had set up, while he was then a leading figure in
the National Union of Students, notable for his Buddy Holly
style glasses and suspected of 'reformism' by revolutionary
students, because he was thought to support the Communist
Party.[434]

In Blackpool, I criticized the commercial focus of the
policy document and stressed social consumption. Arguing
that public services were particularly vital for working-class
women, I referred to the 'Health in Homerton' project in which
the feminist Jo Robinson had gleaned ideas for improving
ante-natal appointments by listening to the complaints of
women in the waiting room. Because they mentioned a lack
of opportunities for discussion, Jo had humanized the room
with 'play facilities for children, more comfortable chairs,
drinks available'.[435] I connected this example to wider efforts by
feminists to democratize social provision and reduce the gap
between recipients and providers. This touched a nerve with
older people at the meeting, who began to talk about their own
experiences.[436]

All this appeared to baffle Jack Straw. Only Jo's cups of
tea seemed to penetrate our chair's body armour. Nodding
emphatically, he asserted with such intemperate zeal how

tea should indeed be delivered to expectant mothers that it conjured up a nightmarish image of tea being poured down their throats throughout the land, willy nilly, drowning out any protests of not being thirsty or perhaps preferring a coffee. I was flabbergasted.

Even more bizarre, when I read the so-called 'report' of our meeting in the *Financial Times,* it did not in any way resemble what had been said or who had been saying it. Being on the periphery of the Labour Party, I did not understand how things operated behind the scenes, and only later learned that the press office would brief journalists on meetings and thus eliminate any critical voices.[437] This astounded me, not only politically, but as an historian. It meant any report of opinions expressed would have to be taken as poppycock.

While in Blackpool, I stayed with Hilary Wainwright at a pseudo-castle of a hotel, replete with turrets, called the Norbreck Hydro. Our stay rapidly began to resemble an episode of Fawlty Towers for it was the kind of hotel where the staff followed strict routines and expected deference from guests. Lips pursed and shoulders stiffened when a polite but persistent Hilary requested healthier modifications to the set breakfast.

Hilary laughed that it was 'kitsch', but I found our stay disconcerting. I had last been there in the early 1950s with my parents when I was ten and had been taught to swim in its pool. My parents, newly prosperous – thanks to the expanding demand for the mining equipment my father sold – had regarded it as 'posh'.[438] Any poshness had become shabby over the years. But the pool was still there and when we swam in it pangs of nostalgia returned me to my childhood.

I had supported Tony Benn's unsuccessful bid to challenge Neil Kinnock for the leadership because I respected and trusted him. But I was not involved with internal Labour politics or part of any organized faction and was friendly with a potpourri of Labour Party people.[439] My links with them had come about through several decades of shared causes and ideas, and I regarded this eclectic mix as 'an affirmation over time'.[440]

Though it was impossible to ignore bitterness at the conference 'to the left and to the right' I persisted in valuing friendships with socialists across political boundaries.[441]

After the Labour Party conference, I shared a platform at the Cheltenham Literature Festival with Jill Craigie, the socialist and feminist film-maker, who had researched the history of women's suffrage. Later that day we both sat listening to her husband, Michael Foot, 'In Conversation' with the lawyer and writer John Mortimer. Eloquence and irony came twirling off their tongues. Such skill with words, delivered with an effortless air, was extraordinary to me. They shook out language like scarves from magicians' sleeves, adeptly casting them into every corner of the hall.[442] Both Jill and Michael shared a gift, as did Tony Benn, of bestowing assurance to others.

Nevertheless, that meeting with Jack Straw on 'consumption' stayed uncomfortably with me. The raft of policies emerging under Neil Kinnock's leadership coincided with a new, less definable cultural ethos which intimated that left-wing socialists were pariahs. When Annie Pike, my book editor, invited me to speak at her Labour Party Women's Section, I realized they, too, were confused by the new policies and demoralized by the blocks on dissent.[443]

After opposing an *exclusive* emphasis upon class, it felt as if now it was being banished from the Labour lexicon. I grumbled in my journal, 'There is a great surge of guff about modernisation and a dismissal of the labour movement. The *Guardian* sneers at workers. Anyone who disagrees is called a fundamentalist. I go around in a rage about it. There is no more mention of exploitation. The conditions of people's work are disregarded.'[444] The uncritical exaltation of individualism irritated me intensely, not because I opposed liberty, but because it was being divorced from the collective mutuality embodied in public ownership and the democratic extension of control over resources.

* * *

I felt caught in 'a kind of circle', doing lectures, writing articles and editing my book *The Past Is Before Us: Feminism in Action*.[445] I was experiencing a lulling familiarity with the words, while beginning to look at what I had written anew. This contradictory sensation was particularly acute because as a participant, I wanted to ensure what had been thought and done was not forgotten and to convey the suppositions about social change many thousands of us had shared. I was driven by a sense that the axes of assumptions were turning. What had seemed so real and living was fading and dissolving. I knew how radical movements could be overlaid by later developments and the extent of their significance confined.

I was working closely with the book editor Annie Pike on the endnotes which documented the text. I had drawn on my stores of ephemera and wanted others to be able to access them. However, many women's liberation publications were not dated or consistent in how they were numbered, while many authors were identified only by their first names. Those forty pages of references made my head spin. But Annie just gripped her pencil and carried on systemizing them.[446]

A series of Renana Jhabvala's downs and ups marked that autumn. I was conferring with Swasti in Brighton about our WIDER project; we had rewritten our report but had heard nothing. We were both suspended in uncertainty. A despondent Swasti wrote that she had met Marja-Liisa at WIDER and talked with Lal but was unable to guess what he planned.[447] This, I would later realize, was not surprising, for Lal was a consummate diplomat, juggling many strands.[448]

Will, along with Jesse Ash and Joe Pipal, was going to 'big' school – Stoke Newington Comprehensive. Hackney was one of the poorest London boroughs and its schools were in chronic disrepair, having been starved of funds by a government that did not care. Things were most definitely worse than in the early 1970s when I had been teaching in an Islington comprehensive and I was worried how Will would fare. Selecting football boots, a symbolic marker of the move, became the focus for all these feelings of apprehension. My worries were accentuated when, early in October, he fell off his bike and then was injured playing football, becoming an outpatient at Homerton Hospital. I became aware of a serious shortage of basic first aid there when the nurse told me he was having to transfer bandages from the teaching hospital.

The impact of the Tories' cuts really registered forcefully that autumn on a visit to Liz Waugh's mother, Lucy, in Hackney's Homerton Hospital. As I stood by her bed I remembered Lucy campaigning for free contraceptives, abortion rights, nurseries and night cleaners in the 1970s. She was as lively and interested in talking about politics as ever, despite being a patient and despite having responsibility for Liz with MS and for young Natasha, her granddaughter, but I was appalled by her ward, recording that Homerton 'seems to lack nurses, tea cups and blankets'.[449] It felt as if the basic fabric of society was being lacerated.

My ambitions of being a freelance journalist had received a blow shortly after the Labour Party Conference. *New Society* had merged with the *New Statesman* and a letter had arrived from the editor, Stuart Weir, saying they were ending my Stand column. Lynne and other feminists, including Catherine Hall, mounted a protest in my defence, pointing to the lack of feminist material in the *New Statesman*, but I never got my column back.[450] I had lost my only regular assignment as a freelance writer in Britain.

Nevertheless, new openings appeared from America. I had acquired a regular slot in the left-wing *Zeta* (later *Z*) magazine which had been started by Michael Albert and Lydia Sargent in 1986 and, wonder of wonders, I could choose my own topics. I wrote article after article in *Z* about the political dilemmas facing the left, and socialist feminists in particular.

I was also able to write a long review of Ros Baxandall's collection of Elizabeth Gurley Flynn's writings, *Words on Fire*, for the new American journal *Rethinking Marxism*. I had learned about the extraordinary woman immortalized by Joe Hill in the song 'Rebel Girl' through my friendship with Ros. As a young woman, Flynn had been to prison, borne a child and entered a stormy love affair with the Italian anarchist Carlo Tresca. As well as defending strikers, Flynn had proposed ways of reorganizing domestic labour. She became a supporter of women's right to birth control, living with the lesbian birth-control advocate Marie Equi. During World War One she was kept under surveillance because of her activism in the Industrial Workers of the World (IWW), later joining the American Communist Party and rising within its ranks.

Ros's introduction to *Words on Fire* revealed Flynn's consciousness of links between personal and social transformation. It tallied with Linda Gordon's findings in *Woman's Body, Woman's Right* and with what I had learned about other early twentieth century rebel women: Alexandra Kollontai, Stella Browne, Dora Russell, Madeleine Pelletier and Hélène Brion in France, all of whom saw a similar correspondence.[451]

Ros had been drawn to Flynn's life and ideas partly through her own rebellious new left politics, but also because, while excoriating 'the horrors of Stalinism', as 'a red diaper baby' she nevertheless felt proud of what her parents and other members of the Communist Party had sacrificed and accomplished.[452] Like Ros, I, too, wanted 'a democratic socialist movement which could combine 'the means of overcoming class exploitation with the other forms of oppression'. Though such a prospect appeared to be growing fainter, I asserted it all the more vehemently, as 'not just a dilemma to be thought about, but an aching need to be acted upon'.[453]

While it was good to write in American left publications, they did not circulate much in Britain. So, when Hilary suggested that I should do a guest issue of *Interlink,* the magazine associated with the non-aligned Chesterfield Conferences, I agreed.

* * *

I had been firing off like a catherine wheel since I returned from India. As the year ended I described feeling 'fragmented and without cohesion'. I had been moving from one thing to another and wrote, 'I don't know how to assimilate all this diverse knowledge from differing areas of activity'.[454] I sensed I was 'drifting intellectually and creatively'.[455]

I might have added 'personally', for I was no nearer resolving the ambivalence that seemed to destine me to fancy only unattainable men. My friends proffered explanations in attempts to reassure me. Sally Alexander, who was becoming increasingly interested in psychology, announced, 'It's our background'.[456] Marsha Rowe consulted astrology and declared that in December Saturn had been in Sagittarius and had gone into Capricorn.[457] Jean McCrindle was less Delphic: adopting a tone of grim pessimism, she opined that passionate sex was incompatible with long-term relationships.[458] But this seemed too gloomy to me. Also, the companionship of love was surely important, even if people in couples did get grumpy and unsexy with one another at times.

Motherhood had become more complicated: even though I had a gang of resourceful allies in fellow parents, there was so much I could not understand about Will's life. He seemed to oscillate between 'pulling me towards him and pushing me away'. Troubled about what to do, I mused, 'I love him so much. But just being a mother isn't enough.'[459]

Noting how he enjoyed films but not plays, I embarked on a cultural mission to introduce Will to the theatre with Ben Jonson's *Bartholomew Fair* and Thomas Dekker's *The Shoemaker's Holiday*. This proved to be a mistake and provoked overt rebellion. My next try was to be more successful when, accompanied by honorary Marx-father James Swinson, we went to see Fiona Shaw in *The Taming of the Shrew*.[460] She played the inhospitable part with such brilliant defiance that Will enjoyed his first glimpse of Shakespeare. Yet only one theatre was ever to be *really* acceptable to my son, the miraculous Hackney Empire, a short walk away on Mare Street. Christmas meant going to its panto packed with children.[461]

11

1989

In January I was back at the Hackney Empire with Will. The old music hall had been rescued from its fate as a Bingo Hall in 1986 by Roland and Claire Muldoon, the socialist founders of CAST touring theatre company. As a result, plays, opera, music and a new style of variety bounced onto its old oak boards. The Empire enlivened our lives and was zealously supported by local rebels, including Nigel Fountain and David Widgery.[462]

Satire with a radical edge boomed during the Thatcher era. I found the virulence of some of it auto-destructive, but liked Dawn French, Jennifer Saunders and Lenny Henry, who took in human foibles with sharp but generous eyes. That night Will and I sat in the front stalls laughing for two hours at Lenny Henry being non-stop funny about Dudley, 'DJ Delbert Wilkins', Reggae and the 'Raggamuffin' style.[463] When he cracked a rude joke, Will leaned over to ask me what it meant. Turning towards him I muttered an ambiguous reply. Spotting us, quick as a flash, Lenny Henry cracked, 'That kid's having to explain that joke to his mum'. The audience rocked with laughter.

Interlink was not proving straightforward. I could persuade friends to write for nothing, but there was no money and no structure for producing a magazine any more. Nigel Fountain came to my rescue. I marvelled at his concentrated speed and noted how little he spoke while subbing. He rolled his sleeves up, left too little time, then proceeded to beat his own deadline. He appeared to thrive on tight limits and a lack of cash. I would have bowed to his superior experience of co-editing *City Limits* with John Fordham, but he insisted on me being the editor.[464]

Together we persuaded Roger Huddle, David Widgery's friend from Rock against Racism, to design it. Computers were looming, but to my relief Roger still put the copy down manually. I visited the designer Ruth Gregory and the photographer Syd Shelton, puzzling them by digging out images they had cast into the bin. They had such high standards; they discarded some really good ones.

Interlink came out in February, published by the Socialist Society and the Conference of Socialist Economists. The magazine had a red cover with 'What, Next?' in large white letters. Our strapline was 'Capitalism is moving so fast, it seems that socialism no longer fits. Yet despite the new look, the exploitation of humanity and nature are real enough. So, what do we make of socialism?'[465]

A key issue was how to approach the impact of new technology upon peoples' work. I wanted to allow space for criticism of the over-simple dichotomy appearing in articles in both the Communist Party's *Marxism Today* and the *Guardian* which postulated that an era of large exploitative 'Fordist' factories were being neatly replaced by 'new times', consisting of small creative 'Post-Fordist' units.[466] This was a personal as well as a political disagreement, for Robin Murray, conscious of the weakness of a left forced onto the defensive, was enthusiastic about their radical possibilities. Swasti was more sceptical, and, in an effort to air the debate more widely, I had gone to interview them in Brighton.[467]

Robin, who was fervently concerned to break with a socialism that adhered limpet-like to disappearing circumstances, stressed, 'We must steer into problems and not away from them'.[468] Swasti was similarly convinced of the need to understand new trends, but more aware of their negative impact on the most vulnerable workers. 'Instead of having hierarchical division within a company you are creating a different kind of hierarchy: those who are part of the company and those *distant* workers.'[469] The small units were more likely to be sweat shops, rather than the democratic co-operative projects Robin admired. She insisted that we had to recognize this unequal division of power in presenting an alternative 'vision of society'.[470]

In her article, 'Time for choice', Mary Kaldor argued that the consequences of the decline of large-scale Fordism and the introduction of new technology were not predetermined. Effective intervention by unions, social movements and governments could affect how changes ensued and she pointed to the differing international forms these were assuming.[471]

Contributors who wrote from direct experience were more pessimistic. I had met Betty Cook through Northern College. Active in Women Against Pit Closures, Betty described working as a 'picker' in a Yorkshire mail-order firm. She detailed how new technology had reduced the physical pressure of her job but diminished the capacity to control the pace of work. Each woman had to 'push, walk, pick, place and throw at the determination of the computer'. So, the pickers had to 'cope with the demands of the computer', rather than the other way round.[472] John Bohanna at Ford, Halewood, regretted that the unions lacked the 'strength and imagination to negotiate the terms of automation'. He regarded 1980s capitalism without illusions, distilling Margaret Thatcher's resolve to make industry 'fitter and leaner', unequivocally, 'I'll be in bed earlier and ache longer – providing I'm in work'.[473]

It was unclear where strategic opposition in defence of workers could come from. There were few indications that the Labour Party was up for contesting what capitalism was about, leading Irene Bruegel to argue that the reliance on market criteria in its Policy Review made its commitment to women's equality unrealizable.[474] Moreover the social movement left had been weakened over the course of the decade. Lynne Segal observed how the prevailing glorification of fragmented identities made it harder to act in a unified way, while Mary Louise Adams questioned the preoccupation with an 'elaboration of personal experience' which was coming to dominate feminist discussion.[475]

Nonetheless, regardless of political setbacks, *Interlink* was publicizing meetings of the Socialist Society and the Conference of Socialist Economists' Working Groups around the country and cultural subversion persisted in unexpected places. I was aware that Juliet Stevenson, along with Fiona Shaw and Harriet Walter, was wrestling with how to relate her feminism to her work in the theatre.[476] When Abigail Thaw interviewed Juliet in *Interlink,* she described the paradox feminists like herself confronted in acting complex characterizations of their parts, while contesting how women were perceived and portrayed.[477]

Despite the sombre mood, we packed a great deal into that issue. Copy ranged from the Independent Broadcasting Authority's ban on The Pogues' 'Streets of Sorrow' for the song's defence of the Guildford Four, framed for a pub bombing they did not do, to celebrating Isaac Julien's film about black homosexuality, *Looking for Langston.* His film penetrated 'the wall of memory', through the sensual grace of images and the rhythmic power of words evoking cultural banishment, 'We are the hunger of shadows in the dark'. Fear stalks desire, 'This kiss could turn to stone'.[478]

Looking for Langston reached beyond left film circuits because it was shown on Channel 4. From 1982 the new channel offered a platform for other radical productions, including the Black Audio Collective's film *Handsworth Songs* (1986) and the mini-series *A Very British Coup* (1988) based on a novel by the Labour politician Chris Mullin about the election of a socialist prime minister.[479] This openness to subversion did not go unnoticed and in his article "Hall of Mirrors', Marc Karlin carefully disentangled the opposing camps.[480]

I found my brief editorial 'realm of responsibility & small power, scary but stimulating'.[481] I was particularly pleased we could reprint the appeal for the seafarers who had been on strike for a year and include an article by Roger Kline about the dangers they faced from cuts and a brutal new shift system the employers were proposing. Linking their predicament with similar threats to safety facing the Fire Brigade and transport workers, he concluded: 'debates about "post-Fordist strategies"' needed 'to be linked to leg-work in support of those groups who were saying enough is enough.'[482]

Inspired by Roger and the seafarers, early in February I legged it to Dover to join other supporters, including a small but dogged contingent of workers from the Government Communications Headquarters (GCHQ), the state intelligence, cyber and security agency. The Conservative government had banned them from unionizing and a minority who resisted were sacked. They responded by persistently showing solidarity with other workers in disputes, including the seafarers.

My arrival caused some embarrassment because messages had been scrambled and there was nowhere for me to stay. Finally, a troubled trade unionist took me to the sole room available at the local Seamen's Mission, where the only other woman in sight was the one in charge of the bar. She cautioned me sternly to make sure I kept my door locked through the night. When I pointed out I was in my mid-forties, she shook her head and declared, 'You don't know seamen' with a confidence that brooked no argument.

* * *

A 'Women for Socialism Conference' on 25 and 26 February attracted left Labour Party women and women in revolutionary groups. It was encouraging to see a mix of young black women as well as white. There was support for Sinn Fein and Palestine, but I felt the stances taken were rather self-consciously 'right on' and somewhat rhetorical. Unlike socialist feminist meetings, the atmosphere did not feel exploratory; it was as if 'socialism' was somehow cut and dried.[483]

Ken Livingstone was at the crux of innumerable Labour Party storms and was about to produce *Livingstone's Labour: A Programme for the Nineties* (1989), which contested not only Labour's economic record and foreign policies, but a failure to negotiate a ceasefire with the PIRA in Ireland. He had also included chapters on women, black people, gays and lesbians and asked me to look at the former. Of course, I concurred with his excellent proposals for full legal equality, childcare, equal pay for work of equal value, state remuneration for carers and funding for women's centres. But I was aghast that Ken bizarrely linked all these to a supposed universal male takeover from goddess-worshipping matriarchies many thousands of years ago and chucked in for good measure the persecution of witches in the sixteenth and seventeenth centuries. My arguments about historical accuracy made little impression, so I hauled in Hermione Harris, whose historical knowledge and research as an anthropologist enabled her to critique both nineteenth-century theories of a supposed universal stage of 'matriarchy', as well as a reductionist interpretation of differing manifestations of witch persecution solely to misogyny. Debating with Ken was great fun, but he was impatient about historical nuances, so the qualifying hints we secured from these battles were derisory. He thanked us both politely, tongue in cheek, for 'detailed and lengthy lists of criticisms and corrections' and for devoting hours of our time 'debating them with me'.[484]

On 4 March I set off for a conference in Sheffield on the casualization of work, organized by the Low Pay Campaign. On the train I happened to meet Tony Benn, who bought me a cup of tea. Though we had met through the GLC and the Chesterfield Socialist Conferences, I was rather shy of him and acutely aware of the stares of other passengers. He soon put me at my ease and somehow I found myself chatting with him about the late nineteenth-century radical workers from Todmorden, Hebden Bridge and Huddersfield, who I had written about during the 1960s in my unfinished PhD on adult education. They had made me aware of the influence of the American campaigner for land nationalization, Henry George. To my amazement Tony wanted to read my thesis. Unfortunately, in lean times, unable to afford photocopying, I had cut it up to turn it into historical articles. With incredible diligence, he would later wade through the tattered pages that had survived, telling me off for destroying the others.

The Low Pay Campaign's Sheffield conference included women from trade unions, community groups, Labour local authorities and researchers fostering international labour links. Among them was Jane Tate, a socialist feminist outreach worker in the Yorkshire and Humberside Low Pay Unit. Jane's work had brought her into contact with large numbers of homeworkers, sewing, soldering, packing and typing for low sums. Since 1988 Jane had been encouraging them to organize through the West Yorkshire Homeworking Group. Two homeworkers from Mixenden spoke on their conditions of work.[485]

One of the homeworkers had three little girls and a baby, aged one, called James. There was no creche at the event and so that afternoon I offered to take them all out so their mother could participate. Spotting a big new shopping centre, I steered them all towards it, proffering ice cream. But while I was preoccupied with paying, James broke free from his sisters and toddled off, attracted by a shallow pool with a small fountain. To my horror I turned round to see that he was crawling into the water. The girls, the ice creams and I rushed to the rescue. When I clasped him in my arms he was perfectly happy but very wet. The women staff mobilized and presented him with a T-shirt with the store's logo. At least he was alive and dry!

However, young James looked like a 1980s Wee Willie Winkie 'in his nicht-gown'. Out of the corner of my eye I spotted a Benetton children's shop. In we all trooped and came out with an excessively elegant one year old, in an excessively expensive baby grower, most likely made by a low-paid Italian homeworker.[486] Back at the conference I stuttered out my confession, while the children described our adventures with glee. To my profound relief, their mother met us with laughter.

Shortly afterwards, when I was invited to an international meeting in Holland where homeworker organizing had taken off, I recommended that Jane and the Yorkshire homeworkers should go instead. The Yorkshire homeworkers' group expanded and quickly began to contribute to the cross-country links in which SEWA played a vital part.[487] I remained in close touch with Jane and other resourceful members in Leeds, Kuldeep Bajwa, Amrit Choda, Linda Devereux and Dian Leppington.

Several socialist feminist networks were focusing on gender and economic development world-wide, including the recently formed Womankind, which had the social anthropologist Kate Young, from the Institute of Development Studies (IDS) at Sussex University, as its first executive director. Womankind had received a generous donation from the philanthropic businessman Sir Alec Reed from the Reed Employment Agency. It was launched at a bizarre, slightly edgy gathering of socialist feminists and perturbed businessmen in dark suits, accompanied by a kernel of brisk and confident businesswomen in smart, brightly coloured ones. Uncertainly, I stood next to a casually elegant Hermione Harris, looking serene, with a group of nervous Reed Employment Agency men clustering around her, marvelling at her ability to put people at their ease.

A few months later, I went to hear Ela Bhatt speak about SEWA at a meeting of Womankind and listened in awe to this small woman in a sari who used words with such acute precision, speaking with concentrated, communicative force.[488] Her greying hair was swept backwards and she carried herself with dignified resolution. When I joined the people waiting to speak with her afterwards, I noted how intently she focused on each one of us and understood how she had become such a powerful and influential organizer. When my turn came, I told her about the meeting with homeworkers in Sheffield; she nodded approvingly.

* * *

The Past is Before Us came out in April. The book had been painful to write, for the present seemed to be gobbling the past. So much was being obscured, even as I turned out the paragraphs. Still, I was glad to have retrieved individual women's voices from all over Britain, tracing how discontents about personal life had opened out into new political and social vistas. I had documented thinking rooted in activity and shown the connections to numerous grassroots struggles at work and in communities which had been so important in women's liberation.

I felt vindicated by a letter from Swasti observing how *The Past is Before Us* combined 'visions (utopia) with strategies'. She saw the significance of the numerous ephemeral sources I had drawn together. 'Your book is about cinema – I mean movement in Greek, but it also has the feel of a cinema.' The chapter on 'The Mother Knot' had particularly affected Swasti and she explained, 'In my case it was motherhood that became the source of a profoundly radical social inspiration'.[489]

While I had wanted to convey the inventive excitement and creative release of women's liberation as a movement, I did not aim just to be celebratory, but to show how innovative perceptions that arise through activity can also leave much unresolved. Liz Heron, the instigator of the collection *Truth Dare or Promise,* caught this in a nutshell in her review for the *Scotsman,* describing *The Past is Before Us* as 'a quizzing of feminism's double binds'.[490]

I was relieved that finally the book was done, but unsure what would be made of it. When I spoke at its launch with Hilary, Lynne and the economist Naila Kabeer at the Institute of Contemporary Arts (ICA), so many friends turned up I was overwhelmed. It was reassuring to have like-minded feminists and socialists gathering once again. However, *The Past Is Before Us* had been long in gestation and it was impossible to deny that a decade of Tory political dominance in Britain had affected cultural assumptions. So much of what we had thought and done in the women's liberation movement of the 1970s was fast being marginalized.

As radical movements, including feminism, had grown weaker, connections which had seemed self-evident had slackened. I grew apprehensive as the decade ended, when the creative paths we had trodden turned slippery and the new worlds we had envisioned slid ever further out of reach.

These shifts manifested themselves through a series of disconnects. I was dismayed to be interviewed by young women in the media who had only come across a feminism concerned simply with equal opportunities for an elite minority. In a local radio interview, when I said that this approach disregarded issues such as homeworkers' pay and conditions, I was met with the response, 'How boring'. I replied they might be boring to her, but not to homeworkers!

To my bewilderment I also found myself in meetings on the book being consulted like a kind of feminist wise woman (or perhaps agony aunt) about sexual behaviour or whether to have a baby or not. Moral guidance is not my forte and I was perplexed because instead of extending outwards, the discussions turned inwards and became purely individual.

Through that summer I travelled far and wide speaking on *The Past is Before Us* in Southampton, Maidstone, Wakefield, Shepley, Denby Dale, Nottingham and Newport as well as London. I sought to assert the positive innovatory politics of the women's liberation movement while also pointing to the questions left hanging by an emphasis upon a single identity and over simple correlations between personal experiences and politics. I was aware the people who came to these meetings wanted something that was more clear-cut. Instead, I became a kind of active listener, trying to understand the mix of uncertainty and openness I encountered. Fortunately, a new crop of socialist feminists was appearing. On one occasion when Lynne and I spoke in Birmingham a young woman approached us and said how glad she was that we were there. Her words made all the toil and tramping on trains worthwhile. My hope was that they would come up with answers.

* * *

Giving a talk on Mary Wollstonecraft at the Institute of Contemporary Arts reanimated me; Sue Crockford caught me in a brief clip for her television film starring Miranda Richardson as Wollstonecraft, *The Rights of Man and the Wrongs of Women* (1989).[491] Watching Sue at work felt like a return, because she had been one of the film-makers who recorded the first Women's Liberation Conference at Oxford in 1970 and our first International Women's Day March in 1971.[492]

Marc Karlin's film *Utopias* was shown on Channel 4 on

1 May. Despite having taken him several years to complete, I thought it remained prescient, probing 'the confusion and bewilderment' that had been gathering on the left over the last few years. I was caught within the same oxymoron as Marc – how to acknowledge the disconnections arising from incipience, while retaining clarity. 'Some people were critical at the lack of coherence. But to be honest, how could coherence be found now for socialists?' I described us as 'disorientated, falling back on the past, losing any sense of the past, denying the past, caricaturing it, berating it'. I ascribed the troubled intensity of these emotions to 'our unhappy present'.[493]

A pressing dilemma was proving divisive. I had heard the writer Salman Rushdie speak at a Socialist Society meeting, just before he was forced into hiding because his life was being threatened after the publication of his novel *The Satanic Verses*. Some people on the left opposed Rushdie on the grounds that his opponents were from working-class Muslim communities, but in May Southall Black Sisters, along with other feminists, took a stand against the denial of human rights which could be found within every absolutist interpretation of religion, forming a courageous new group, Women Against Fundamentalism.[494]

On 4 June my disorientation was accentuated by the killing of demonstrators claiming greater democracy in Tiananmen Square by the Chinese police and soldiers. Despite admiring many things that had been done by the Communists in China, I identified with the protesters and was still troubled and grieving for them when I went to hear Li Shizheng, known as Duo Duo, read his poetry. He was a dignified and delicate reader, but I could not understand the imagery in his writing. He had been influenced by a loose network labelled the 'Misty poets' who adopted intricate metaphors from European writers and were regarded with suspicion by the authorities. This was surely unreasonable, given that Mao had been so influenced by the Romantics, who were surely ancestors of the Misties. The tragedy of Tiananmen Square seared Duo Duo so painfully that for many years he did not return to China.

In contrast, the Soviet leader Mikhail Gorbachev did not attempt to suppress rebellions in Hungary and Poland with armed force and over the course of the year I watched as one country after another broke away from the Soviet orbit. Power based on fear appeared to crumble. Initially it seemed as if this assertion of democracy was unequivocally positive, but gradually flickers of doubt began to surface as it became evident that anti-feminism, nationalism and an uncritical enthusiasm about capitalism were also strands in dissidence. It began to look like a choice between the devil and the deep blue sea.

The third Socialist Conference was at Sheffield University's Octogen Centre on the weekend of the 17 to 18 June. I missed the conviviality of Chesterfield as a place but gravitated with enthusiasm to a workshop led by the socialist feminist economist Diane Elson. A large crowd of us sat outside on the grass to listen as Diane stressed the material significance of women's activity in the household. Demonstrating that rethinking the market had been a weakness in socialist economics, she focused on the need to encourage *social* forms of consumption, rather than simply falling back on the existing terms set by capitalism.[495]

Her arguments for encouraging the socialization of the market resonated with me partly because I was becoming increasingly aware how important controlling prices and reorganizing consumption had been for working-class women historically.[496] More recently too I had seen how successful Twin Trading had been in defending small producers' interests in the global market.

The workshop became stormy because Diane was challenged by a small but vociferous contingent of revolutionary men who bone-headedly considered attempting to change distribution was somehow inherently 'reformist'. Discussion was impossible until the economist Trevor Evans, who was in the audience, spoke up. I had last seen Trevor in the mid-1970s when he had been a student squatter in Brixton with Will's father, Paul. He had worked for several years in Nicaragua and had observed the problems they had encountered there in relation to the market.

Both he and Diane were able to put economic issues in a global context.

I did a bit of small-scale local socializing of the market with Paul by selling some of our books at bargain basement prices on a stall for Stoke Newington Comprehensive's school fair. Paul, now a psychoanalyst, had cleared out his social science books and these were seized enthusiastically by young Afro-Caribbean mothers who were studying for degrees. Conversation was difficult on our five-hour stint as we happened to be next to the loudest sound system I had ever heard. A variant of hip-hop had hit Hackney and those speakers belted out speedy repetitive beats non-stop. One of the mothers said, 'It's Jungle'.

Will went on holiday with Paul that year and early in August I accompanied Lynne, Peter Osborne and his brother-in-law, Mehmet Ali Dikerdem, a specialist on the Middle East, to Italy for two weeks. Will's name was still on my passport; 'Where's the bambino?' enquired the Italian passport official at the airport, puzzled by an unaccompanied mother. At the seaside town of Follonica, we swam, had long inconclusive talks about politics and ate spaghetti, sitting at the long wooden tables of the local Communist festivals. I read Joan Sangster's reflective history of women in the Canadian left, *Dreams of Equality*, the science fantasy novel *The Chronicles of Morgaine* and a biography of Dorothy Parker.[497] The extreme lives of early twentieth century bohemians reassured me that my own was not as chaotic as theirs. They just seemed to have been rather better-heeled.

Back in London I struggled without success to write a science fantasy novel and worked on a clutter of doomed film scripts and proposals.

* * *

I still worried that in the absence of any definable women's movement, we lacked a collective context where ideas could be distilled. Yet, as 1989 drew to its close, a feminist-influenced critique of social and economic policies continued to gather momentum and expanded in diffuse ways we had not initially envisaged. Moreover, feminist ideas were entering influential institutional crannies as more women moved into jobs in the public sector, trade unions, local government, the arts, as well as professions like medicine, law and the universities. So, in a sense we were still doing what Audrey Wise had described as generalizing feminism and feminizing a male dominated culture.

Along with other feminists in adult and higher education I had contributed to the growth of 'women's studies'. My feelings about the consolidation of a separate strand of knowledge were mixed. Women's studies represented an undoubted gain, yet I perceived it as at once a source of preservation and of potential constraint. While I appreciated that the resources of the universities enriched study, making valuable in-depth approaches possible, I feared that because academia tended to be self-regarding, there were also strong pressures to isolate political thought from action. I was conscious too that an exclusive focus on women's predicament might blinker us to the subordination of others and thus fence us in. Two journals, *Feminist Review* and *History Workshop Journal*, became important reference points for me, because in different ways they countered these polarities.

The concept of a sex/gender system had arisen in the mid-1970s in an effort to acknowledge both biology and culture, and had proved fruitful as a means of extending a feminist perspective *beyond* simply highlighting 'women'. 'Gender' made it possible to examine masculinity, as well as the social relations of power within which women were subordinated, while demonstrating how social categories such as class or 'race' were also 'gendered'.

But like all abstract perspectives, it could also generate its own kind of confinement. I was becoming uneasy that an *exclusive* focus on gender could inadvertently occlude women's participation in movements against class-based injustice, slavery, colonialism or racism. Thanks to Ros and other friends such as Elaine Scott, Barbara Winslow and Linda Gordon, I had begun to collect books and articles on the history of African American women, but realized how little I knew about histories of women of African, Afro-Caribbean and Asian descent in Britain. The few books I could find were mainly about men.[498]

Students on my MA course at Kent were trying to find out about the British Empire's treatment of women slaves, and Delia Jarrett-Macauley was soon to start a pioneering black women's studies course in the MA at Kent which resulted in the book she edited, *Reconstructing Womanhood, Reconstructing Feminism: Writings on Black Women*.[499] A post-graduate historian at London University, Paula Spenser, who was studying how British imperial law had impinged on prostitution in India, alerted me to the complexities of gender in the history of colonialism.

Looking at gender in relation to other forms of social subordination and *connecting* personal experience, thought and action opened a means of exploring not simply the history of feminism, but more diverse women's movements for political, social and economic emancipation. My links to women in the miners' strike combined with my friendship with Radha Kumar, Kumari Jayawardena and Swasti Mitter had alerted me to these in Britain and elsewhere. When a telephone call came from the American political philosopher Roger Gottlieb asking for a book on women's global social movements, I said 'Yes' and *Women in Movement: Feminism and Social Action* was to result.[500]

* * *

I spoke on the history of feminism and *The Past Is Before Us* in Athens on the weekend of 23 and 24 September.[501] Curiously, our meeting was regarded as national news and TV cameras arrived to film it. I was personally happy to meet up with socialist feminist friends there again, but the atmosphere in Greece was less upbeat than on my previous visit, for the centre-left leader, Andreas Papandreou, was embroiled in scandals and the right was on the rise. The most intense memory I brought back with me was an outdoor exhibition of photographs of Iraqi Kurds documenting how Saddam Hussein's regime had killed thousands upon thousands of people. Seeing the terrible images put any problems of mine into perspective.

So did the dogged tenacity of older left-wingers. On 8 October

I went to the memorial for one of the early Trotskyists, Harry Wicks, at London's Conway Hall. Born in 1905, he had become a railway worker and joined the Communist Party. He had met Trotsky, worked with CLR James, been in the left of the Labour Party and had subsequently linked up with the Socialist Workers' Party.[502]

I sat remembering a meeting chaired by Michael Ward in the early 1980s where Harry had given an illuminating talk on the socialist movement in Battersea during the 1920s. The borough had elected the left-wing Indian anti-colonialist Shapurji Saklatvala, first as their Labour and then as their Communist MP and Harry had told us how Saklatvala used to report back to a public meeting in the borough each week on the doings of Parliament. When I asked him about labour movement support for Battersea's early birth control clinic, he had explained how a driving force had been a member of the Women's Cooperative Guild who had worked as a servant for the actress Ellen Terry. Having learned about contraception among the bohemians, she had brought the knowledge back to women in Battersea.[503]

Later in October I spent a few days at WIDER and was able to talk in depth with Kumari Jayawardena about our project on women's organizing around work. On my return I became locked in a furious argument on the plane with a businessman about the impact of Tory policies upon working-class people in Hackney and Liverpool. He had repeated 'Hackney and Liverpool' as if the denizens of both were too despicable to be even considered.

I was disagreeing with people on the left as well and my long-held inclination towards broad alliances was creaking badly. Not only was I at odds with Communists around *Marxism Today*, at a conference organized by the Labour group around *Tribune*, when I spoke about the equivocal role of the state, the Labour MP Harriet Harman had caricatured this as some bizarre theory I had invented. There was little time to reflect on why I was now in conflict with people with whom I had previously co-existed because, yet again, I was over-committed that autumn, hoisted on my own variegated enthusiasms. On 9 November I lectured in Milton Keynes for the Open University on French Revolutionary Women. On the weekend of the 10th Will and I stayed with John and Joan Bohanna in Liverpool where I spoke on Alice Wheeldon.[504]

Then, on Monday 13 November, I went to Brighton.[505] Naila Kabeer had invited me to speak at the Institute of Development Studies (IDS) to her course of women government workers, organizers and activists from developing countries. In the morning I talked about 'Women and the State' and in the afternoon we discussed whether there could be said to be specifically 'Women's Values'. The class consisted of an interesting group of women, several of whom were from various countries in Africa.

I stayed on to watch the American documentary *Rosie the Riveter* about women workers in World War Two. Those American 'Rosies' communicated powerfully to the class. The African women were especially affected by the fate of the women workers who had lost their jobs after the war. When one remarked sympathetically, 'They didn't even have land to return to,' I was jolted by her recognition of land as a fall back. My father had been raised on a small farm, but the links had long gone and for me, as a British city dweller, land had never registered as a resource. Members of the class also observed ruefully on how lack of footage would make anything similar impossible to make in their own countries. I had not grasped before how the preservation of memory on film depended so crucially on where you came from.

It was evening when I caught the train back from Victoria. Three burly men in belted fawn raincoats were swaggering up and down the aisle. They were drunk and offensive, peering down into my face as I read. Crouched in the corner across the aisle was a young black man who looked like a student. When we reached the station, they began taunting and harassing him on the platform. He was terrified of them and ran towards the underground. They started to pursue him, shouting racist insults.

I made a quick decision to try to delay them. Because we were on a busy station concourse and because I was white, I figured I was less vulnerable than he was. So, I stood in the way of these three men saying quietly that I thought their remarks were 'nothing to be proud of'. I expected a torrent of abuse which would gain him a few minutes to get on a tube. Instead, the burly, bearded man facing me did not hesitate. In one split second, a large fist covered with signet rings was in front of my face. And that split second, I knew I had got it wrong. These men were not just drunk, they were trained to fight.

On films people duck. Instead, I stood like a transfixed rabbit as the blow struck my jaw, leaving me stunned and bloody. They were gone, running in the direction of the tube entrance. I turned round to face a young white man of about eighteen, who had seen what had happened. Taking my arm, he helped me find the station master, a tall, proud black man who initially regarded me as if I was white-woman bother with an air of stern authority. Between us we managed to explain what had happened, whereupon he told the young man to take me to the transport police. They were tucked away in an office, monitoring the station on screens.

The policeman took out a very large form and filled it up laboriously. While he was doing this, a report came in of another 'incident' in the underground station. I feared for the young black man in the underground and I felt I had failed him. Ashamed and helpless I got on the 38 bus from Victoria to Hackney, covering my messy face with a scarf. I learned from the dentist that the stump of my crowned tooth had gone and so had its root. Will's sensible response was to tell me not to get into conflicts without 'back up'. Henceforth I followed his advice.

'This has been a grim autumn,' I wrote, in my journal that November.[506] However, my mother had always insisted that 'every cloud has a silver lining' and, indeed, some good things did happen. Coming back from giving a talk at Essex University on 20 November, I happened to meet an elderly Jewish socialist taxi driver who was fiercely anti-racist and a supporter of Tony Benn. He talked to me for a long time and put me back together again. More emotional 'back up' came from Naila, Delia and Kumari who communicated empathy and power over the telephone.[507]

Also, I believed I had prospects. For several months I had been happily meeting with the left-wing film-maker Sally Hibbin, who had produced the acclaimed TV series 'A Very British Coup'. We were researching a series of labour history videos for the TUC.[508] Moreover, my conversations with Kumari had been encouraging and WIDER had at last responded positively to our project about women's organizing at work. On the 27 November, I recorded in jubilation, 'Helsinki is happening'.[509]

I was due to speak on 'Women and the State' at the *Rethinking Marxism* Conference at Amherst in Massachusetts on 1 December. I caught flu and set off with a temperature. Fortunately, the plane was nearly empty, and I was able to lie down through the flight. Ros drove us both from New York to Amherst in freezing weather and I managed to deliver my talk. I was feverish and my memories of the conference are hazy, apart from being reunited with the genial Canadian Marxist thinker Leo Panitch, who had studied with Ralph Miliband at LSE and was now co-editing the journal *Socialist Register*. Kindly, the anthropologist Frédérique Apffel-Marglin and the economist Steve Marglin took me to their home for the weekend, put me to bed and gave me lemon and honey, enabling me to deliver a lecture at Hartford University in Connecticut and then go on to a meeting about *Women in Movement* with Roger Gottlieb at Massachusetts' Worcester Polytechic Institute.

Back with Ros in New York, I braced myself for a crop of talks. These began on the 6 December at New York University. Later that day I went on to do another at Barnard College, where I was welcomed enthusiastically by the historian Temma Kaplan, whose writings on both anarchism and feminism I admired. The following morning, I went to Baruch, invited by

Bell Gale Chevigny.[510] I had read *The Woman and the Myth*, her study of the life and writings of Margaret Fuller, the nineteenth-century transcendentalist, and longed to discuss the woman Bell had depicted as having 'to create a life not yet possible and a self whose nature was without local example'.[511] But Bell perceived I was groggy and hoarse and settled me on a bench to rest before the class. I was discovered there by an administrator who assumed the supine mound was a ne'er do well student recovering from a feckless night. She admonished me for lying down and sternly told me to sit up in a chair. Voiceless, I feebly obeyed.

I had a final day of lectures on Friday 8 December, speaking between 11 and 12 at Hunter College and then between 6 and 9 at the City University graduate school, where a large crowd had gathered in the lecture hall.[512] By the time people came up to comment, my voice had dwindled to a whisper. The last person in the queue was a young, shy Chinese American woman. To my great relief she dropped her initial manner of formal respect and sweetly responded to me as a person who was just ill and weary.

The next day was a Saturday, so I could relax with Harry and Elaine Scott and Liz and Stuart Ewen, for once meeting them in winter clothes rather than on the beach. Harry was in an ebullient mood because he was about to start working for New York's first African American Mayor, David Dinkins. On the Sunday, my socialist feminist friend, the historian Barbara Winslow, nobly drove through snow and ice out to Rutgers where Dorothy and Edward Thompson had been teaching.[513] Edward, exhausted by his work for European Nuclear Disarmament, had collapsed with pneumonia and was seriously ill in hospital.

Dorothy was isolated and relieved to see us. She had been walking through the snow to visit Edward each day and bearing the anxiety alone. Dorothy could be warm and encouraging but was rarely effusive. However, when we arrived she took me aside and embraced me, saying how grateful she was that Barbara had been able to get me there. Edward was slowly getting better, but

I was shocked by how frail he looked on his hospital bed. He nevertheless managed to muster the strength to grumble about the hospital mores and the American capitalist system to boot.

I returned home to a hectic Christmas in Hackney crowded with visits from friends. And, in my 1989 diary, just above the 'January 1990' section, I wrote myself a memo, 'Remember not to accept talks in Jan & Feb'.[514]

Afterword

Of course I did not keep my resolution. How could I? New causes erupted. Ravers rebelled for the 'Right to Party'; ecological opposition was mounted against new roads and a mass rebellion contested Margaret Thatcher's efforts to introduce the inequitable poll taxes. She resigned in November 1990, after losing the support of prominent Conservative ministers. Her successor, John Major, propagated Conservatism in more dulcet tones, but there was to be no return to a post-war capitalism alleviated by social reforms. Over the next two years many towns and cities were to see violent rebellions in which people on the largely white council estates became involved.

I demonstrated against the first Gulf War in 1991 and the following year I joined an estimated 150,000 marching through London in pounding rain in support of the miners once again. Never has a flapjack tasted so good as it did that day. I munched it gratefully, walking in the wake of a large contingent of Anglican priests in black, the water glistening as it dripped down their silver regalia.

Indefatigably, Hilary launched a new left magazine, *Red Pepper,* in 1993, which linked the new generation defending fun and trees with the older socialist left. Instead of the customary trudge of 1960s veterans like us, these younger rebels walked lightly and moved swiftly, sometimes accompanied by dogs with ecological strings tied to their collars, rather than leather leads. The atmosphere of protest had, in some indefinable way, altered. The early 1990s felt transitional – between times – for, of course, we could not see what was to come.

Those years were personally frightening for me because I developed repetitive strain injury and was unable to write.

Desperate, I managed to dictate a short book, *Homeworkers' Worldwide*.[515] In 1994, *Dignity and Daily Bread,* the collection of essays that Swasti and I had edited on women's organizing from the meeting at WIDER, was published and I became involved in efforts to foster international grassroots links between women workers.[516]

Encouraged by my agent Faith Evans and Margaret Bluman at Penguin, I clumsily began using an early model of Dragon Dictate on the early chapters of *A Century of Women.* Revising them as soon as I could write again, I traced how the splintering shards of women's aspirations for freedom and fulfilment had been propelled into politics, work, daily life, personal relations and culture in Britain and the United States. In the updated paperback edition (1999), I described my search as an historian as 'an effort to reveal suppressed possibilities – those understandings that time rushes past which can be a means of releasing aspiration'.[517]

My circumstances changed dramatically in 1995 because I began working in the Sociology Department at the University of Manchester. Through a group of left academics, including Huw Beynon and Diane Elson, social sciences at Manchester had developed a strong emphasis on labour and gender studies. I was able to contribute work I had done on homeworking and poor women's livelihood struggles.[518] This was a major move in my life and personally a happy one.

I was becoming aware that new radical movements were emerging globally. Someone sent me a video of the gigantic 1999 demonstration in Seattle where environmentalists, trades unionists, indigenous groups, NGOs and students converged in protest against the capitalist bias of international institutions like the World Trade Organization. As I watched it, I felt that I was seeing the kernel of *Beyond the Fragments* manifest and multiplied.[519] But how to extend this extraordinary spirit of resistance into a new reality? This was just one of many questions without an answer.

As the years rolled by, I continued to ponder the political

questions that still puzzled me. How to acknowledge and assert differing circumstances of oppression without taking cover behind restrictive barriers? How to enable people to combine in powerful, yet non-hierarchal, groupings? How to bring personal feelings of oppression into politics without landing in a rigid, external moralism? How best to combine participatory and representative democracy? How to safeguard existing state welfare, while countering the repressive power of the state in capitalism? How to ground utopias in known desires? How to nurture present aspirations and foster more beyond? How to make a new world possible and create a new kind of politics. And, in the process, how to celebrate the tree of life, while not rejecting vital openings created by thoughts in the past?

These thoughts had been stimulated by organizing with others as a socialist feminist, but without any concerted movement the understandings we had shared came to seem by the way – a bundle of preoccupations from another era. This was partly because of external circumstances, but also because going backwards can be psychologically painful. A knowledge of time-subsequent can crash into memories of time-past, sharpening a sense of sadness when so much of what was striven for has been lost without any signs of reclamation or reconstitution. Marc Karlin was right about how unprotected memories can get cast away, making remembering appear an endangered folly. Though I did not dump them, my aspirations for collective answers, along with the riddles they had provoked, were bottled, preserved and thus contained.

During the 2000s I returned to the later years of the nineteenth and early twentieth century, picking up on the history of socialism and sexual emancipation in a biography of Edward Carpenter, whose expansive life had long intrigued me. It was published in 2008 and, I am chuffed to say, was awarded the Lambda Literary Award for Gay Memoir/ Biography in the US and shortlisted for the James Tait Black Memorial Prize in the UK.[520]

It led me to explore lesser-known rebels who were part of

Carpenter's unconventional circle in *Rebel Crossings: New Women, Free Lovers, and Radicals in Britain and the United States* (2016). This took me to members of the Bristol Socialist Society, who, during the 1880s, had been deeply influenced by Edward Carpenter and had participated in the upsurge of 'new unionism' which reached out beyond the craft unions.

By the time *Rebel Crossings* was published the political combination of socialism and feminism had become muffled. A culture defined by the right had sought to silence all manifestations of egalitarian radicalism, either overtly by force, or covertly with contemptuous ridicule. So, ours is a history that has become silted over, not simply by the passage of time but because the forces of those who opposed us triumphed.

I felt driven by a sense of urgency to document aspects of my own life and thus to touch on the lives of some of the people I have known, respected and loved, in an effort to subvert the debilitating forgetfulness which prevails. In *Daring to Hope* (2021) I focused on the 1970s, when I was involved with the new movement for women's liberation and became a mother. The 1980s however were a period when radical social movements in Britain were forced onto the defensive by an assertive right. Nevertheless, my personal account in *Reasons to Rebel* reveals how feminists and socialists still continued to devise new ways of resisting and describes protesters cohering, despite the odds being against us. I have sought to reckon with defeats honestly, while remembering Raymond Williams' counsel on 'making hope practical, rather than despair convincing'.[521]

My aim in writing about my own life experience is to nudge further enquiry and encourage the testimonies of others who seek to move from our unequal society in thrall to capital, to one based on meeting people's needs mutually. My yearning is to bring a smile of recognition across the generations, revive submerged visions and strengthen the resolve of those in left movements from below to keep on keeping on.

NOTES

INTRODUCTION

1   See Sheila Rowbotham, *Promise of a Dream: Remembering the Sixties*,
     Verso, London, 2019. (First published by Allen Lane and Penguin,
     2000).
2   Sheila Rowbotham, *Daring to Hope: My Life in the 1970s*, Verso,
     London, 2021.
3   Unofficial Reform Committee, *The Miners' Next Step: Being a Suggested
     Outlining Scheme for the Reorganisation of the Federation*, (pamphlet),
     Tonypandy, 1912. Reprinted, Pluto, London 1972, p. 14.
4   Sheila Rowbotham, Lynne Segal and Hilary Wainwright, *Beyond The
     Fragments: Feminism and the Making of Socialism*, 1st edition, booklet
     published by Newcastle Socialist Centre and Islington Community
     Press, London, 1979, (2nd extended edition, 1979, 1980, 1981. 3rd
     edition, Merlin Press, London, 2013.)
5   Margaret Thatcher, *The Downing Street Years*, HarperCollins, London,
     1993, p. 38.
6   See Dina Copelman, Interview with Sheila Rowbotham in eds. Henry
     Abelove, Betsy Blackmar, Peter Dimock, and Jonathan Schneer,
     MARHO, The Radical Historians Organization, *Visions of History*,
     Pantheon Books, New York, 1984 and Rowbotham, *Daring to Hope*,
     p. 285. See also Sheila Rowbotham, Papers in the Women's Library,
     London School of Economics, 'Beyond the Fragments', 7SHR/C/2, Box
     7 Folder1of 2, LSE.). A further collection has been deposited by Julian
     Harber in Calderdale Archives, West Yorkshire Archive Services in
     Halifax. These are closed until 2030.
7   Joint Letter on Beyond the Fragments, 3 December,1979, Martin Stott,
     Private Collection.
8   On Jean McCrindle see Rowbotham, *Promise of a Dream* and *Daring
     to Hope;* on Kenny Bell see Hilary Wainwright, 'Kenny Bell. From Loss
     to Living Legacy, *Red Pepper*, 28 August 2011 and Hilary Wainwright,
     Obituary Kenny Bell, *Guardian*, 4 October 2011.

Chapter 1. 1980 January to July

9   See Sally Groves, Vernon Merritt, *Trico: A Victory To Remember*,
     Lawrence & Wishart, London, 2018, pp. 51, 73, 76, 98, 169; Sundari
     Anitha, Ruth Pearson, *Striking Women: Struggles & Strategies of South
     Asian Women Workers from Grunwick to Gate Gourmet*, Lawrence &
     Wishart, London, 2018, p. 124.
10   Sheila Rowbotham, Diary (SRD), 29 January 1980, Sheila Rowbotham,
     Talk on Beyond the Fragments, Brent, Notebook 7ANG 2000/12 Box1
     of 2, 317, 7ANG/B/01/-02. LSE.On the US see Sara Evans, *Personal
     Politics: The Roots of Women's Liberation in the Civil Rights Movement
     and the New Left*, Knopf, New York, 1979; Wini Breines, *Community*

and Organization in the New Left:1962-1968:The Great Refusal, Praeger, New York, 1982.

11 Sue Finch and Market Nursery supporters, *Not So Much a Nursery,* (pamphlet) London, c. 1977. SR. I am grateful to Sue Finch for sending me a copy of this.

12 Andrew Puddephatt, Appeal Market Nursery 1980. 7SHR/D/3. Box 8, Folder 2 of 2. LSE.

13 SRD , 9 Feb, 1980; Sheila Rowbotham to Martin Stott, 2 March, 1980. (Papers of Martin Stott).

14 I describe meeting the Thompsons in Rowbotham, *Promise of a Dream,* pp. 55-65, 74-76.

15 SRD, 9 March, 1980; on the demonstration see https://steelvoices.file. wordpress.com/2015/01/0016-2.jpg

16 SRD, 12, 14, 15 March, 1980.

17 See Rowbotham, *Promise of a Dream,* pp. 212-13.

18 Audrey Wise, in ed. Peter Hain, *The Debate of the Decade: The Crisis and the Future of the Left,* Pluto Press, London, 1980 p. 77.

19 Wise in ed. Hain, *The Debate of the Decade,* p. 75.

20 Sheila Rowbotham, in ed. Hain, *The Debate of the Decade,* pp. 65-7.

21 Lynne Segal, in ed. Hain, *The Debate of the Decade,* pp. 65-7.

22 SRD, 21 March, 1980.

23 Rowbotham, *Daring to Hope,* pp. 282-3.

24 E.P. Thompson, *Protest and Survive,* (pamphlet) Campaign for Nuclear Disarmament and Bertrand Russell Peace Foundation, Spokesman, Nottingham, 1980, pp. 32-33.

25 See Richard Taylor, 'Thompson and the Peace Movement: from CND in the 1950s and 60s to END in the 1980s', in Roger Fieldhouse and Richard Taylor, *E.P. Thompson and English Radicalism,* Manchester University Press, Manchester, 2013, pp. 181-201.

26 Letters from John and Joan Bohanna are in my papers at the Women's Library, LSE.

27 Ray Challinor, *The Origins of British Bolshevism,* Croom Helm, London, 1977, pp. 144-9.

28 Chloe Mason's efforts brought the case to the Criminal Cases Review Commission. But in 2022 they responded that though the evidence submitted to them 'may raise a real possibility that these convictions would be overturned', they would not refer the case to the Court of Appeal owing to the cost and length of time since the trial. https:// alicewheeldon.org/criminalcases-review-commission#Downloads

29 Ron Rose Introduction to E.P. Thompson, *Warwick University Ltd,* Spokesman, Nottingham, 2nd edition, 2014, pp. xvii-xix; see also E.P. Thompson, 'The Business University', *New Society,* February 19, 1970.

30 Sheila Rowbotham, *Friends of Alice Wheeldon: the Anti-War Activist Accused of Plotting to Kill Lloyd George,* Pluto Press, London, First edition 1986; 2nd edition, 2015.

31 SRD, 28 May 1980.

32 SRD, 17-22 June 1980.

33 Now 'The Washhouse Pottery'.

34 SRD, I July 1980.

35 SRD, 30 July 1980.

36 See Rowbotham, *Daring to Hope*, pp. 155-157; Sheila Rowbotham, Rosalyn Baxandall, *Guardian*, 30 November 2015; Rosalyn Fraad Baxandall, 'Catching the Fire' in eds, Rachel Blau Du Plessis and Ann Snitow, *The Feminist Memoir Project*, Three Rivers Press, Random House, New York, 1998.

CHAPTER 2. 1980 August to December.

37 See *Beyond the Fragments Bulletin*, (*BFB*)No. 1, January, 1981, pp. 1-23; List of Stalls and Folder of letters on Beyond the Fragments, 7SHR, add 1/2011/25, Box 1 of 9, LSE.

38 Mike Cooley, *BFB*, No. 1, January 1981, p. 4.

39 John Bohanna (second) *BFB*, No. 1, January, 1981, p. 17.

40 Barbara Castle, Cardiff, *BFB*, No. 1, January, 1981, p. 17.

41 Rowbotham, interviewed by Copelman, (1981) in MARHO, *Visions of History*, p. 64.

42 Introduction, *BFB*, No. 1, January, 1981, p. 2.

43 Hilary Wainwright and Joanna de Groot, 'A Society of Socialists', *BFB*, No. 2, June 1981, pp. 17-19.

44 'Report from Liverpool Socialist Forum', *BFB*, No. 1, January, 1981, pp. 20-1.

45 Jane Barker, Jobs from Health – Workers' Plans for Better Health, CAITS (pamphlet) London, 1980; on the broader context see Ursula Huws 'The fading of the collective dream/ Reflections on twenty years' research on information technology and women's employment', in eds. Swasti Mitter and Sheila Rowbotham, *Women Encounter Technology: Changing Patterns of Employment in the Third World*, UNU/INTECH, Routledge, London, 1995.

46 Sheila Rowbotham, 'More Than Just Cogs in the Machine', *New Society*, 11 September, 1980, reprinted in Sheila Rowbotham, *Dreams and Dilemmas*, Virago, London, 1983, pp. 338-342; Marianne Herzog, *From Hand to Mouth: Women and Piecework*, Penguin, London, 1980.

47 Rowbotham, 'More Than Just Cogs in the Machine,' *Dreams and Dilemmas*, p. 340.

48 Herzog, *From Hand to Mouth*, p. 140.

49 Rowbotham, 'More Than Just Cogs in the Machine, *Dreams and Dilemmas*, pp. 341-342.

50 SRD, 21 September, 1980.

51 Sheila Rowbotham, Lectures, 1980, 7SHR/2010/36, Box 18, LSE.

52 Ed. Zillah Eisenstein, *Capitalist Patriarchy and the Case for Socialist Feminism*, Monthly Review Press, New York, 1979, Sheila Rowbotham, 'Dissolving the Hyphen', *New Statesman*, 21 September 1979.

53 On Michael Leibson, see Rowbotham, *Daring to Hope*, pp. 25, 214, 287.

54 SRD, 13 November 1980.

55 SRD, 24 November 1980.

56 SRD, 29 November 1980.

57 Sheila Rowbotham, 'Sally on Saturday,' (wrongly dated as summer 1981) in Rowbotham, *Dreams and Dilemmas*, p. 129.

58 SRD, 5 December 1980.

59 SRD, 1,2,3, December 1980.

60 The London to Edinburgh Return Group, *In and Against the State*, Pluto Press, London, 1980. (Originally a pamphlet, 1979) On the Conference of Socialist Economists see Hugo Radice, 'A Short History of the CSE,' *Capital & Class*, 10 Spring, 1980 and Michael Barratt Brown, *Seekers: A Twentieth Century Life*, Spokesman, Nottingham, 2013, p. 123.

61 Sheila Rowbotham, 'Mother, Child and the State', *New Society*, October, 1981, reprinted in Rowbotham, *Dreams and Dilemmas*, pp. 130-35.

62 See 'State Intervention in Industry', *BFB*, No. 1, January, 1981, p. 19.

63 Hilary Wainwright, 'A New Trade Unionism in the Making?' *BFB*, No. 2, June 1981, p. 10.

64 Leaflet, Dorothy Thompson, Modern Social History Seminar, Spring Term, 1980, 7SHR C/2, Folder 1 of 2, LSE.

65 SRD, 8 December 1980.

66 SRD, 10 December 1980.

CHAPTER 3 1981

67 The Big Red Diary's Utopias inserts were produced by Jean McNair and the Directory by Terry Illott.

68 Aidan White, Introduction Big Red Diary 1981, Utopias, Pluto Press, London, 1981, no page numbers.

69 See ed., John Merrick, *Workshop of the World: Essays in People's History* by Raphael Samuel, Verso London, 2024.

70 *Tributes for the Memorial of Raphael Samuel, 1934-1996*, (pamphlet) no editor, publisher or date; on the history of the Fed see, Tom Woodin, *Working Class Writing and Publishing in the late Twentieth Century*, Manchester University Press, Manchester, 2018; Liz Heron, 'Giving People a Voice', *The Times Educational Supplement*, 13 June, 1980.

71 Sheila Rowbotham, 'Travellers in a Strange Country', *History Workshop Journal*, No. 12, Autumn, 1981, reprinted in Rowbotham, *Dreams and Dilemmas*, pp. 267-305.

72 Faith Evans to Sheila Rowbotham, 16 May, 1979, 7SHR , add 1, 2011/25, Box 2 of 9. LSE; Faith Evans to Sheila Rowbotham, 23 December,1980, 7SHR, add 1,2011/25, box 2 of 9, LSE.

73 SRD,17 March, 1981.

74 Sheila Rowbotham, 'Introduction', to Olga Meier and Faith Evans, *The Daughters of Karl Marx: Family Correspondence, 1866-1898*, Andre Deutsch, London, 1982, pp. xvii-xl.

75   SRD, 28 to 30 April,1981.

76   Colin Ward, *The Child in the City*, Architectural Press, 1978, Penguin, London, 1979.

77   Sheila Rowbotham, Typed mss. of article submitted unsuccessfully to *Cosmopolitan*, 1981. SR.

78   SRD, 16 May, 1981.

79   SRD, 10 May, 3 June, 17, 18 October 1981, SR; Conference on Alternative Strategies for the Labour Movement, 18 October,1981, 7SHR/D/3, folder 1-2, LSE; Report of October 1981 Conference from members of the Conference of Socialist Economists and Beyond the Fragments, *BFB*, No. 3, Spring, 1982, p. 20.

80   'Union Official Victimised', *BFB*, No. 2, June 1981, p. 21, SR.

81   Mike Ward, 'Jobs and Workers' Plans' 7-30, Labour and Trades Hall, SRD, 10 June,1981, SR; Sheila Rowbotham, Notes on Mike Ward's talk at the meeting organized by Hackney Trades Council, on the back of a leaflet about Hackney Trades Council, Women's Sub- Committee, 1981, 7SHR/D/3, Folder 2 of 2, LSE. See also Michael Ward, *Municipal Socialism: The London Labour Party at County Hall 1934-81*, Wandsworth Community Publications, London 1981.

82   On the Institute for Workers' Control (IWC) see Rowbotham, *Daring to Hope*, pp. 14, 43, 49, 137.

83   Sheila Rowbotham, London, Meeting on GLC, July, 1981, *BFB*, No. 3, Spring, 1982, p. 20.

84   Eds, Maureen Mackintosh and Hilary Wainwright, *A Taste of Power: The Politics of Local Economics*, Verso, London, 1987, p. 106.

85   Sheila Rowbotham, 'Reclaim the Moon', Rowbotham, *Dreams and Dilemmas*, pp. 348-49.

86   SRD, 3, 4,5 July, 1981. SR.

87   Information from Wikipedia 1981 England riots; Anandi Ramamurthy, Bradford 12: Self-Defence is No Offence, https://libcom.org/ history/ Bradford-12-self-defence-no-offence.

88   Pratibha Parmar, 'A Revolutionary Anger', in ed. Ann Curno et al, *Women in Collective Action*, Association of Community Workers, London, 1982, p. 93.

89   Rowbotham, 'Mother, Child and the State', *New Society*, October, 1981, reprinted in Rowbotham, *Dreams and Dilemmas*, pp. 130-35.

90   Hilary Wainwright, 'A New Trade Unionism in the Making?' *BFB*, No. 2 June 1981, p. 10, SR.

91   Shop Stewards' Combine Committees and Trade Councils, *A Declaration, Popular Planning for Social Need: An Alternative to Monetarism* (pamphlet) September, 1981, p. 9, quoted in Sheila Rowbotham, 'Women Power and Consciousness,' in Rowbotham, *Dreams and Dilemmas*, pp. 148-9.

92   See Huws, 'The fading of the collective dream?' in eds, Mitter and Rowbotham, *Women Encounter Technology*, pp. 322-26.

93   Socialism, Democracy and Feminist Politics, Labour Party Conference, 1 October, 1981, 7SHR, D/3, Folder 1-2, LSE; 'Local Reports', Brighton,

Labour Party Conference, 1 October1981, *BFB*, No. 3, Spring, 1982, p. 19.

94   Tony Manwaring, 'Events', *BFB*, No.2, June 1981, p. 21.

95   Sheila Rowbotham, 'Local Reports', London, October 1981, 'Conference on Alternative Strategies for the Labour Movement', *BFB*, No. 3, Spring 1982, p. 20

96   Anna Coote, 'The Sexual Division of Labour and Relations in the Family', paper given at Conference on Alternative Strategies for the Labour Movement, October 1981, extracts in *BFB*, no.3, Spring 1982, pp. 5-6. Victor Anderson and Anna Coote are cited in Rowbotham, 'Women, Power and Consciousness', in Rowbotham, *Dreams and Dilemmas*, pp. 149, 359. See also Jean Cousins and Anna Coote, *Family in the Firing Line*, (pamphlet), NCCL/CPAG, London, 1982.

97   *SRD*, 28 October, 11 and 18 November, 1981.

98   Rowbotham, 'Local Reports, London', *BFB*, No. 3, Spring 1982, pp 20-21.

99   Gloden Dallas, 'Local Reports, Halifax', *BFB*, No 3, Spring 1982, pp. 19-20.

100 See Ann Pettitt, *Walking to Greenham*, Hanno, Dinas Powys, 2006, pp. 134-41.

101 Rowbotham, 'Women, Power and Consciousness', in Rowbotham, *Dreams and Dilemmas*, p 143. (I gave this talk in New York, Amsterdam and the UK during 1981 and 1982).

102 Rowbotham, 'Women Power and Consciousness', pp. 152-54.

103 Rowbotham, 'Women, Power and Consciousness', pp. 136, 158.

104 Rowbotham, 'Women, Power and Consciousness', p. 158.

105 Rowbotham, 'Women, Power and Consciousness', pp. 158-59.

106 *SRD*, 30, 31 October, 1 and 2 November 1981.

107 Sheila Rowbotham, 'A New Kind of Socialism' and Dave Feickert, 'Liberating Time and Energy Strategies' in *BFB*, No. 2, June 1980, pp. 4-6, 7-8.

108 Sheila Rowbotham, 'Local Reports, London', *BFB*, No. 3, Spring 1982, p. 21.

109 See Rowbotham, *Promise of a Dream*, pp. 180-2, 192-95, 198, 201-5.

110 Ed. Renate Hinz, *Käthe Kollwitz: Graphics Posters Drawings*, Writers and Readers Publishing Cooperative, London, 1981. On Writers and Readers see Chris Searle, *Isaac and I: A Life in Poetry*, Five Leaves, Nottingham, 2017, pp. 256-62.

111 Sheila Rowbotham, 'Loss', Autumn 1981, *Dreams and Dilemmas*, p. vii. I describe my mother's death in *Promise of a Dream*, pp, 105-9.

CHAPTER 4. 1982

112 *SRD*, 14, 15 January 1982.

113 Ros Baxandall to Sheila Rowbotham, 8 February, 1982, 7SHR add 1, 2011/25, Box 8 of 9, LSE.

114 *SRD*, 17 January 1982.

115 SRD, 20 January, 1982.
116 Marina Lewycka, 'A Fare Question', *BFB*, No.3, Spring, 1982, pp. 8-9.
117 Ed. Holly Aylett, *Marc Karlin: Look Again*, Liverpool University Press, Marc Karlin Archive, Liverpool, 2015, pp. 65-87, 309.
118 SRD, 27 February 27, 2 March, 1982.
119 See Ward, *Municipal Socialism*; Max Jäggi, Roger Müller and Sil Schmid, *Red Bologna*, Writers' and Readers' Publishing Cooperative, London, 1977.
120 See Ken Livingstone, *Livingstone's Labour: A Programme for the Nineties*, Unwin Hyman, London, 1989, pp. 90-91.
121 Mackintosh, Heron, 'Women's Work', in eds Mackintosh and Wainwright, *A Taste of Power*, p. 106.
122 Michael Ward, 'Robin and the GLC', https://robinmurray.co.uk
123 John Palmer, "Mike Cooley Obituary', *The Guardian*, 17 September, 2020.
124 Hilary Wainwright, *The Workers Report on Vickers*, Pluto Press, London 1979, Hilary Wainwright & Dave Elliott, *The Lucas Plan. A new trade unionism in the making?* (First edition 1982) Republished by Spokesman, Nottingham, 2018.
125 Shop Stewards' Combine Committees and Trade Councils, *A Declaration, Popular Planning for Social Need: An Alternative to Monetarism* (pamphlet) September, 1981.
126 SRD, 28 April, 1982.
127 Sheila Rowbotham, 'Feminism and the Making of Socialism', *BFB*, No. 3, Spring 1982.
128 SRD, 29 March 29 to April 9, and 1 May 1982.
129 Lectures, Amsterdam, April, 1982, 7SHR 2010/ 36, Box 18, LSE; Rowbotham, Diary, March 30 to April 8, 1982; SR. Rowbotham, SRD, 1 May 1982.
130 See Sheila Rowbotham, *The Past is Before Us: Feminism in Action since the 1960s*, Pandora, London 1989, Penguin, London, 1990.
131 See Rowbotham, *Promise of a Dream*, pp. 139-41.
132 SRD, 1 May 1982.
133 SRD, 8, 14,15 June 1982.
134 Rowbotham, 'Against the Grain', *Dreams and Dilemmas*, p. 349.
135 SRD, 18 May,1982; Rowbotham, *Dreams and Dilemmas*, p. 354.
136 Rowbotham, *Dreams and Dilemmas*, p. 351.
137 Rowbotham, *Dreams and Dilemmas*, p. 354.
138 Rowbotham, *Dreams and Dilemmas*, pp. 353-54.
139 See Guide to the Grace and Max Granich Papers and Photographs TAM 255. Tamiment Library, New York.
140 SRD, 25 September 1982.
141 Susan Sharpe, *Just Like a Girl*, Penguin, London, 1976; Susan Sharpe, *Double Identity: The Lives of Working Mothers*, Penguin, London, 1984.
142 David Phillips, *Do –it-yourself surveys: a handbook for beginners*, Polytechnic of North London, Survey Research Unit, London 1982, notice in *BFB*, No. 3, Spring 1982, p. 22.

143 SRD,18 to 24 October 1982.
144 SRD, 17, 19 November 1982.
145 Kumari Jayawardena, *Feminism and Nationalism in the Third World*, International Institute of Social Studies, The Hague, 1982, New edition, Verso, London, 2017.
146 SRD, 22 November 1982.
147 'London As It Might Be: Understanding the Power Structure', *BFB*, No. 4, Winter, 1982-83, p. 9.
148 On the 1969 Convention see Rowbotham, *Promise of a Dream*, pp. 226-7, 232-3.
149 Michael Barratt Brown, 'Stephen Bodington: Polymath for the Future. Obituary', *Guardian*,1 January 1990.
150 Stephen Bodington, 'Control of Resources', *BFB*, No. 4, Winter, 1982-83, pp. 6-7.
151 See Rowbotham, *Promise of a Dream*, pp. 181-82, 192-96.

CHAPTER 5 1983

152 I owe the memory of the red tie to Hilary Wainwright, The Economics of Labour: Robin Murray, Industrial Strategy and the Popular Planning Unit', https://robinmurray.co.uk
153 SRD 25 February, 1983.
154 *Jobs For A Change*, (Booklet), Front cover, GLC, London 1983, SR.
155 *Jobs For A Change*, (Booklet), Inside back cover.
156 'Lambeth Toys'. Jobs for a Change, (*JFAC*), April, 1983, p. 1.
157 Tom Durkin, *JFAC*, June, 1983, pp. 1 and 3.
158 SRD, 20 April, 1983.
159 Dave Benlow, quoted in "Tricked, Cheated and Bullied"', *JFAC*, June, 1983, p. 6; on the impact of privatization on London in 1983 see also *JFAC*, Special Edition, Public Sevices, November, 1983.
160 Micky Langley, quoted in '"Tricked, Cheated and Bullied"', *JFAC*, June, 1983, p. 6.
161 SRD 13 April, 1983; André Gorz, Hilary Wainwright and Elizabeth Wilson, 'Farewell to the Working Class? ICA, 13 April, 1983 The British Library Sound Archive.
162 'Resource Centres', *JFAC*, June, 1983, p. 5; Maureen Mackintosh, Liz Heron, 'Women's Work', in eds, Maureen Mackintosh and Hilary Wainwright, *A Taste of Power: The Politics of Local Economics*, Verso, London, 1987, pp. 116, 118-23; SRD, 17, 20, 22, 25 January, 1 February, 1983.
163 Lorna, quoted in 'A Sense of Self-Worth', *JFAC*, June, 1983, p. 8. On London Women's Employment Projects see ed. Ann Curno, et al, Women in Collective Action, The Association of Community Workers, 1983, pp 55-64.
164 Judy Wilcox and Jenny Williams, 'Susie Parsons, Obituary', *Guardian*, 22 June, 2015.

165 GLC, Westway Laundry, 7SHR C/C 317, Box 1 of 21, 7/ANG 2000/12 7ANg /B/01/-02, LSE.

166 Ed. Ellen Malos, *The Politics of Housework*, Allison & Busby, London, 1980.

167 Sheila Rowbotham, Housework Debates, GLC Economic Policy Unit no date, 7SHR 317 Box 1 of 21, 7/ANG200/12 7ANG/B01/-02. LSE.

168 Ed. Lynne Segal, *What Is To Be Done About The Family?* Penguin, London, 1983.

169 SRD, Notes, 1983.

170 SRD, 10-21 February 1983. On Kodak see Dave Spooner, 'On the side of the Workers? The GLC and Transnational Firms', in eds. Mackintosh and Wainwright, *A Taste of Power*, pp. 264-65.

171 SRD, 8-19 March 1983.

172 SRD, 17 March 1983.

173 SRD, 18 March 1983. The title comes from a poem and a collection of poems written by a Workers' Educational Association class, Knowle West Community Council, Bristol Broadsides, (pamphlet) Bristol, 1978. See Sheila Rowbotham, 'Shush Mum's Writing', *Socialist History* 17, 2000, pp. 1-21.

174 SRD, 8 April 1983; Angela V. John, *History Workshop Journal*, Vol. 16, Issue 1, Autumn, 1983, p. 176; I am grateful to Angela John (email 13 September, 2022) for clarification of the Conference's theme.

175 SRD, 16 April 1984.

176 Jill Liddington, 'The Women's Peace Crusade: The History of a Forgotten Campaign', ed. Dorothy Thompson, *Over Our Dead Bodies: Women Against the Bomb*, Virago London 1983, pp. 180-198.

177 Lynne Segal, *Making Trouble: Life and Politics*, Serpent's Tale, London 2007, p. 106.

178 See Rowbotham, *Daring to Hope*, pp. 84-85, 104, 108.

179 SRD, 7 April 1983.

180 See Sheila Rowbotham, 'Robin, a lodestone and a lodestar', https://robinmurray.co.uk

181 SRD, 4 June 1983.

182 Thatcher, *The Downing Street Years*, p. 306.

183 SRD, 6 July 1983.

184 Jane Paul, *Where There's Muck There's Money*, (booklet) Industry and Employment Branch, Greater London Council, 1986, SR.

185 Paul, *Where There's Muck There's Money*, pp. 38, 68, SR; 'Equal Opportunities', *JFAC*, Special Edition, Keep GLC Working for London, No. 6, February, 1984, p. 11.

186 Sheila Rowbotham, LIS. Childcare, Introduction pp. 72, 74. Typed mss. SR.

187 Sheila Rowbotham, Folder on Hackney, 7SHR, add 1. 2011/25, Box 4 of 9 LSE.

188 SRD, 8, 23 June 1983.

189 SRD, 7 June 1983.

190 SRD, 14 July 1983.

191 Jill Liddington, 'Gloden Dallas 1943–1983', *History Workshop Journal*, 1984, no. 17, pp. 213-14.
192 Thatcher, *The Downing Street Years*, pp. 305-6.
193 John Lister, 'How Thatcher Unleashed the NHS Outsourcing Wave', https//tribunemag.co.uk/2020/12/thatcher-nhs-outsourcing-wave.
194 Ken Livingstone, Leader's report, 19 July, quoted in *JFAC*, Special Edition, Public Services, November, 1983, p. 1
195 'Message from Ken Livingstone', *JFAC*, Special Edition, The London Industrial Strategy, September, 1983, p. 1.
196 Sheila Rowbotham, 'Our Health in Whose Hands? Health Emergencies and the Struggle for Better Health Care in London', eds, Mackintosh & Wainwright, *A Taste of Power*, pp. 332-333.
197 'How to fight?', *JFAC*, Special Edition, Public Services, November, 1983, p. 7.
198 'British Telecom', *JFAC*, Special Edition, The London Industrial Strategy, September,1983, p. 3; see also Hilary Wainwright, *The Economics of Labour, Robin Murray, Industrial Strategy and the Popular Planning Unit*, https://robinmurray.co.uk.
199 Spooner, 'On the side of the Workers?', eds, Mackintosh and Wainwright, *A Taste of Power*, p. 266.
200 These covered transport, docks, house building, cable, software, energy, engineering, food, furniture, clothing, multinationals, along with the cultural industries, printing, publishing, audio visual media, shops, offices, cleaning and domestic labour. See *JFAC*, Special Edition, The London Industrial Strategy, September,1983, pp. 2-9.
201 'Just a labour of love?' and 'Who's minding the kids? *JFAC*, Special Edition on the London Industrial Strategy, September 1983, p. 10.
202 Sheila Rowbotham, 'Child Care – Meeting Needs and Making Jobs', Economic Policy Group Strategy Document No. 14, (pamphlet) September, 1983, SR, p. 3.
203 Sheila Rowbotham, 'Value of Care', *JFAC*, Special Edition, Public Services, November, 1983, pp. 2-7.
204 See Gail Lewis, 'From Deepest Kilburn' in ed. Liz Heron, *Truth, Dare or Promise: Girls Growing Up in the Fifties*, Virago, London, 1985, pp. 213-36.
205 SRD, 8 September 1983.
206 Sheila Rowbotham, 'Our Lance' in ed. Ursula Owen, *Fathers: Reflections by Daughters*, Virago, London 1983, p. 203.
207 Rowbotham, 'Our Lance' p. 216.
208 SRD, 31 October 1983.
209 5, 10 November 1983. SR.
210 SRD, 16,18,19, 21 December 1983.
211 SRD, 25 December 1983.
212 Sheila Rowbotham, 'Bonfires in our own backyard', *Chartist*, No.98, January/February, 1984, pp. 20-21.

CHAPTER 6 1984

213 SRD, 21 February 1984.
214 Sheila Rowbotham, 'Passion off the Pedestal', *City Limits*, March 2-8 1984, p. 21.
215 Rowbotham, 'Passion off the Pedestal', p. 21.
216 Rowbotham, *Promise of a Dream*, pp. 193-95.
217 'Save the GLC', *JFAC*, Special Edition, Keep the GLC Working for London, February 1984, p. 1.
218 John Hoyland, 'Reggae on the Rates: The Jobs for a Change Festivals', eds, Maureen Mackintosh & Hilary Wainwright, *A Taste of Power: The Politics of Local Economics,* pp 371-74.
219 SRD, 28 February 1984.
220 SRD, 12 March, 1984; *JFAC*, Special Edition, London Transport, No.7, April 1984
221 SRD, 13 March 1984.
222 Sheila Rowbotham, 'Hopes Dreams and Dirty Nappies', *Marxism Today*, December, 1984 reprinted in *Practice* Winter, 1986, p. 138.
223 SRD, 20 March, 1984. See ed., Collective Design/Projects, *Very Nice Work If You Can Get It: The Socially Useful Production Debate,* Spokesman, Nottingham, 1985.
224 Roger Coleman and Ian Tod, Interview with Mike Cooley', *William Morris Today*, Institute of Contemporary Arts, London 1984, p. 112.
225 SRD, 17 March 1984.
226 Eds. James Curran, Ivor C. Gaber and Julian Petley, *Culture Wars: The Media and the British Left,* Routledge, London, 2nd edition, 2019, p. 35.
227 Sheila Rowbotham interviews Jean McCrindle, 'More Than Just a Memory: Some Political Implications of Women's Involvement in the Miners' Strike, 1984-85', *Feminist Review,* No. 23, Summer 1986, p. 110.
228 This is based on my memory of Joan Bohanna's description, and clarified in September 2020 by Eileen Turnbull. John Bohanna and Eileen Turnbull were to participate in the campaign for the vindication of the wrongly convicted North Wales building workers. Eileen Turnbull, *A Very British Conspiracy: The Shrewsbury 24 and the Campaign for Justice,* Verso, London, 2022, pp. 129-30.
229 SRD, 17, 19 April 1984.
230 *JFAC.* Special Editions, 'London's Black Workers, May, 1984, Pension Funds, May 1984.
231 'Give Us A Job', *JFAC,* June 1984, p. 1.
232 Anne Scargill quoted in Hoyland, 'Reggae on the Rates', eds, Mackintosh & Wainwright, *A Taste of Power,* Hoyland, pp. 384-5.
233 See Simon Price, 'Reissue of the Week, Redskins' 'Neither Washington Nor Moscow', *The Quietus,* 14 January 2022. Online.
234 Rowbotham interviews McCrindle, p. 115.
235 SRD, 12 June 1984.
236 Information from Shelley Adams, August 2020.

237 Sheila Rowbotham, Notes on Miners' Strike, Soft blue notebook, 7SHR 2010/ 36. Box 18. LSE.
238 SRD, 11 August 1984. SR.
239 Interview, 'London Can Work' JFAC, No. 13, no date, p. 8; SRD, 27 September 1984.
240 Michael Ward, foreword, ed, Rodney Mace, *Taking Stock: A Documentary History of the Greater London Council's Supplies Department.* GLC, London, 1984, p. 3; 'Support Services', *JFAC,* February, 1984, p. 4.
241 Winifred Holtby, 'Prefactory Letter to Alderman Mrs Holtby', *South Riding: An English Landscape,* First edition 1936, reprinted, William Collins, London, 1949, pp. v-vi.
242 SRD, 26 June 1984.
243 Sheila Rowbotham and Jeffrey Weeks, *Socialism and the New Life*, Pluto Press, London,1977.
244 SRD, 7 September 1984.
245 Rowbotham , *Daring to Hope*, p. 134.
246 Anna McGonnigle, quoted in Sheila Rowbotham, 'What do Women Want? *Feminist Review*, No 20, June 1985, p. 65.
247 Marx told Engels of his mother's comment on his 50th birthday in 1868 when he was particularly broke. David McLellan, *Karl Marx: His Life and Thought*, Macmillan, London, 1973, p. 356.
248 Hester Eisenstein, *Contemporary Feminist Thought,* Unwin Paperbacks, London 1984, p. 144.
249 Sheila Rowbotham, 'What Do Women Want?, *Dalhousie Review,* Volume 64, Number 4, Winter, 1984-85, p. 649.
250 Rowbotham, 'What Do Women Want? p. 663.
251 Temma Kaplan to Sheila Rowbotham, no date, 7SHR add1 2011/25, Box 3 of 9.
252 Pete Turner's death in 2003 was from asbestos. He had been connected to Committee of 100 and to the lively and thoughtful magazine edited by Colin Ward, *Anarchy*, No.4, June 1964; Obituary, 'A Lifetime of Struggle', *Freedom*, 24 January, 2004; Arthur Moyes, Pete Turner, http://libcom.org/history/articles/1935-2004-pete-turner Report by Construction Safety Campaign http:www.labournet/ukunion/0401/ turner1.htmlPeter Turner04/01/04. I am grateful to Julian Putkowsi for these references.
253 On the GLC and Ford see Spooner, 'On the side of the Workers?' in eds. Mackintosh and Wainwright, *A Taste of Power* pp. 265-69.
254 On transport see Maureen Mackintosh, 'Public Engineering: The GLC and the Transport Unions' and Dave Welsh, 'Jobs and People's Lives: One Person Operation on Buses and Tubes', eds, Mackintosh and Wainwright, *A Taste of Power,* pp. 20-45, 46-79.
255 Rosina Stanford, 'The Right to Reply', *JFAC,* No. 8, February 1984, p. 5.
256 See Hilary Wainwright, 'The Economics of Labour: Robin Murray, Industrial Strategy and the Popular Planning Unit' https:// robinmurray.co.uk/glc-ppu

257 See Lliane Phillips, 'Docklands for the People', eds, Mackintosh and
     Wainwright, *A Taste of Power,* p. 320; see also *The People's Plan for the
     Royal Docks,* GLC, 1983.
258 SRD, 10 December 1984. SR.
259 Sheila Rowbotham, 'Hopes, Dreams and Dirty Nappies' *Marxism
     Today,* December 1984, reprinted in *Practice,* Winter, 1986, pp. 136,
     132.
260 SRD, 21 and 24 December 1984.

CHAPTER 7 1985

261 'Miners' Families Appeal for Women Against Pit Closures', 7SHR,
     Orange Folder, Box 39. LSE.
262 SRD, 21 January 1985; Karl Dallas, 'The Multi-Cultural Man,' in
     Programme for Ewan MacCall's 70th Birthday Celebration Folk
     Concert, Royal Festival Hall. Working Class Movement Library
     (WCML) online.
263 On their relationship and work together see Peggy Seeger, *First Time
     Ever: A Memoir,* Faber & Faber, London, 2017.
264 See Raphael Samuel, 'Obituary of Ewan MacColl', *The Independent,*
     30 October 1989. SR.
265 SRD, 24 January 1985. SR.
266 Obie Bing, 'Report on Coal Use in the Utilities' and 'Solidarity in
     Miners' Strike', 7SHR. Box 4 of 9, add 2011/25, LSE.
267 SRD, 29 January 1985.
268 Winston Beckford, 'Playing for the Love of it', *JFAC,* 'Power Cuts in
     January', No 14 (no date), 1985, p. 9.
269 SRD, 8 February 1985.
270 SRD, 26 February 1985.
271 Keith Harper, 'Pit strike ends in defiance and tears', *Guardian,* 4 March,
     1985.
272 Margaret Widgery to Sheila Rowbotham, 13 March, 1985, 7SHR, Box 4
     of 9, add 1, 2011/25. LSE.
273 See Doreen Massey and Hilary Wainwright, 'Beyond the Coalfields', in
     ed. Huw Beynon, *Digging Deeper,* Verso, London, 1985; reprinted in
     eds. David Featherstone and Diarmaid Kelliher, *Doreen Massey: Selected
     Political Writings,* Lawrence and Wishart, London, 2022.
274 SRD, 8, 9 March1985.
275 *JFAC,* 'A New Deal for London,' March, 1985, p.12; robinmurray.
     co.uk/ glc-ppu.
276 Spooner, 'On the side of the Workers? The GLC and Transnational
     Firms' in eds. Mackintosh and Wainwright, *A Taste of Power,* pp. 265-
     269.
277 SRD 1 October 1985; Sheila Rowbotham, Notebook, 1980s, 7SHR, Box
     39, LSE.

278 Barratt Brown, *Seekers*, pp. 183-94.
279 Marc Karlin, 'Filmography' in ed., Aylett, *Marc Karlin, Look Again*, p. 309.
280 Hermione Harris, 'A Shared Experience', in ed., Aylett, *Marc Karlin, Look Again* p. 129; I describe the background to our friendship, in *Promise of a Dream* and *Daring to Hope*.
281 'Voyages', 'The Making of a Nation', 'In Their Time', 'Changes' were shown in autumn 1985 on Channel 4. 'Scenes from a Revolution', in May 1991. Karlin, 'Filmography' in ed., Aylett, *Marc Karlin, Look Again*, pp. 309-10.
282 SRD, 31 March 1985.
283 SRD, 11 April 1985.
284 SRD, 11 May 1985.
285 See Rowbotham, *Daring to Hope*, pp. 84, 104, 108.
286 SRD, 6 June 1985.
287 Siân James, quoted in Diarmaid Kelliher, 'Solidarity and sexuality: lesbians and gays support for the miners, 1984-5 *History Workshop Journal*, 77(1), pp. 240-262; http://eprints.gla.ac.uk/155165/ p. 10, University of Glasgow.
288 Neil Kinnock and Tony Benn at Conference at County Hall, *JFAC*, Special Summer Issue, No.18, no date, 1985. https://robinmurray.co.uk/ glc-ppu
289 See Charles Foster, 'Robin Murray and the London Industrial Strategy', https://robinmurray.co.uk
290 Robin Murray, 'Introduction', *The London Industrial Strategy*, (LIS) Greater London Council, 1985, p. 6.
291 Robin Jenkins, a development sociologist and Sandy Hunt, a nutritionist also guided the Economic Policy on food policy. Tim Lang, 'The Food Problem and the GLC'. https://robinmurray.co.uk
292 Michael Ward, Preface to the LIS, p. viii.
293 Sheila Rowbotham, Interview with Ben Birnbaum, 'Craft Patterns', *JFAC*, Special Summer Issue, No. 18, no date, 1985, https://robinmurray.co.uk/ glc-ppu
294 SRD, 30 May 1985.
295 'Who Will Care for the Natterjack Toad?', *JFAC*, No.18, 1985, https://robinmurray.co.uk/ glc-ppu) robinmurray.co.uk/ glc-ppu.
296 Sheila Rowbotham, 'Who needs a new economics?' *JFAC*, No.18, no date, https://robinmurray.co.uk/ glc-ppu.
297 Mike Cooley, 'Things We Know But Cannot Tell', *JFAC*, No. 18, no date, 1985, https:// robinmurray.co.uk
298 John Hoyland, 'Reggae on the Rates: The Jobs for a Change Festivals', eds. Mackintosh & Wainwright, *A Taste of Power*, pp. 375-76, 385-87.
299 Hoyland, 'Reggae on the Rates, pp. 382-83.
300 See Joy Sable, 'Facing the Music: The Future of the Contemporary Dance Theatre at Sadlers' Wells *Jobs for a Change*, No. 18, no date, 1985, https://robinmurray.co.uk

301   Ruth Milkman, 'Feminism and Labor since the 1960s' in ed. Ruth
      Milkman, *Women, Work and Protest*, Routledge and Kegan Paul,
      Boston, 1985, pp 308-9.

302   Rosalyn Baxandall and Elizabeth Ewen, 'From Civilization to
      Barbarism', eds, Stephen Resnick and Richard D. Wolff, *Rethinking
      Marxism: Struggles in Marxist Theory -Essays for Harry Magdoff and
      Paul Sweezy*, Autonomedia, 1985, p. 14.

303   Baxandall and Ewen, 'From Civilization to Barbarism', p. 12.

304   SRD, 16 August, 1985; Sheila Rowbotham, Issues for the Next
      Generation Conference, Introductory talk, Toronto, 1985, Typed Mss.
      SR

305   Ante Ciliga, *The Russian Enigma*, Ink Links, London, 1979, p. 92.

306   Sheila Rowbotham, 'Picking Up the Pieces', *New Socialist*, October,
      1985, reprinted in Raymond Williams Society blog, March 27, 2020, as
      'Radical Resources', pp. 1-3.

307   Rowbotham, 'Radical Resources', p. 3.

308   The transcripts, which I checked and corrected for typing errors, along
      with the tapes, were incorporated with Michael Ward's Archive on the
      GLC and donated to London Metropolitan Archives, City of London in
      2000; see also Mackintosh & Wainwright, *A Taste of Power*.

309   Shamis Diri quoted in Rowbotham, 'Our Health in Whose Hands? pp.
      353-354.

310   Margery Bane, in Rowbotham, 'Our Health in Whose Hands? p. 364.

311   Lily Cook, quoted in Rowbotham, 'Our Health in Whose Hands? p.
      355.

312   Rowbotham, 'Our Health in Whose Hands? pp. 356-357.

313   Lucy de Groot, quoted in Rowbotham, 'Our Health in Whose Hands?
      p. 344.

314   SRD, 26 November, 1985.

315   Sheila Rowbotham, 'Feminism and Democracy', eds. David Held and
      Christopher Pollitt, *New Forms of Democracy*, Sage Publications in
      association with the Open University, London, 1986, pp. 78-109.

316   SRD, 5 December 1985.

317   See Kumari Jayawardena, *Doreen Wickremasinghe: A Western Radical
      in Sri Lanke*, pamphlet, Women's Education and Resource Centre,
      Colombo 1991; Sheila Rowbotham, *Edward Carpenter: A Life of Liberty
      and Love*, Verso, London, 2008, p. 445.

318   Sally Alexander to Sheila Rowbotham, Saturday, no date, 1985, 7/SHR/
      surrey Box 4-21. LSE.

CHAPTER 8 1986

319   Emma Goldman, *Living My Life* Vol. 1, Pluto Press, London, 1987, p. 5.

320   Sheila Rowbotham and Hilary Wainwright, Manuscript interview with
      Ken Livingstone, January 1986, Sheila Rowbotham Papers, Women's
      Library , LSE.

321 Sheila Rowbotham, Handwritten manuscript of talk to San Diego State students, 10 February 1986, SR.

322 SRD,14 February, 1986.

323 Michael Pooler, *Red Pepper*, 20 October 2011; The *Guardian*, Rupert Murdoch and the battle of Wapping: 25 years on.

324 SRD, 8 March 1986.

325 Filmography, in ed., Aylett, *Marc Karlin, Look Again*, p. 309.

326 I have been unable to establish the year of Edward Thompson's speech at Burford. Jonathan Bloom and Brand Thumin who helped to make the film, narrowed the year down to 1980 or 1981.There is a hint that Will and I visited the Thompsons in Worcester on Friday 16 May 1980 in a note of a Paddington train in my diary.

327 E.P. Thompson quoted in ed., Aylett, *Marc Karlin, Look Again*, p. 81.

328 Marc Karlin to Hermione Harris, no date in ed. Aylett, *Marc Karlin, Look Again*, p. 74; see also Sheila Rowbotham, 'Interview with Marc Karlin', in Sheila Rowbotham and Huw Beynon, *Looking at Class: Film Television and the Working Class*, Rivers Oram, London, 2001, pp. 144-145.

329 See Gary Younge, 'Ambalavaner Sivanandan Obituary', *Guardian*, 7 February, 2018.

330 Ambalavaner Sivanandan, in 'Utopias' quoted in ed. Aylett, *Marc Karlin: Look Again*, p.159.

331 This archive was preserved first in the basement of Conway Hall and then in the Extra Mural Library of London University, thanks to the feminist Mary Kennedy. In 2000 Michael Ward and I agreed that it should be combined with material he was donating to the London Metropolitan Archives. Because photographers filed their pictures, while musicians preserved the posters of their GLC gigs a record of some of this extraordinary creativity can now be found online.

332 SRD, 18 March 1986.

333 Wikipedia records that Chris Duffield was later to be appointed as Chief Executive of the Corporation of London and Chief Executive of the Police Authority.

334 *Beneath the Veneer: London furniture workers report on the collapse of their industry and spell out what should be done to save it.* static1. squarespace.com and robinmurray.co.uk; Hilary Wainwright, 'Planning from Above; Planning from Below: A Case Study', eds, Mackintosh and Wainwright, *A Taste of Power*, pp. 215-39.

335 Maureen Mackintosh and Hilary Wainwright, *A Taste of Power: The Politics of Local Economics.* Verso, 1987.

336 'Bread and Roses' appeared as a slogan in American women's suffrage and trade union women's struggles in the early 20th century; it was a poem by James Oppenheim, in 1911, put to music in the 1970s.

337 Ken Livingstone quoted in Hoyland, 'Reggae on the Rates', eds, Mackintosh & Wainwright, *A Taste of Power*, pp. 396-97.

338 'His Worship Takes the Plunge', *Sunday Sun* (Newcastle) 25 June 1922. (I am grateful to Mike Richardson for this reference).

339 Hilary Wainwright to Sheila Rowbotham, no date, (summer 1986), 7SHR,/ add1, 2011/25, Box3 of 9, LSE; Hilary Wainwright, *Labour: A Tale of Two Parties,* Hogarth Press, London 1987.
340 SRD, 12 April 1986.
341 SRD, 14-15 May 1986.
342 SRD, 29 May 1986.
343 SRD, 31 May 1986.
344 See Paul Salveson, *With Walt Whitman in Bolton: Spirituality, Sex and Socialism,* Little Northern Books, 2008.
345 Mandana Hendessi, Fourteen Thousand Women Meet: Report from Nairobi, Socialist-Feminism, Out of the Blue, *Feminist Review,* No. 23, Summer 1986, p. 148.
346 Susan Ardill and Sue O'Sullivan, 'Upsetting the Applecart: Difference, Desire and Lesbian SM', *Feminist Review,* No. 23, Summer 1986, p. 30.
347 Ardill and O'Sullivan, 'Upsetting the Applecart', p. 34.
348 Ardill and O'Sullivan, 'Upsetting the Applecart', pp. 32-33.
349 Dora Russell, *The Right To Be Happy,* Garden City Publishing, New York 1927.
350 SRD, 30 September 1986.
351 SRD, 18 October 1986.
352 Swasti Mitter, *Common Fate, Common Bond: Women in the Global Economy,* Pluto Press, London, 1986, p. 146.
353 Mitter, *Common Fate, Common Bond,* pp. 149-152, Swasti Mitter, On organising women in casualised work, i Appendix IV: Homeworkers' Charter in the United Kingdom, in eds, Sheila Rowbotham and Swasti Mitter, *Dignity and Daily Bread: New Forms of Economic Organising among Poor Women in the Third World and the First,* Routledge, London, 1994, pp. 47-48.
354 'Policy adopted by the 1984 National Conference on Homeworking', London Industrial Strategy, pp. 434-35.
355 Swasti Mitter, New Technology and the Rise of Manufacturing Homework: A Case Study in the UK Clothing Industry, 1984. Unpublished paper commissioned by the GLC, cited in 'Homeworking', London Industrial Strategy, pp. 421-23.
356 Mitter, *Common Fate, Common Bond,* p. 125.
357 Mitter, *Common Fate, Common Bond,* p. 80.
358 Mitter, *Common Fate, Common Bond,* pp. 178-179.
359 SRD, 26 September, 14 October, 8 November 1986; on Bhopal, see Radha Kumar, *The History of Doing: An Illustrated Account of Movements for Women's Rights and Feminism in India, 1800-1990,* Kali for Women New Delhi and Verso, London, 1993, pp. 187-90.
360 SRD, 25, 26, 27 November 1986.
361 SRD, 29, 30 November 1986.
362 SRD , 1, 2, 3, 4 December 1986.
363 SRD, 12 December 1986.
364 Thatcher, *The Downing Street Years,* p. 590.

365 John Milton, 'The Areopagitica' in ed., Douglas Bush, *The Portable Milton*, Viking Press, New York, 19 63 p. 155.

CHAPTER 9 1987

366 Rowbotham, Introduction, *The Past Is Before Us*, p. xi.
367 Robin Blackburn, 'Nicolas Krasso: 1930-1986' *New Left Review*, No. 155, January/February 1986.
368 SRD , 27 January 1987; on the Institute of Women (Instituto de la Mujer) see ed., Monica Threlfall, *Mapping the Women's Movement, Feminist Politics and Transformation in the North*, Verso, London, 1996, pp. 124-5.
369 Fernando Claudin, *The Communist Movement: From Comintern to Cominform*, Penguin, London, 1975.
370 See Rowbotham, *Daring to Hope*, p. 282
371 SRD, 10 January 1987; on the continuing campaign see Helen Penn, '*Be realistic, demand the impossible*': *A Memoir of Work in Child Care and Education*, Routledge, London, 2018.
372 I later wrote on the impact of OPO. SRD 29 October 1987.
373 SRD, 13 March 1987.
374 See Sheila Rowbotham, *A New World for Women: Stella Browne-Socialist Feminist*, Pluto, London, 1977.
375 Ed., Jane S. Jaquette, *The Women's Movement in Latin America: Transition to Democracy*, Unwin Hyman, Boston, 1989.
376 Sheila Rowbotham on *The Star*, in Paper Tiger Television Archive, Deconstructing the News Industry, https//papertiger.org
377 See Sheila Rowbotham, '"Commanding the Heart" Edward Carpenter and Friends', *History Today*, Vol 37, September 1987, reprinted in ed., Gordon Marsden, *Victorian Values*, Longman, London, 1990.
378 Eventually resulting in *Edward Carpenter: A Life of Liberty and Love* and *Rebel Crossings: New Women, Free Lovers, and Radicals in Britain and the United States*, Verso, London, 2016.
379 SRD, 5 July, 1987.
380 See Eric Hobsbawm, *Age of Extremes: The Short Twentieth Century*, 1914-1991, Preface and Acknowledgements, Michael Joseph, London,1994, p. x.
381 See Amartya Sen, *Home in the World: A Memoir*, Allen Lane, London, 2021, pp. 265, 276.
382 See Amartya Sen, *Food, Economics and Entitlement*, WIDER Working Paper, 1/1986, UNU WIDER, Helsinki; Sen, *Home in the World*, pp. 117-18, 168.
383 SRD, 26 and 27 July, 1987; UNU/WIDER conference on poverty, undernutrition and living standards, Helsinki, July 1987, Papers of Professor Eric Hobsbawm, Warwick Modern Records Centre.
384 Bengt Sundkler died before he could complete his book, *A History of the Church in Africa*. It was to be published in 2000 with Christopher Steed by Cambridge University Press; see Marja-Liisa Swantz, *Beyond*

the Forestline: The Life and Letters of Bengt Sundkler, Studia Missionalia, Gracewing, Leominster, Herefordshire, 2002.

385 Hermione Harris, *Yoruba in Diaspora: An African Church in London,* Palgrave Macmillan, 2006.

386 SRD, 20 August, 1987; Radha Kumar, 'Family and factory: Women in the Bombay cotton textile industry 1919-1939', *Indian Economic and Social History Review,* No. 1, Vol.20, 1983; see also. Radha Kumar, *City Lives: Women Workers in the Bombay Textile Industry,* PhD Thesis, Department of History, Jawaharial Nehru University, Delhi, 1992.

387 On Tony Benn and Ralph Miliband's influence on the inception of the Chesterfield conferences in the late 1980s see Michael Newman, *Ralph Miliband and the Politics of the New Left,* Merlin Press, London, 2002, pp. 299-308.

388 Swasti Mitter to Sheila Rowbotham, 30 September, 1987, 7SHR, add 1, 2011/25, Box 4 of 9, LSE.

389 SRD, 24-25 October 1987.

390 Information on the workshop on Women's International Links and the Labour Movement, Chesterfield, 24 October 1987, Typed report, SR; Anne Scargill and Betty Cook refer to some of the international links that developed in the miners' strike in their book with Ian Clayton, *Anne and Betty: United By The Struggle,* Route Publishing, Pontefract, 2020.

391 Information on the workshop on Women's International Links and the Labour Movement, Chesterfield, 24 October 1987, Typed report, SR.

392 SRD, 31 October 1987.

393 The account of our visit to India that follows in this chapter is drawn from my handwritten journal (SRJ) between 18 to 31 December 1987.

394 See Radha Kumar, *The History of Doing: An Illustrated Account of Movements for Women's Rights and Feminism in India, 1800-1990,* Kali for Women New Delhi and Verso, London, 1993, pp. 173-81.

395 Urvashi Butalia, was later to write, *The Other Side of Silence: Voices from the Partition of India,* Duke University Press, Durham, North Carolina, 2000.

396 Kumar, *The History of Doing,* p. 97; see also Stree Shakti Sanghatana (Lalita K., Vasantha Kannabiran, Rama Melkote, Uma Maheshwari, Susie Tharu, and Veena Shatrugna), *We Were Making History: Life Stories of Women in the Telangana Peoples' Struggle,* Kali for Women, New Delhi and Zed Books, London, 1989.

CHAPTER 10. 1988

397 SRJ, 5 and 10 January 1988.

398 SRD, 2-5 January and 11 January 1988.

399 On the background to SEWA see Renana Jhabvala, 'Self-Employed Women's Association' in eds, Sheila Rowbotham and Swasti Mitter, *Dignity and Daily Bread,* Routledge, London 1994, pp. 114-38; see also Radha Kumar, *The History of Doing,* Verso, London, pp. 102-3, 193.

400 Policy Adopted by the 1984 National Conference on Homeworking, Homeworkers' Charter, Recommendations by the National Steering Group on homeworkers, Proposals for action, LIS London Industrial Strategy, pp. 434-9.

401 See Jhabvala, 'Self-Employed Women's Association', pp.114-38.

402 SRJ, 10 February 1988, for an account of Renana Jhabvala's conviction on the need for an international campaign on homeworking. On the development of links during the 1990s see Sheila Rowbotham, 'Weapons of the Weak', *The European Journal of Women's Studies*, Vol. 5, 1998, pp. 453-63.

403 SRJ, 10 February 1988.

404 SRD, 15 and 16 January 1988.

405 SRD, 18 January 1988. SRJ, 10 February 1988.

406 SRD, 29 January 1988.

407 SRJ, 10 February 1988.

408 Thatcher, *The Downing Street Years*, pp. 5, 60, 590-92.

409 See Jeffrey Weeks, *Between Worlds: A Queer Boy From the Valleys*, Parthian,Cardigan, 2021, p. 177.

410 Lynne Segal, *Is The Future Female? Troubled Thoughts on Contemporary Feminism*, Virago, London, 1987.

411 SRD, 17 February 1988.

412 SRD, 5 February 1988.

413 SRD, 12 February 1988.

414 See Florence Binard, 'Beyond Invisibility and Bias: English Women's and Gender Studies in France', in ed., Renate Hass, *Rewriting Academia: The Development of Anglicist Women's and Gender Studies of Continental Europe*, Peter Lang, Bern, 2018; Françoise Barret-Ducrocq, *Love in the Time of Victoria*, Verso, London, 1991.

415 SRJ, 10 February 1988.

416 SRD, 26 March 1988.

417 SRJ, 9 March 1988.

418 SRD,30 April 1988.

419 Sheila Rowbotham, in 'Utopias' quoted in ed., Aylett, *Marc Karlin: Look Again*, p. 159.

420 SRJ, 3 May 1988, SR.

421 *Women and the Economy*, Women's Studies Unit (WSU) The Polytechnic of North London, duplicated pamphlet, London, 1988, SR, lists the full programme of speakers and their papers.

422 Sheila Rowbotham,' Woman's place is in another economy', *Guardian*, 9 May 1988.

423 Mary Louise Adams, 'There's No Place Like Home: On the Place of Identity in Feminist Politics', *Feminist Review*, Spring 1989, No. 31, p. 32.

424 See Hilary Wainwright, 'Writing off the left, Open letter to the SWP', *Socialist Worker Review*, No. 105, January 1988, Marxists' Internet Archive; Hilary Wainwright, 'The alternative media and transformative

politics: The case of Red Pepper magazine', *Progressive Review* , Vol. 27 (4), Institute of Public Policy Research, (IPPR).

425 Sheila Rowbotham to Ros Baxandall, Tuesday 14 June 1988, (postmark 15 June) RBP in SL.

426 Sheila Rowbotham to Ros Baxandall, Tuesday 14 June , 1988 (postmark 15 June,1988 RBP in SL.

427 SRD, 17 June 1988.

428 Sheila Rowbotham, A New Vision of Society' in eds, Juliet Ash and Elizabeth Wilson, *Chic Thrills: A Fashion Reader*, Pandora Press, 1992.

429 SRJ,17 August 1988.

430 Sheila Rowbotham, 'Rainbow Politics', *New Statesman & Society*, 2 September 1988.

431 SRD, 23, 24, 25 September 1988.

432 Inez McCormack, 'Introduction to *Women's Voices*', eds. Women's Committee of National Union of Public Employees, Attic Press, Dublin,1992, p. 7; see Mary Robinson, 'Inez McCormack, Obituary', *Guardian*, 1 February 2013.

433 See Rowbotham, *Promise of a Dream*, pp. 58-59.

434 See Rowbotham, *Promise of a Dream*, pp. 192-94.

435 See Jo Robinson, *Health in Homerton: Report on the First Year*, (pamphlet) Homerton Health Centre Project, London, September, 1981, p. 11, quoted in Sheila Rowbotham, *The Past is Before Us: Feminism in Action*, London, Pandora 1989, Penguin, 1990, pp. 124-125.

436 SRJ, 5 October 1988.

437 Sheila Rowbotham to Ros Baxandall, 20 October 1988. RBP in SL.

438 SRJ, 5 October 1988.

439 SRJ, 5 October 1988.

440 SRJ, 5 October 1988.

441 SRJ, 5 October 1988.

442 SRD, 4 and 16 October 1988.

443 SRJ, 5 October 1988.

444 SRJ, 12 October 1988.

445 SRJ, 5 October 1988.

446 This source material is in the Women's Library, LSE.

447 Swasti Mitter to Sheila Rowbotham, no date 1988, 7SHR/ Surrey/ Box 4 of 9, 21. LSE.

448 See Ajit Singh, 'Legacies – Lal Jayawardena: Crafting Development Policy', *Development and Change*, vol. 6, no. 36, 2005.

449 SRJ, 30 November 1988.

450 SRJ, 23 November 1988.

451 Baxandall, *Words on Fire*; Linda Gordon, *Woman's Body Woman's Right*, New York, Grossman, 1976; Claude Maignien, *Madeleine Pelletier*, Paris, Editions Syros, 1978; Hélène Brion, *La voie feministe*, Paris, Editions Syros, 1978.

452 Baxandall, *Words on Fire:* p. viii.

453 Sheila Rowbotham, 'Rosalyn Baxandall's *Words on Fire* and the Question of Syndicalism', *Rethinking Marxism: a journal of political economy and social analysis,* Winter 1988, Volume 1, Number 4, p. 34.
454 SRJ, 30 November 1988.
455 SRJ, 14 December 1988.
456 SRJ, 12 October 1988.
457 SRJ, 14 December 1988.
458 SRJ, 10 February 1988.
459 SRJ, 14 December 1988.
460 SRJ, 23 November 1988.
461 SRD, 11 December and 20 December 1988.

CHAPTER 11 1989

462 Nigel Fountain, *Lost Empires: The Phenomenon of Theatres Past, Present & Future,* Cassell Illustrated, London, 2005, pp. 16-17, 148-56; Roland Muldoon, *Taking On The Empire: How We Saved The Hackney Empire For Popular Theatre,* Just Press, London, 2013.
463 SRD, Note at the end of 1988.
464 SRJ, 12 February 1989.
465 *Interlink,* front cover, March 1989. SR.
466 See Sheila Rowbotham, Editorial *Interlink* March 1989, p. 5; Sheila Rowbotham, 'Left out of the argument by ideological gift-wrap', *Guardian,* 20 February 1989; Hilary Wainwright, 'Pyramids of power need a push: reply to Geoff Mulgan', *Interlink,* March 1989, p. 25.
467 SRJ, 14 December 1988.
468 Robin Murray, 'A step ahead: Combining economic strategy with vision', *Interlink,* March 1989, p. 14; see also Robin Murray 'Life After Henry (Ford) in the New Times edition of *Marxism Today,* October, 1988.
469 Swasti Mitter, 'A step ahead: Combining economic strategy with vision', *Interlink,* March 1989, p. 13.
470 Swasti Mitter, 'A step ahead', p. 13.
471 Mary Kaldor, 'Time for Choice', *Interlink,* March 1989, p. 14.
472 Betty Cook, 'When computers command', *Interlink,* March 1989, pp. 17-18; see also Anne Scargill and Betty Cook with Ian Clayton, *Anne and Betty.*
473 John Bohanna, 'Hanging on at Halewood', *Interlink,* March, 1989, p. 15.
474 Irene Bruegel, 'Needs more than a surface gloss', *Interlink,* March, 1989, pp. 19-20; on Labour's Policy Review, see eds, Curran, Gaber and Petley, *Culture Wars,* pp. 154-164.
475 Lynne Segal, 'Still seeking a union' and Mary Louise Adams, 'Probing the personal.' *Interlink,* March 1989, pp. 26-27.
476 On their feminism see eds, Carol Rutter and Faith Evans, *Clamorous Voices: Shakespeare's Women Today* (1988).

477 Abigail Thaw, 'New readings for old lines', *Interlink,* March, 1989, pp. 34-35.
478 On The Pogues, *Interlink,* March 1989. p. 9; on Isaac Julien's 'Looking for Langston', see Sheila Rowbotham, *Interlink,* March 1989, p. 8.
479 On the historical context see Curran, Gaber and Petley, *Culture Wars.*
480 Marc Karlin, 'Hall of Mirrors', *Interlink,* March, 1989 pp. 31-33.
481 SRJ, 12 February 1989.
482 Roger Kline, 'When savings mean sacrifice,' *Interlink,* March, 1989
483 Women for Socialism' Conference, 25-26 February, 1989, Contact, Irene Breugel, Notice in *Interlink,* March, 1989, p. 40.
484 Ken Livingstone, Preface, *Livingstone's Labour: A Programme for the Nineties,* p. ix.
485 West Yorkshire Homeworking Group, *A Penny A Bag,* Yorkshire and Humberside Low Pay Unit, 1990, pp. 2 and 7.
486 See Pauline Conroy Jackson, 'Beyond Benetton; Homeworking Italian Style, *Yorkshire & Humberside Low Pay Unit Newsletter,* No. 10, July 1990.
487 See Sheila Rowbotham, *Homeworkers Worldwide,* Merlin, London, 1993, pp. 9-17.
488 SRD, 18 September 1989.
489 Swasti Mitter to Sheila Rowbotham, 9 July 1989, 7SHR/surrey/ Box 4 of 9, 21. LSE.
490 Liz Heron quoted on the cover of Sheila Rowbotham, *The Past is Before Us,* Penguin, London, 1990.
491 See Caitlin Adams and Anna Davin, Obituary of Sue Crockford, *Guardian,* 12 August 2019.
492 See Rowbotham, *Daring to Hope,* p. 21; the film *A Woman's Place* is on YouTube, London Community Video Archive.
493 SRJ, 10 May 1989. SR.
494 Southall Black Sisters,1979-1989, *Against the Grain – a celebration of survival and struggle,* 'Our History', p. 7.
495 See Diane Elson, 'Market Socialism or Socialization of the Market', *New Left Review,* No. 172, Nov/Dec,1988.
496 See Sheila Rowbotham, 'Facets of Emancipation: Women in Movement from the Eighteenth Century to the Present', in eds, Sheila Rowbotham and Stephanie Linkogle, *Women Resist Globalization: Mobilizing for Livelihood and Rights,* Zed Books, London, 2001.
497 SRJ, 'Mon'. (early August) 1989.
498 The exception is the comprehensive overview by Beverley Bryan, Stella Dadzie & Suzanne Scafe, *The Heart of the Race,* London, Virago, 1985.
499 Ed. Delia Jarrett Macauley, *Reconstructing Womanhood, Reconstructing Feminism: Writings on Black Women,* Routledge, London, 1996.
500 Sheila Rowbotham, *Women In Movement: Feminism and Social Action,* Routledge, London, 1992.
501 SRD, 23 and 24 September 1989.
502 See Harry Wicks, *Growing Up in Battersea 1910 -1924,* (Pamphlet) ed. Sean Creighton, Battersea and Wandsworth Labour and Social History,

Newsletter No 15 1988; Harry Wicks, (with Logie Barrow) *Keeping My Head: The Memoirs of a British Bolshevik,* Socialist Platform, London, 1992.

503 Rowbotham, *A New World for Women,* pp. 52-53.
504 SRD, 9-12 November 1989.
505 SRD, 13 November 1989.
506 SRJ, 17 November 1989.
507 SRD, 20 November to 25 November 1989, SRJ, 27 November 1989.
508 Sally Hibbin continued to produce films and TV series but the TUC videos never happened.
509 SRJ, 27 November 1989.
510 SRD, 6 and 7 December 1989,
511 Bell Gale Chevigny, Introduction, *The Woman and the Myth: Margaret Fuller's Life and Writings,* The Feminist Press, Old Westbury, New York, 1976, p. 6.
512 SRD, 8 December 1989.
513 SRD, 9 and 10 December 1989.
514 Note in SRD 1989.

AFTERWORD

515 See Rowbotham, *Homeworkers World Wide* and Sheila Rowbotham, *Women in Movement,* Routledge, London, 1992.
516 Eds. Sheila Rowbotham and Swasti Mitter, *Dignity and Daily Bread: New forms of economic organizing among poor women in the Third World and the First,* Routledge, London, 1995.
517 See Sheila Rowbotham, *A Century of Women,* Viking, New York 1997; second edition, Penguin, London, 1999, p. 590.
518 Eds, Sheila Rowbotham and Stephanie Linkogle, *Women Resist Globalization: Mobilizing for Livelihood and Rights,* Zed Books, London, 2001.
519 See Alexander Cockburn, Jeffrey St. Clair, Alan Secula, *5 Days That Shook the World: Seattle and Beyond,* Verso, London, 2000.
520 See Rowbotham, *Edward Carpenter: A Life of Liberty and Love.*
521 An email on 30 December 2021, from Nancy Krieger, (who I met through Ros Baxandall) alerted me to this quote from Raymond Williams, *Resources of Hope,* London, Verso 1989. p. 209.

Index of Names

Index of Organisations

Transport and General Workers' Union (TGWU), 125, 137
Twin Trading, 134-35, 165, 195-96, 240
Tyneside CND, 79

Ulster Polytechnic, 14
Union Carbide, 174
Union of Construction and Allied Technical Trades (UCATT), 80
Union of Shop, Distributive and Allied Workers (USDAW), 11
Union of the Physically Impaired Against Segregation (UPIAS), 23
UNISON, 83
United Nations University's, World Institute for Development Economic Research (UNU WIDER), 169, 187-88, 190
United Nations, 169, 188
University of Aalborg, 71
University of Aarhus, 71
University of Amsterdam, 38, 64, 69, 70
University of Manchester, 251
University of Roskilde, 71
University of Toronto, 51
University of Uppsala, 192
Utility Workers of America, 130-31

Virago, feminist book publishers, 55, 65, 87, 99, 101, 107, 127, 137

Wandsworth Council, 59, 81, 96
War on Want, 23, 173

Warwick University
West Yorkshire Homeworking Group, 235
Westway Laundry, 83, 177
Women Against Fundamentalism, 239
Women Against Pit Closures, 112, 114-15, 122, 129, 133, 158, 161, 194, 215, 231
Women for Nicaragua, 195
Women Working Worldwide, 173-74
Women's Committee (GLC), 42, 59, 92-93, 107, 151
Women's Cooperative Guild, 88, 95, 244
Women's Liberation Movement, 2, 29, 70, 102, 134, 148, 154, 168, 172, 179, 210, 237-38
Workers' Beer Company, 165
Workers' Educational Association (WEA), 50, 57, 71, 195
Workers' Revolutionary Party (WRP), 88
World Trade Organization (WTO), 251

York University, 16
Yorkshire and Humberside Low Pay Unit, 235
Yorkshire District of the Communist Party, 23
Young Communist League, 10, 115, 130
Young Socialist group, 179

About the Author

Reasons to Rebel covers the years 1980 to 1989 and follows two earlier memoirs by Sheila Rowbotham, *Promise of a Dream* and *Daring to Hope* which reveal her life and influences during the 1960s and 70s.

Becoming a socialist as a student, Sheila Rowbotham helped to start the British women's liberation movement in 1969. Her early works, *Women Resistance and Revolution: Woman's Consciousness, Man's World* and *Hidden from History* gained an international readership. Later books, *Women in Movement: Feminism and Social Action, Dreamers of a New Day: Women Who Invented the Twentieth Century* and *A Century of Women: The History of Women in Britain and the United States*, could draw on a growing body of feminist historical studies.

Sheila Rowbotham's publications have been widely translated in Europe and beyond, appearing in languages that include Arabic, Hebrew, Japanese, Korean and Turkish. They range from studies of the late nineteenth and early twentieth centuries to contemporary political commentary. In 1979 she collaborated with Lynne Segal and Hilary Wainwright on *Beyond the Fragments: Feminism and the Making of Socialism* which was published by Merlin Press, as was her *Homeworkers Worldwide* in 1993.

She went on to write a biography, *Edward Carpenter: A Life of Liberty and Love*. Published by Verso, this was shortlisted for the James Tait Black Memorial Prize and awarded the Lambda Literary Award for Gay Biography in 2008. Her *Rebel Crossings: New Women, Free Lovers and Radicals in Britain and the United States* dived further into the archives, uncovering a small group of little known socialists and anarchists living within a similar political milieu to Carpenter, who migrated from Britain to the United States. The research for this was partly funded by an award from the Eccles Centre for American Studies (British Library) in 2012.

After teaching in schools and further education, combined with a short stint on a biscuit stall in Ridley Road market, from 1995 to 2010 Sheila Rowbotham was employed at Manchester University where she became a Professor in Labour Studies. She has lectured widely in Europe, the United States, Canada, India and Brazil and has received Honorary Degrees from the Universities of Bristol, London Metropolitan, Sheffield and Rouen in France.